Keeping *the* Campfires *Going*

NATIVE WOMEN'S ACTIVISM IN URBAN COMMUNITIES

EDITED BY

Susan Applegate Krouse
and Heather A. Howard

D0869501

UNIVERSITY OF NEBRASKA PRESS
LINCOLN AND LONDON

Library of Congress Cataloging-in-Publication Data
Keeping the campfires going: Native women's activism in urban communities / edited by Susan Applegate Krouse and Heather A. Howard.
p. cm.
Includes bibliographical references and index.
ISBN 978-0-8032-2050-8 (pbk. : alk. paper)
1. Indian women–United States– Political activity–History–20th century. 2. Indian women–Canada– Political activity–History–20th century. 3. Women political activists–United States–History– 20th century. 4. Women political activists–Canada–History–20th century. 5. Community life–United States–History–20th century. 6. Community life–Canada– History–20th century. 7. City and town life–United States–History– 20th century. 8. City and town life–Canada–History–20th century. 9. United States–Ethnic relations– History–20th century. 10. Canada– Ethnic relations–History–20th century. I. Krouse, Susan Applegate, 1955– II. Howard, Heather A.
E98.w8k446 2009
305.48′897–dc22
2009004626

Set in Scala by Bob Reitz.
Designed by Nathan Putens.

Contents

Acknowledgments   vii

Introduction
**SUSAN APPLEGATE KROUSE AND
HEATHER A. HOWARD**   ix

1   Urban Clan Mothers: Key Households in Cities
    SUSAN LOBO   1

2   Gender and Community Organization
    Leadership in the Chicago Indian Community
    ANNE TERRY STRAUS AND DEBRA VALENTINO   22

3   Indigenous Agendas and Activist Genders:
    Chicago's American Indian Center, Social Welfare,
    and Native American Women's Urban Leadership
    GRANT ARNDT   34

4   "Assisting Our Own": Urban Migration,
    Self-Governance, and Native Women's Organizing
    in Thunder Bay, Ontario, 1972–1989
    NANCY JANOVICEK   56

5   Their Spirits Live within Us: Aboriginal
    Women in Downtown Eastside
    Vancouver Emerging into Visibility
    DARA CULHANE   76

6 "How Will I Sew My Baskets?": Women Vendors, Market Art, and Incipient Political Activism in Anchorage, Alaska

MOLLY LEE 93

7 Women's Class Strategies as Activism in Native Community Building in Toronto, 1950–1975

HEATHER A. HOWARD 105

8 Creating Change, Reclaiming Indian Space in Post–World War II Seattle: The American Indian Women's Service League and the Seattle Indian Center, 1958–1978

MARY C. WRIGHT 125

9 What Came Out of the Takeovers: Women's Activism and the Indian Community School of Milwaukee

SUSAN APPLEGATE KROUSE 146

10 Telling Paula Starr: Native American Woman as Urban Indian Icon

JOAN WEIBEL-ORLANDO 163

Contributors 189

Index 193

Acknowledgments

Six of these essays are reprinted from the *American Indian Quarterly*, volume 27, numbers 3 & 4 (Fall 2003) by permission of the University of Nebraska Press. Copyright © 2004 University of Nebraska Press. They are:

Anne Terry Straus and Debra Valentino, "Gender and Community Organization Leadership in the Chicago Indian Community," pp. 523–32.

Nancy Janovicek, "'Assisting Our Own': Urban Migration, Self-Governance, and Native Women's Organizing in Thunder Bay, Ontario, 1972–1989," pp. 548–65.

Dara Culhane, "Their Spirits Live within Us: Aboriginal Women in Downtown Eastside Vancouver Emerging into Visibility," pp. 593–606.

Molly Lee, "'How Will I Sew My Baskets?' Women Vendors, Market Art, and Incipient Political Activism in Anchorage, Alaska," pp. 583–92.

Heather Howard-Bobiwash, "Women's Class Strategies as Activism in Native Community Building in Toronto, 1950–1975," pp. 566–82.

Susan Applegate Krouse, "What Came Out of the Takeovers: Women's Activism and the Indian Community School of Milwaukee," pp. 533–47.

"Urban Clan Mothers: Key Households in Cities" by Susan Lobo is reprinted from the *American Indian Quarterly*, volume 27, numbers 3 & 4 (Fall 2003) by permission of the author. Copyright © 2004 Susan Lobo.

Introduction

SUSAN APPLEGATE KROUSE AND
HEATHER A. HOWARD

In the twentieth century, Native peoples in North America went from being a rural to an urban population, changing their marriage patterns, family structures, and community organizations, as well as their levels and kinds of education and employment. Research on Indians was a fundamental part of the development of the discipline of anthropology in North America, but the rural to urban migration of Indian people has been largely overlooked by anthropologists. Sociologists, historians, and educators, often more concerned with urban populations, have also neglected Indians in cities, focusing instead on other populations. Research on urban American and Canadian Indians began in the 1960s with a focus on assimilation and the assumption that urban Indians would blend into their urban surroundings. By the 1970s researchers acknowledged the continuing presence of Indians in cities and began looking at the organizations they created there. Not until the 1990s did the focus begin to shift to the vibrant communities that Indian people have created in cities. Even today, the insights those communities could offer on cultural transformation and continuity, and social action and resistance, have not been fully explored.

A further neglected aspect of these urban areas has been the central role of Indian women in generating and sustaining community cultural and social life. While a general body of literature on Native women has grown in the last thirty years, only a fraction of this literature has examined Native women's activism, and it is virtually silent on activism in an urban context.

The chapters in this collection examine Indian women's community work and activism in urban contexts in the United States and Canada. Women's activism has been crucial to building Native communities in cities, not only through their direct participation in political and social movements, but also through their roles behind the scenes, as keepers of tradition, educators of children, and pioneers in city life. Native women have adapted traditional ways to the realities of city life. These traditions have provided the strength and foundation for the networks and organizations that are often the backbones of urban Native communities. Native women have been instrumental in the shaping of identity and community in the city, in mobilizing resources to benefit their communities, and in fighting the poverty and discrimination that too often afflict Indian peoples. In this sense the women whose stories are told in this volume have kept the campfires going, ensuring stability and continuity based in Native cultural and social practice, while also tending to the flames of resistance and asserting tribal sovereignty. Native women's experiences of rural to urban migration, the scope of their educational and employment opportunities in the city, and their relationships with non-Native individuals and organizations can provide insights into the power dynamics of race, class, and gender in the processes of cultural and individual adaptation to urbanization.

What have previous studies told us about urban Indians, particularly women? The first studies of Indians in cities appeared in the 1960s and focused primarily on how well Indians were assimilating into urban American or Canadian life. Hurt, for example, reported on a five-year study of Indian adjustment to the urban environment of Yankton, South Dakota.[1] Many of these first studies reflected the emphasis of the U.S. federal program of relocation, formalized in 1952 and designed to move Indians away from tribal communities and into urban life. Ablon looked specifically at relocated Indian people in San Francisco.[2] Assimilation studies continued to dominate urban Indian research well into the 1970s, with Chadwick and Stauss examining Seattle, and Margon and Sorkin looking more broadly at U.S. urban areas.[3] Related to assimilation, pan-Indianism became a topic for research at the same time. Hirabayashi, Willard, and Kemnitzer, for example, used data from San Francisco to examine pan-Indian identity, organizations, and social networks in urban areas.[4] The important role of women in pan-Indian networks remained unexamined by scholars, at least as late as 1980, according to Green.[5]

Other studies, also beginning in the 1960s, looked at poverty, social class, and social mobility more specifically, including Dowling on Green Bay, Dosman on Saskatoon, and Sealey and Kirkness on Indians and Métis in Canadian prairie cities.[6] Frideres then used Dosman's social classes to look more broadly at urban Indians across all of Canada.[7] Stanbury attempted to measure the success or failure of Native urbanization, concluding that there was "substantial evidence that Indians living off reserves engage in a range of behaviour that contributes to the maintenance of their distinctive cultural identity."[8] Stanbury's is one of the few studies that examine the development and viability of urban Indian communities; others would not appear until twenty years later. Ryan's examination of the struggle of Calgary's urban Indians provided a critical analysis of the structures of poverty and racism of Canadian society, moving away from the culture-bound, success-or-failure framework for understanding issues faced by Native people in cities.[9]

Urban Indian organizations are the subject of a number of studies, beginning with Price and continuing with Fiske in Los Angeles, both of whom saw an evolutionary sequence of stages in the development of organizations.[10] Price's model, however, failed to account for the persistence of simple organizations like Indian bars over time, as more complex urban Indian institutions develop. Fiske revised this model to incorporate various types of organizations and to include the impact of Native kinship and friendship structures and the influence of federal policy on urban Indian institutions.

Liebow further expanded on the model to look at the way that urban institutions shape communities.[11] Shoemaker discussed how organizations offered choices for Indians in Minneapolis in how they expressed their ethnic identity.[12]

In the 1970s a few studies emerged that examined Native people in urban areas as sociopolitical ethnic communities, moving beyond urbanization as something that happens to or victimizes Indian people to recognizing them as active agents in creating new communities. Guilleman's study of Boston underscored the importance of reservation and urban networks in Native community building.[13] Hansen's study of Seattle looked at the political dynamics of community formation, including relations between developing Indian organizations and national institutions.[14]

A new wave of research since the 1990s has begun to elaborate on the idea of community as a source of empowerment and cultural generation, and on the experiences of Indians in the city.[15] In particular, Weibel-Orlando provided a way to look at community in the dispersed Los Angeles Native community, with a focus on urban Indian organizations and their leaders. She emphasized the flexible, multi-sited character of the community, in the absence of a geographically discernable "Indian" neighborhood.[16]

Many of these studies were produced by members of the urban Indian communities themselves, or in close collaboration with the researchers. Lobo and Peters's edited collection included essays by anthropologists, historians, and community members, along with creative works by urban Indian people.[17] Lobo extended the collaborative model with a wide-ranging history of the Oakland, California, Native community, assembled by Native women who have been the core of the community's Intertribal Friendship House.[18]

More recent studies have begun to look at other issues that impact Indians not only in cities but on reservations as well. These studies situate Native peoples' experiences of the city in relation to broader accounts of urbanization. Beck, for example reviewed significant events in the history of the Chicago Indian community that have contributed to self-determination for that population. This is not political self-determination, as with tribal communities on reservations, but rather an urban community's own identity and voice.[19] Rosenthal discussed organizations in Portland and the impact of changing federal Indian policy on the development of those urban organizations, calling our attention to issues beyond the urban boundaries.[20] Thrush describes the participation of Native peoples in the urbanization of Seattle and its surrounding landscape, from prior to the first non-Indian settlement to the present.[21] Moving beyond the conceptualization of Native urban history as a late twentieth-century phenomenon, Thrush challenges the boundaries of urban history and concepts of the agency of Native people in relation to that history.

Using observations beginning in the 1970s and spanning twenty years, Metcalf noted the problems associated with using an acculturation model to understand Navajo women in San Francisco. She looked at the impact of federal relocation policy in this community and called for more comparative studies of Navajo women in different cities.[22] Other studies have focused on the adjustments women have made to urban life, such as Fogel-Chance's work on sharing networks among urban Inupiag women in Anchorage and Griffen's work with Navajos in Flagstaff.[23] Joe and Miller also look at Navajos and other Native women in Tucson and their adaptation to the city.[24]

The legal and political status of Native women in Canada has also impacted urbanization and needs to be further examined. Weaver provided a history of Canadian Native policy and its negative impact on Indian women.[25] Until 1985, Native women lost their federal Indian status when they married nonstatus or non-Native men. These women were then forced to leave their home reserves, resulting in slightly larger numbers of women than men migrating from rural reserves to urban areas, beginning as early as the 1890s. These women impacted community development in Canadian cities. A report for Status of Women Canada by Dion Stout and Kipling in 1998 recommended that priority be given to studying "Aboriginal women's rural-urban migration patterns and the differential experiences of First Nations, Inuit and Metis female migrants."[26] The authors further suggested that researchers should look at how Native women are involved in community politics and economic development, in both specifically women's organizations and larger community groups.

This volume looks at both Canada and the United States, as we uncover and critique the significance of Native women's contributions to the structures of urban Indian communities. In particular, we explore how communities emerged from women's participation in both social movements organized around Native rights and in rural to urban migration movements spawned by socioeconomic exigency. Green pointed out that scholars looking at Native women need to do more than chronicle the status of women and their problems. Women, she suggested, "do not, on the whole, document change; they make change."[27] Certainly that is the case with the Indian women represented in this book.

Our focus on the complex and active participation of Native women in shaping urban experiences seeks to problematize not only existing ideas about Native women but also those about urbanization and the construction of Native identity. As Joan Weibel-Orlando wrote in her introduction to the papers in this volume originally published as a special issue of *American Indian Quarterly*, "Urban space . . . has been and continues to be the sociopolitical terrain in which cultural innovation can occur and in which engendered community actions and roles can be challenged and reassigned."[28] The chapters in this book underscore the leadership of Native women in these processes of cultural innovation, in a context in which studies specifically of urban Indian women have been late-coming and are still limited.

Our specific case studies range geographically across North America, including Anchorage, Chicago, Los Angeles, Milwaukee, San Francisco, Seattle, Thunder Bay, Toronto, and Vancouver. The cities cluster down the Pacific Coast of North America and around the Great Lakes, reflecting both aboriginal and recent populations. The Indian populations in these cities include members of tribes native to the area and people from outside the area, brought to cities by formal relocation programs and informal social networks, as escapes from domestic violence and poverty, and as avenues to greater education and employment.

A number of themes emerge from these chapters, as the authors consider women's activism in urban Indian communities—kinship, class, migration, place, violence, public events, and gendered leadership. We begin with Susan Lobo's examination of urban clan mothers, with its emphasis on *kinship*, real and fictive, in sustaining community life. In what she identifies as "low-keyed activism," Lobo details the significance of "key households" headed by middle-aged and elder women in the San Francisco Bay Area Native community. The anchoring places provided by these women illustrate that unlike many other ethnic communities, urban Native communities are not often defined by geographically bound enclaves, but rather by constantly changing webs of social relations. Urban Native communities are distinctive in that they are multitribal, fluid, and flexible. The mobility of Native people between urban and rural, as well as between social, cultural, and political spaces that define the urban Native community, also challenges conventional understandings of community. Women like those described in Lobo's chapter mediate all of these factors, serving simultaneously as stabilizers and facilitators of the locomotive dynamics, which are the life of the urban Native community.

Class has been largely ignored by scholars looking at urban Indians, leading to an assumption that all Native people in cities live in poverty, or that those who attain upward economic mobility do so at the expense of assimilation and disengagement from the Native community. Heather A. Howard points out that as Native women in Toronto became more affluent, they also found and used new opportunities to secure resources for community building in the city. These women formed organizations modeled on, and in alliance with, white women's clubs and volunteer associations.

In contrast both to the mainstream feminist movement and to the male-dominated Red Power movement, the women in Howard's study did not overtly articulate gender-specific or Native-specific oppression as motivating their actions, which nonetheless served to address concerns such as poverty, homelessness, health disparities, joblessness, and high rates of incarceration. These Native women were instrumental in the acquisition of a building for a community center, organizing and delivering social services, countering assimilative or negative imagery of Native people in the city, and influencing national policy concerning Native urbanization, all work that Howard reframes as activism.

Rural to urban *migration* is the focus of several chapters here, including Howard's on Toronto, where women moved to the city for greater opportunities. Nancy Janovicek considers a darker reason that women came to cities, specifically to escape abuse at home. Molly Lee points out that migration is not just one way but often involves movement back and forth, for varying reasons and amounts of time.

Making a *place* for Indian people becomes an issue in several communities examined here. Mary C. Wright chronicles how women searched for a home for the Seattle Indian Center, and Susan Applegate Krouse recounts the struggle by women for a permanent location for the Milwaukee Indian Community School. Janovicek and Lobo also emphasize the importance of place for Native women, both formal space such as a shelter and informal gathering space such as the homes of urban clan mothers. Like Lobo, Wright describes the role Native women played in providing a "base camp" in the city for Native activists. However, she also details how women took their "household" role to the public sphere through their participation in 1960s and 1970s Indian protest activism and in their leadership in the establishment of Native organizations. Both Wright and Krouse examine the ways in which Native women saw their work as one of reclaiming Native space by occupying and taking over places that seemed marginal—like Native people themselves—but that they then turned into places of central meaning to the Native community. In both cases Native women not only "symbolically reclaimed colonized space," as Wright describes it, but they also established long-term structures, which form the foundations of the Native communities in Seattle and Milwaukee.

While connected to the relatively short-lived Native protest movements of the 1960s and 1970s, Krouse articulates the need to recognize the long-term legacy of Native women's work, which resulted from the specific type of engagement they took in relation to actions such as takeovers and occupations. In the case described by Krouse, the takeover of an abandoned Coast Guard Station was initiated by the American Indian Movement, an action of relatively short term. However, the legitimacy of the protesters' claims to the federal property was bolstered by Native women's establishment of a school there, a move that was motivated more by community need than by the desire to make a political statement. Krouse chronicles the subsequent struggles and successes of the women who organized, maintained, and continue to sustain the Milwaukee Indian Community School into the present.

Violence against women is an all-too-common problem in Native communities, both reservation and urban. Janovicek's research on Thunder Bay points out the cultural and legal issues compounding domestic abuse. In founding Beendigen, an emergency shelter for Native women and their children, Native women activists consciously emphasized Native identity in their delivery of social services in the urban setting. Their mandate to address domestic violence through culturally specific and appropriate frameworks underscored Native cultural pride, which in turn formed the foundations of urban Native community and self-determination in Thunder Bay. Rather than viewing violence (as well as poverty and other social problems) as results of a fundamental incompatibility between Native culture and the modern world, the Beendigen women demonstrated the commensurability of Native culture with urban life, and how it provides a more successful way of addressing social problems faced by Native people than non-Indian approaches. Women and their families at Beendigen access social support networks that replicate the support traditionally provided by the Native extended family. Like Lobo, Janovicek highlights the importance of kinship for Native people, as adapted to the urban context, and in which women are central. Importantly, Janovicek also situates the Beendigen women's work in relation and contrast to national policy issues, as well as the concerns and goals of the mainstream women's movement.

Resistance to the pathologization of Native culture in relation to social problems is also the subject of Dara Culhane's analysis of how violence against street women led to community action in Vancouver's Downtown Eastside, an inner-city neighborhood in which survival—and death—are dependent upon drug trafficking and the sex trade. Native women are disproportionately represented in the population of the neighborhood. High rates of HIV and violence characterize the Downtown Eastside; however, the most significant trait of the neighborhood, which came to public attention in recent years, is the overwhelming number of "disappeared" Native women. Culhane describes the annual Valentine's Day march, organized primarily by Native women and in which Eastside residents and others protest conditions in the neighborhood through a focus on the many dead and missing women.

Culhane foregrounds the discourse of the women activists in which the problems of the Eastside are articulated in terms of the structures of racism, social and economic inequality, and oppression, which sustain the colonialism of Canadian society. Even in this world where the elders are those who make it past the age of forty-five, the Native social institution of kinship can be found, whether in the day-to-day work of the "Street Moms" of the Downtown Eastside or in the expressions of remembrance. During the march the names of the dead and missing women are listed as mothers, daughters, sisters, and aunties, while their names inscribe the "women's lives on the land and in place."

Where Wright, Krouse, and Culhane describe how Native women organize *public events* as part of their activism, Molly Lee considers the juxtaposition of a Native craft market and a political protest in Anchorage, and the role that women are starting to play in the political arena—a role she describes as "incipient activism." While more recent than other urban migrations, the migration of Native people to Anchorage has resulted from a need to go where education and work are found. As Lee describes, however, the relative newness of Native urban migration in Alaska is also grounded in particular historical, legal, and economic circumstances, especially those surrounding Native peoples' land-based subsistence. Lee draws attention to the interdependence of rural subsistence, craft production, and urban marketing. She describes the primacy of "sharing networks"—at the center of which are women—to Native people both within the city and between rural and urban communities.

All of the chapters contribute to our understanding of *gendered leadership*. Anne Terry Straus and Debra Valentino lay out the historical background for changes in men's and women's leadership in Chicago, and Grant Arndt provides additional context for the creation of a role for women's leadership in social welfare work in that community. While the women in Straus and Valentino's essay took on less public roles during most of the early years of organization building, like Lobo's key householders they clearly sustained the networks that were the lifeline of the Chicago Native community. These women were, in Straus and Valentino's words, "absolutely essential . . . through influence rather than official status." These authors also connect Native women's eventual repositioning in public leadership roles with their attainment of higher education, an important personal and collective goal motivating many of the women described in this book.

Joan Weibel-Orlando's specific consideration of Paula Starr's rise to leadership positions in the Los Angeles Indian community pays special attention to this connection to education. Weibel-Orlando's life history approach also provides important glimpses of the distinctive manner in which Native women connect the personal with the political. In contrast to conventional feminist readings of women's transition from the private to the public sphere, Paula Starr demonstrates how Native women's public leadership may be largely informed by her personal experience, as well as that of her family, extended kin, and nation. Starr connects, rather than separates, the intimate, often emotionally charged events of her life—"turning points and defining moments" in Weibel-Orlando's analysis—to her daily action as a key decision maker in the Los Angeles Native community.

Weibel-Orlando contextualizes Paula Starr's development through a close examination of the personalization of broader structural influences, such as the impact of Indian policy on displacement, poverty, and social dysfunction in Native families, as well as the rise of Native social movements in the 1960s and 1970s. In this vein of close analysis, Grant Arndt adds to the Straus and Valentino chapter a gendered examination of the particular moment in Native American organizing in Chicago in which a shift occurred from male to female leadership, and a corresponding turn to social welfare concerns. Focusing on the history of the American Indian Center, Arndt argues that this turn reflects the essentialized view that women are better suited to social welfare work, and that Native women in particular are culturally compelled to assume roles of caring, adapting traditional female roles to the urban setting through the provision of social services. In contrast to Janovicek's chapter on the specific formation of services addressing domestic violence, Arndt's account details multiple dimensions of the struggles that took place within the broader Native community and with outsiders. These struggles shaped the gendered transition of leadership of the American Indian Center in relation to the growth of the Native community and its needs and the availability of funding sources, as well as fostering the development of Native discourses on the gendered division of labor.

Wright, Howard, Krouse, and Culhane also provide examples of individual Native women leaders and how their efforts shaped their communities. Not all leadership is so overt, however, and other chapters emphasize the idea of incipient activism, where women are working, often behind the scenes, to build a base for future leadership, especially women's leadership. Lee notes the reticence of craft women to become more politically active, although they are becoming increasingly more vocal, particularly on issues that affect their families and communities. Howard notes that Native women in Toronto become leaders not for themselves, but because they are looking out for their families.

We originally brought some of these chapters together in a session at the 2001 American Anthropological Association's annual meetings, which included papers by Howard, Krouse, Lee, Lobo, and Straus and Valentino, with discussion by Weibel-Orlando. We then expanded that session into a special issue of *American Indian Quarterly* published in 2003, adding the articles by Culhane and Janovicek to the papers from the AAA session and an introduction by Weibel-Orlando.[29] This book expands again to include the chapters by Arndt and Wright and a new contribution by Weibel-Orlando.

In her introduction to the special issue of *American Indian Quarterly*, Joan Weibel-Orlando challenged us as researchers not just to look at the efforts of Indian women in their urban communities but to engage in "a holistic and engendered interpretation of historical processes" in our ethnographic accounts of urban Indian communities. She notes that this kind of research would "consciously explore not only both sides of the traditional male hegemony versus female suppression paradigm, but the full spectrum of gender identifications and their relative impact on social and political behavior." Specifically, she points out that "to be ethnographically holistic, the writers need also to take into account the political and economic context within which any social action takes place."[30] The contexts she suggests we consider include the international women's movement; the mandates of federal, state, and local funding agencies; and traditional and nontraditional roles for Native men and women. She also notes the need to expand our ethnographies of urban Indian communities and the work of women in those cities.

Our hope is that this volume begins to address some of the concerns so rightfully raised by Joan Weibel-Orlando. Her chapter here provides a life history of one woman activist, contextualized in the larger history of the Los Angeles Indian community. The new chapters included here expand our coverage geographically to Seattle (Wright) and provide more historical depth to the investigation of gendered leadership in Chicago (Arndt).

Other researchers are also contributing to a more holistic investigation of American Indian women and men in cities. Anthologies such as *Native Chicago* edited by Terry Straus and Grant Arndt and *American Indians and the Urban Experience* edited by Susan Lobo and Kurt Peters provide greater voice to urban Indian people by examining historical and contemporary issues impacting them and their communities.[31] Renya Ramirez's recent book, *Native Hubs: Culture, Community, and Belonging in Silicon Valley and Beyond*, looks at the ways that Native people connect across time and space in the large urban areas of central California, and focuses particularly on women community leaders.[32]

The stories of urban Indian communities, those of women and of men, need to be told. Their experiences in building community can help us to understand the experiences of Native people in cities and of other rural to urban migrants in an increasingly urban world. As this volume demonstrates, the dynamics of Native peoples' lives in cities are diverse, complex, and multilayered, and yet they also share a number of commonalities. *Keeping the Campfires Going* tells stories of Native women's activism in urban areas, which represents a central dimension of urban Indian community life and history. There are more stories waiting to be told.

Notes

1 Wesley R. Hurt Jr., "The Urbanization of the Yankton Indians," *Human Organization* 20:4 (1962): 226–31.

2 Joan Ablon, "Relocated American Indians in the San Francisco Bay Area: Social Interaction and Indian Identity," *Human Organization* 23:4 (1964): 296–304.

3 Bruce A. Chadwick and Joseph H. Stauss, "The Assimilation of American Indians into Urban Society: The Seattle Case," *Human Organization* 34:4 (1975): 359–69; Arthur Margon, "Indians and Immigrants: A Comparison of Groups New to the City," *Journal of Ethnic Studies* 4:4 (1977): 17–28; Alan L. Sorkin, *The Urban American Indian* (Lexington MA: Lexington Books, 1978).

4 James Hirabayashi, William Willard, and Luis Kemnitzer, "Pan-Indianism in the Urban Setting," in *The Anthropology of Urban Environments*, ed. Thomas Weaver and Douglas White (Boulder CO: Society for Applied Anthropology, 1972), 77–87.

5 Rayna Green, "Native American Women," *Signs* 6:2 (1980): 248–67.

6 John H. Dowling, "A 'Rural' Indian Community in an Urban Setting," *Human Organization* 27:3 (1968): 236–40; Edgar J. Dosman, *Indians: The Urban Dilemma* (Toronto: McClelland and Stewart, 1972); D. Bruce Sealey and Verna J. Kirkness, eds. *Indians without Tipis: A Resource Book by Indians and Métis* (Winnipeg: Project Canada West, 1973).

7 James S. Frideres, *Canada's Indians: Contemporary Conflicts* (Scarborough ON: Prentice-Hall of Canada, 1974).

8 William T. Stanbury, *Success and Failure: Indians in Urban Society* (Vancouver: University of British Columbia Press, 1975), 241.

9 Joan Ryan, *Wall of Words: The Betrayal of the Urban Indian* (Toronto: PMA Books, 1978).

10 John A. Price, "The Migration and Adaptation of American Indians to Los Angeles," *Human Organization* 27:2 (1968): 168–75; John A. Price, "U.S. and Canadian Indian Urban Ethnic Institutions," *Urban Anthropology* 4:1 (1975): 35–52; Shirley J. Fiske, "Urban Indian Institutions: A Reappraisal from Los Angeles," *Urban Anthropology* 8:2 (1979): 149–71.

11 Edward D. Liebow, "Urban Indian Institutions in Phoenix: Transformation from Headquarters City to Community," *Journal of Ethnic Studies* 18:4 (1991): 1–27.

12 Nancy Shoemaker, "Urban Indians and Ethnic Choices: American Indian Organizations in Minneapolis, 1920–1950," *Western Historical Quarterly* 19:4 (1988): 431–47.

13 Jeanne Guillemin, *Urban Renegades: The Cultural Strategy of American Indians* (New York: Columbia University Press, 1975).

14 Karen Tranberg Hansen, "Ethnic Group Policy and the Politics of Sex: The Seattle Indian Case," *Urban Anthropology* 8:1 (1979): 29–47.

15 Edmund Jefferson Danziger Jr., *Survival and Regeneration: Detroit's Ameri-*

can Indian Community (Detroit: Wayne State University Press, 1991);
Frances Sanderson and Heather Howard-Bobiwash, eds. *The Meeting Place:
Aboriginal Life in Toronto* (Toronto: Native Canadian Centre of Toronto,
1997); Terry Straus and Grant P. Arndt, eds. *Native Chicago* (Master of
Arts Program in Social Sciences, University of Chicago; Chicago: McNaugh-
ton and Gunn, 1998); Joan Weibel-Orlando, *Indian Country, L.A.: Main-
taining Ethnic Community in Complex Society* (Urbana: University of Illinois
Press, 1999 [1991]); Susan Lobo and Kurt Peters, eds. *American Indians
and the Urban Experience* (Walnut Creek CA: Altamira Press, 2001); Susan
Lobo, ed. *Urban Voices: The Bay Area American Indian Community* (Tucson:
University of Arizona Press, 2002); Craig Proulx, *Reclaiming Aboriginal
Justice, Identity and Community* (Saskatoon SA: Purich, 2003); Coll Thrush,
Native Seattle: Histories from the Crossing-Over Place (Seattle: University of
Washington Press, 2007).

16 Weibel-Orlando, *Indian Country, L.A.*

17 Lobo and Peters, *American Indians.*

18 Lobo, *Urban Voices.*

19 David R. M. Beck, "Developing a Voice: The Evolution of Self-Determination
in an Urban Indian Community," *Wicazo Sa Review* 17:2 (2002): 117–41.

20 Nicolas G. Rosenthal, "Repositioning Indianness: Native American
Organizations in Portland, Oregon, 1959–1975," *Pacific Historical Review*
71:3 (1992): 415–38.

21 Thrush, *Native Seattle.*

22 Ann Metcalf, "Navajo Women in the City: Lessons from a Quarter-Century
of Relocation," *American Indian Quarterly* 6:1/2 (1992): 71–89.

23 Nancy Fogel-Chance, "Living in Both Worlds: 'Modernity' and 'Tradition'
among North Slope Inupiaq Women in Anchorage," *Arctic Anthropology*
30:1 (1993): 94–108; Joyce Griffen, "Life Is Harder Here: The Case of the
Urban Navajo Woman," *American Indian Quarterly* 6:1/2 (1992): 90–
104.

24 Jennie R. Joe and Dorothy Lonewolf Miller, "Cultural Survival and Con-
temporary American Indian Women in the City," in *Women of Color in
U.S. Society*, ed. Maxine Baca Zinn and Bonnie Thornton Dill (Philadelphia:
Temple University Press, 1994).

25 Sally Weaver, "First Nations Women and Government Policy, 1970–1992:
Discrimination and Conflict," in *Changing Patterns: Women in Canada*,
ed. Sandra Burt, Lorraine Code, and Lindsay Dorney (Toronto: McClelland
& Steward, 1993) 92–150.

26 Madeleine Dion Stout and Gregory D. Kipling, *Aboriginal Women in Canada: Strategic Research Directions for Policy Development* (Ottawa: Research Directorate Status of Women Canada, 1998) 7–8.

27 Green, "Native American Women," 263.

28 Joan Weibel-Orlando, "Introduction," *American Indian Quarterly* 27: 3/4 (Summer/Fall 2003): 491–504.

29 Susan Applegate Krouse and Heather Howard-Bobiwash, eds. "Keeping the Campfires Going: Urban American Indian Women's Community Work and Activism," *American Indian Quarterly* 27: 3/4 (Summer/Fall 2003): 489–90.

30 Weibel-Orlando, "Introduction," 500.

31 Straus and Arndt, *Native Chicago*; Lobo and Peters, *American Indians*.

32 Renya Ramirez, *Native Hubs: Culture, Community, and Belonging in Silicon Valley and Beyond* (Durham NC: Duke University Press, 2007).

KEEPING THE CAMPFIRES GOING

1 Urban Clan Mothers

Key Households in Cities

SUSAN LOBO

American Indian communities in urban areas are characteristically fluid networks based on relationships. Residence is dispersed, but nodes on the community network include the many American Indian organizations found in urban areas, seasonal or intermittent events or activities, and sites that hold connotations of special significance. In many instances these "sites" are the "key households" headed by older respected and influential Indian women, here referred to as Urban Clan Mothers. It is these key households that provide a degree of permanence in the swirl of constant shifts and changes in the highly fluid urban Indian communities. These household gathering spots often provide short-term or extended housing and food for many people, health and healing practices and advice, a location for ceremony, emotional and spiritual support, entertainment, and transportation and communication resources. They are also often vital spots of linkage with more rural communities and tribal homelands. The women who head these key households and extend many services to urban community members are strong but low-profile activists. They are the focus of this chapter. Their presence and sustaining actions are one of the essential foundations for community stability and vitality.

A summary discussion of social context and the structuring of urban Indian communities is necessary here in order fully to understand both the role and the importance of women who come to function in urban areas in ways that are similar to that of clan mothers in many traditional tribal homelands.

Although each urban Indian community is distinctive, there are a number of common features or characteristics that are found in most urban Indian communities. The salient characteristics of the Bay Area Indian community and many other urban Indian communities are that they are multitribal and therefore multicultural; are dispersed residentially; comprise a network of individuals, families, and organizations; encompass a number of economic levels; are multigenerational; and are extremely fluid. On a general level, urban Indian communities answer needs for affirming and expressing identity, create contexts for carrying out the necessary activities of community life, and provide a wide range of circumstances and symbols that encourage "Indian" relationships at the family and community level. The fluid, and therefore flexible, nature of the urban Indian community contributes to its resiliency and persistence, as well as its invisibility from an outside perspective. Indian people living in urban areas rarely cluster in ethnically homogeneous geographic locations, unless there are historically established villages or communities that have been engulfed by the expanding metropolis.[1] In sum, Indian urban communities differ substantially from more visible ethnic-based neighborhoods.

The role of Urban Clan Mothers and why they and their households are so crucial can best be understood within the context and through a clear delineation of urban Indian community social structuring and community dynamics. Indian people living in urban areas understand this structuring; their survival often depends on it.[2] The discussion that follows summarizes the rationale for having a clear picture of the nature of urban Indian communities, as well as some of the characteristics of urban communities.

This discussion is based on long-term fieldwork since the 1970s in the San Francisco Bay Area American Indian community and less extensive work in other urban Indian communities throughout the United States. The fieldwork includes the standard anthropological tradition of immersion—that is, through participant observation, extensive note-taking, and interviews, but more importantly through years of applied work in a number of Bay Area Indian organizations. This has allowed me to more fully gain insights into relationship dynamics, process, appropriate cadence, and protocols, while at the same time making a contribution to community well-being through collaborative project work. Though the majority of the research on which this discussion is based was carried out in the San Francisco Bay Area, much of what is presented here can be generalized to reflect urban Indian communities in the United States and Canada.

Urban Indian Community Social Structure

The San Francisco Bay Area is the home of approximately 50,000 American Indian people, according to the 2000 census. This is a large, diverse, and active Indian community that, although long established, began to increase in numbers during the 1950s as a result of the federally sponsored relocation program. Many of those now living in this multitribal Indian community in the Bay Area are the descendants of those who came to the area during the relocation period. In the 2001 *San Francisco Bay Area American Indian Resource Directory* there were fifty-seven Indian-run organizations.[3] These provide social services, educational activities, health care, recreational and cultural activities, and job training. Every weekend there are events and activities that bring the community together: powwows, workshops, concerts, demonstrations, and healing ceremonies.

The structuring of urban Indian communities as essentially a network of relations is in contrast to the more commonly held conceptualization of a community seen as a geographically based cluster of residences and commercial enterprises with accompanying shared cultural attributes. The application of this standard definition of community to urban American Indian communities by researchers, and including the U.S. Census Bureau, distorts reality and limits an understanding of many aspects of community dynamics, including the essential role played by Urban Clan Mothers.

Much of the literature from the 1960s and 1970s focused on questions of assimilation and carried with it an assumption that Indian people living in cities cluster in particular neighborhoods, most frequently termed *ghettos* or *Indian enclaves*.[4] This body of literature followed on the increased migration to urban areas by Indian people as a result of the federal relocation program and often had an implicit agenda of assessing the pros and cons of the effectiveness of the relocation program. This was done not by evaluating the program itself but by looking at the degree to which Indian people had "successfully" assimilated, in terms of the goals and standards generated by the program. In many instances there was a blaming-the-victims approach when aspects of the relocation program failed to attain its goals. Political policy and funding were tied to and reflected this body of literature. The majority of those carrying out research and writing in the years following relocation applied many assumptions, such as the nature of urban Indian communities, and some utilized long-standing stereotypes about American Indians that biased their work. When the funding died for relocation and also for research related to assimilation themes, most of the research and writing on Indians living in urban areas ceased to exist as well. Only in the mid-1990s has a fresh, primarily qualitative approach to urban research emerged.[5]

The assumption by some researchers that Indian people in cities must live clustered in urban neighborhoods, ghettos, or enclaves, and that this is synonymous with an Indian community, still continues to persist, however, as with Fixico's frequent reference to "the Indian Ghetto."[6] Utilizing this standard definition of community and the assumptions on which it is based can have profound and potentially negative impacts, not only on discerning reality as Indian people know it and live it, but on policy as well. For example, in addition to the influence on relocation policy and the relocation program discussed above, Lobo indicates the ways that U.S. census methodology, based on assumptions that urban Indian communities are located in circumscribed neighborhoods similar to urban

Chinatowns, rather than being dispersed and network based, has been a key contributing factor to census undercounts and miscounts of Indian people in urban areas.[7]

Urban Indian communities, because they are dispersed and based on a network of relations, for the most part, may be invisible or misunderstood from the outside and to outsiders, but they are anything but invisible to those who participate in them. They are viable communities but structured on an American Indian–derived model of community or tribe, rather than a European-derived one. Likewise Jojola notes, "This 'invisibility' [of Indian people in Albuquerque] is consistent with findings from other major urban centers including reports developed for the urban Indian populations in Los Angeles, Oakland, and St. Louis, to name a few."[8]

Two important factors that shape urban communities and are crucial to understanding the role of Urban Clan Mothers are, first, whether an urban area was a destination city of the federal relocation program and, second, the degree of proximity to reservation homelands. Those cities such as Oakland, Los Angeles, and New York that were relocation sites tend to have a more tribally heterogeneous population, compared to those that were not relocation cities and that grew through self-motivated migration from nearby reservations. Also, those urban Indian communities such as Tucson that are close to reservation homelands tend to have a different configuration of Indian organizations, compared to those that are more distant from homelands, since the availability of services such as health care may be found nearby "at home," rather than "in town." For these urban Indian communities there is the opportunity for frequent participation in nearby reservation tribal activities, politics, and family responsibilities, compared to those urban areas that may be hundreds or thousands of miles from "home." The creation of multitribal communities far from tribal homelands, as seen in the Bay Area, has led to a proliferation of greatly needed community organizations in these urban Indian communities. The support provided by Urban Clan Mothers in urban Indian communities distant from tribal homelands is as vital to community well-being as are the formal organizations.

Fluid Indian Communities, Individual Mobility Patterns, and Urban Clan Mothers

Community-wide patterns of fluidity and mobility patterns of individuals are also closely tied to the role of women who head key households. These households are the stopping points, the locations of stability for highly mobile individuals, and are situated within communities that are structurally very fluid. Social scientists who have worked in urban contexts have mentioned in passing the very fluid nature of urban Indian communities.[9] These same authors have also documented, to some extent, the individual mobility patterns characterized by the coming and going from home reservations to cities for employment and education and the returning to reservation homes for ceremony and family responsibilities. In all urban Indian communities, people frequently travel back and forth from city to home. However, those living near tribal homelands have the opportunity to do so most frequently, or even as Jojola describes in reference to Albuquerque, to commute daily from a home pueblo to work in the city.[10]

We are beginning to see more in-depth inquiries into what is meant by this term *fluid*. For example, writings by Ackerman, Bonvillain, and Salo are some of the ethnographic works on American Indian mobility patterns.[11] Knack also speaks of "social fluidity."[12] Jojola's survey of the urban Indian population of Albuquerque describes the cyclical return patterns to home reservation areas. A long-time participant in the Bay Area Indian community often referred to it as a "floating craps game": always action, always moving, never the same on any given day from what it was the day before, yet with shared knowledge of the underlying rules and protocols.[13]

It has been noted by Lobo, and by Straus and Valentino, that in some respects urban Indian communities reflect pre-reservation/

pre-European contact, or more traditional structural characteristics.[14] Because urban Indian communities are not bounded geographically as a reservation community is, the community itself may exhibit physical fluidity to expand and contract geographically as resources become available, to move into resource-rich niches, and to reflect seasonal opportunities. Also, in urban areas social and political boundaries are less rigid and more fluid than on reservations because, for example, membership is not tied exclusively to a charter of blood-quantum or genealogical criteria. Nor is there a formal over-arching political structure, equivalent to a tribal council that governs the entire urban community.

In the Bay Area Indian community it is principally the Indian-run organizations, a few other non-Indian organizations, and events and sites of significance that constitute the nodes on the social network. As Ramirez says in relation to the Indian community in San Jose, California, which is part of the Bay Area community, "These gathering sites support agency, structures of feeling, and social change. In these gathering spaces the imagination is freed to create an inclusive, democratic world, which people can work to realize."[15] The majority of the Indian organizations in the Bay Area, and in other urban Indian communities, were primarily founded by and are currently staffed by women. Most organizations are in continual flux, able to disassemble and reassemble. Many women move from organization to organization as each organization expands, shrinks, or closes; yet these women in the long run continue to provide needed core services within the Indian community. Most often it is the women who staff and are on the boards of these organizations, whether as cooks, receptionists, counselors, or directors, and who also in more informal ways maintain key households and function as Urban Clan Mothers. Thus, there are multiple ways in which people are linked and are in contact with one another. Through all this motion, this fluidity, an underlying network of connectedness allows for social and cultural continuity.

In addition to the patterns of fluidity of the community itself, individuals in the Bay Area American Indian community and other urban communities are highly mobile as well. This pattern is reflected in longstanding cultural traditions held by some tribes and is similar to what is found on many reservation homelands. Ackerman in reference to Colville reservation residents says, "The latter are still living by the rules that most hunter-gathers employ—you have a home territory, loosely defined and encompassing a wide area, but you move around a lot; not just inside home territory, but often outside it in order to make a living."[16] When there is movement, there are also the places where one stops moving, for a day or for extended periods. These are the key households, headed by women in urban communities that provide the anchor points where those on the move stop over. As one Bay Area individual indicated in reference to his aunt's home, where he frequently stayed for long periods of time during visits from South Dakota, "This is our encampment out here." Poverty, lack of affordable housing, ceremonial and social responsibilities, and the complications of substance abuse and other health-related issues are strong underlying factors for mobility in many cases. Yet, for many there is also an active cultural and personal preference to remain on the move. Ramirez in reference to the Indian community in San Jose, California, finds that much of the social science literature dealing with American Indian migration to cities and movement within cities is ethnocentric and based on the negative concept of "rootlessness," rather than appreciating the positive associations of mobility held by many Indian people.[17]

Key Households Provide Stability in a Highly Mobile Population

As with other aspects of the urban Indian community, household composition itself is fluid. Household shifts are common and expected as relatives often make prolonged visits to and from rural and reservation homelands, as single mothers take in boyfriends, or as nieces or nephews stay temporarily or for long periods of time. Children may leave crowded situations to go stay with grandparents, or with aunties or uncles, or other relatives, either in the city or elsewhere. Some adult couples, who live on the streets or in vehicles, may place their children to sleep over with relatives. Household size and composition also have a seasonal aspect since many Indian people living in the Bay Area are "on the road" during the late spring and summer months, and relatives from tribal homelands likewise visit the city: on the powwow circuit, attending ceremonies, or visiting relatives.

Some of the types of mobility noted by Salo in the Indian community in Los Angeles include the following: "frequent and lengthy stays with relatives on reservations and in various urban areas, as well as attendance at pow-wows, tournaments, rodeos and ceremonial events. Many also participate in migratory labor, including fishing in Alaska, and agricultural work and fire fighting throughout the western states."[18] There are many forms of mobility: mobility by those living in established residential units, but who travel extensively for weeks or months at a time for important life cycle, ceremonial, or kin responsibilities. As they travel through the Bay Area, they know there are key households and Urban Clan Mothers that will welcome them in their journeys. There are those who are without an established home and are highly mobile, living on the streets and staying from time to time in the homes of women who have taken on the role of Urban Clan Mothers. There are those who have ambiguous residences or consider themselves as having a number of simultaneous residences, perhaps one being in a key household. Others may cycle between various institutional settings and the streets, relatives' homes or those of Urban Clan Mothers. People travel for fun as well and to see new places or visit friends and family.

In the Bay Area Indian community there is wide latitude of acceptance of the many ways that individual mobility takes place. Although tribes differ regarding the degree of affinity for travel, movement is frequently spoken of in the Bay Area Indian community as "just a part of our way of life." To be on the move is valued, unless it is the result of extreme duress.

There are some Indian people who travel widely because of a spiritual and cultural dedication, and who consider the Bay Area their home, or at least one of their homes. These are the people who are respected for their cultural understandings and the necessary work they do for Native rights or the spiritual well-being of Indian people. One such woman said, "All of my travels are for political, personal, spiritual and professional reasons." When she is in the Bay Area the key households extend their hospitality to her.

Some people have set up a long-term routine of movement within the Bay Area that includes frequent stops at a key household and a special kin-like relationship with the woman whose house it is. For example, "Antelope" is one of those people. Now in his mid-forties, he has lived a traveling life throughout the western states and in his old childhood neighborhood. Here he sleeps on the streets, rotating between two secret spots, or stays at the home of an elderly woman who is an Urban Clan Mother and has known him since he was a child. At her home he often sleeps, eats, and hangs out talking to friends and watching the television. Though Antelope is not a consanguineal kinsman of hers, this household is what he calls his extended family. She keeps track of his coming and going and general well-being and also feels free to ask for his assistance with the grandchildren or in doing some shopping and carrying the groceries for her. He wrote a poem:

My life is freedom, and it's lived that way,
My goal is peace and it stays that way,
I don't need violence, and I don't really hate.
I'm like a spirit that rides the wind,
I just drift in and out again.

Many American Indians, both on rural and reservation lands and in urban areas, view themselves as having multiple homes, so that one lives simultaneously in more than one place. This may include cycling between rural and urban areas, or within the urban area itself, and often a key household is one of their homes. Bonvillian, in regard to the St. Regis Mohawk Reservation, says, "Other people may live simultaneously in more than one household on a temporary, fluid basis. They can claim rights to residence in multiple houses because of established kinship relations."[19] Ramirez, writing of two Indian women living in San Jose, California, says, "They seem to have multiple homes. Jane and her two sisters describe their journey from Fresno to San Jose to Farmington as 'follow the leader'. For them, there is much travel between different urban areas and 'home', their reservation. Thus, their senses of culture and community cannot be bounded in space to include only San Jose, but includes many points of location."[20]

In the Bay Area Indian community, Indian families, especially extended families, may utilize the resources of a number of residential spots with a wide array of often shifting and flexible sleeping, eating, and financial or general living arrangements. An extended family may share a household or may be spread throughout the city in various households. Most often an Urban Clan Mother's home, a key household, may be the central home base for this shifting set of extended kin.

In urban areas there are many forms of activism carried out by American Indian women in addition to the more visible and standard definitions of activism such as public speaking and organizing demonstrations or occupations. For example, Hoikkala discusses the prominent role played by many Indian women in creating and sustaining Indian organizations in Phoenix, particularly those focusing on education, health, including substance abuse prevention and treatment, and family welfare.[21] Somewhat less visible, but just as crucial as expressing a form of social activism, are the key households that have been created and sustained by women. These households play a vital function for the extended family, for highly mobile individuals within the urban Indian community, and for those who circulate through or visit the city. The stable households they have created and maintain serve as fixed and welcoming anchors in the otherwise highly fluid and complex urban Indian community.

These households are similar to what Ackerman identified on the Colville reservation as "anchor" households and are headed by women functioning as clan mothers. Similar arrangements and social roles for middle-aged and elderly women are typically found as well on many other reservations throughout the United States. Women providing for the community well-being have taken on an urban form.[22] In the Bay Area Indian community these key households are headed almost exclusively by mature women of long-standing respect and influence in the community who have become homeowners or have arranged for secure long-term inexpensive leases. They are most frequently women with large extended families. Many of these women are also active in leadership positions in the local Indian community organizations or work in the organizations as well, though this is not always the case. Some women who have established key households focus their efforts on making their homes a safe and stable haven for many people and many activities. The number of people sleeping in one of these key households can be extremely high. One woman commented that "every morning I've got my alligator farm to look at when I get up" in reference to the number of people rolled up in blankets on her apartment floor. Temporary visits by those who are considered "couch surfers" may become permanent, or at least as permanent as any living arrangement in the Bay Area Indian community.

Many people float or circulate through these households, knowing they will be welcomed with a place to sleep, if only on the floor, and a meal and shower. People on the road know that these households are dependable stopover points. One such house has a sweat lodge in the back yard, and another an extensive vegetable garden. There is a strong correlation between home ownership and the continuity of these key households. This fact further underlies the economic basis for household stability or instability. Those who purchased houses years before now have comparatively low housing costs and a sense of housing security, while those who pay the current high rents face housing insecurity and tend for that reason to be forced to move frequently.

There is no generic label used in the Bay Area urban Indian community for key households. Rather they are referred to as "Sarah's house," or Clara's or Magee's. One person in the community commented that these houses where people congregate in the city are like "our Clan Mother Camps that we set up back home when we come together [during summer Sun Dance]." As noted by Jojola and also seen in the Bay Area, "informal and casual networks" serve many of the basic survival needs of those who are homeless, either by choice or economic circumstances and who prefer "to maintain their anonymity rather than bear the scrutiny of non-Indians" at social service agencies.[23] These key households in the Bay Area fulfill many of the necessary survival functions that otherwise might be carried out by non-Indian social service agencies.

For example, one woman who is the head of a key household migrated to the Bay Area as a young woman. She worked as a formally trained social worker at various Indian organizations for many years. Now she is a grandmother and great-grandmother. Defining her role as a community member and elder along with that of a social worker, she carries out her professional mandates to encompass the values of the community. Her home is not only the place where her children, sometimes their spouses, her grandchildren, and her great-grandchildren call home, but also the place where traveling visitors from "back home" always are welcomed, and where some of her clients live who are in need of a temporary place to stay. Although she declines to consider herself a politically involved person, she ran for the board of a prominent Indian organization. As a reflection of the recognition and respect for her long service within the community and her role both professionally and personally, she received many more votes than any of the other candidates. The basis for her leadership vote of confidence was an acknowledgment of the respect and influence that she has earned. The women who are the heads of these key households provide shelter, food, and other necessities of a home in the same way that a mother or auntie would "back home" on the reservation. These key households are an important nexus in the Bay Area Indian community network and crucial to understanding the structuring of the community.

One Urban Clan Mother, although owning a house where many people often stayed, carried out most of her activities, not at home, but in the kitchen of one of the major Indian organizations where she was the cook. "Delphina's" kitchen was known throughout the Bay Area Indian community as the place to go to dip into the stream of information and communication that constantly flowed. Others might have referred to it as gossip, but women who spent hours in the kitchen knew that it was important for them to remain informed about who was doing what, when, where, and with whom in order to assist in keeping the community in balance and to play a mediating role should conflicts develop. During the day, and often in the evening, Delphina's kitchen was the place to go to find out what was happening in the community. Delphina never spoke in public, nor sat on boards. Yet she held great influence and respect in the community, and her kitchen was a key or anchor point. She was a grandmother who everyone knew, and she had seen and experienced "everything" in life.

In the offices on the floor above Delphina's kitchen, the social workers met with clients on a wide range of personal matters. Many clients then frequently came downstairs to help in Delphina's kitchen. Here they could make fry bread or cut up vegetables for the senior lunch or a community dinner. And talk. There was always something cooking, and Delphina was likewise always ready to listen sympathetically, to hear about one's problems and dreams, and to laugh together with her visitors and helpers about life's cruel ironies. During this time working in the kitchen, everyone was working together, contributing to the well-being of the community by preparing food. People always felt warm, safe, and cared for in Delphina's kitchen.

Another woman who maintained a key household in the Bay Area American Indian community had been very active politically during the 1970s, participating in land takeovers, demonstrations, spiritual runs, and long-distance walks for Indian rights. Her house was frequently filled, not only with her children and grandchildren, but also with many on the move from distant places. She decided that it was important for the young women in her household and their friends to start a drum. A young women's drum was highly unusual, and some felt that this was only a male prerogative. However, "Darlene" saw this as very important for "her girls." She organized the drum and lent her support for many years. It became generally recognized that the drum and her efforts were in the best interest of these young women, and she was given respect and support for her decision to start the drum.

"Bernice" carried out her important role in the community through establishing and maintaining a household that provided a home base to many: members of the family and both those in need of temporary shelter and those coming into the Bay Area Indian community to take care of activities of spiritual and cultural necessity. This particular case study derived from research carried out in 2000–2001 that was funded through a grant from the U.S. Census Bureau.[24] Bernice and others in various households who participated in this research maintained a journal of the activities in their household for a period of six weeks. As a part of the study women who were the heads of five key households kept journals, as did twenty-seven highly mobile individuals. Interviews were carried out with additional individuals as well. The short case study presented here is also contextualized as a result of over fifteen years of my acquaintance with Bernice and her household.

Bernice and her late husband, "Clarence," were fortunate to have joined a housing cooperative over twenty years ago. They had a comfortable two bedroom flat in a Victorian duplex in the Bay Area. Their tenancy was secure, and over the years Bernice was active on the cooperative board of directors. Although they never had a surplus of money, they both worked and lived adequately. Clarence lived in the Bay Area most of his life, and Bernice came "out from South Dakota on relocation" as a teenager. Clarence passed away six years ago. Bernice was considered one of the founding mothers of the Bay Area Indian community and in the spring of 2000 was in her mid-sixties. Over the years Clarence's nephew had stayed with them for periods of time, and the youngest of Bernice's three daughters by an earlier "Indian marriage" lived with them since childhood. Bernice's two other daughters lived out of town, but one often made extended visits, along with her three children in order to take care of medical treatment in the city for herself and one of her children.

Bernice's household was the center of much community activity since she was repeatedly on the board of a number of Indian organizations and her housing cooperative. Committee meetings and potlucks and many informal get-togethers were held in her flat. Bernice also followed her traditional Lakota spiritual practices and therefore often hosted medicine people who came out from South Dakota for ceremonies, some of which were held at her home. People from throughout the urban community often came to visit her during times of crisis in their lives. During these conversations with her, often over a cup of strong coffee with donuts or fry bread, Bernice gently gave advice in the form of stories regarding others that had found themselves in similar situations. Relatives from "back home," especially those who traveled the powwow circuit, often made Bernice's home their base of operations for months at a time after the first powwow of the season at Stanford University on Mother's Day weekend in mid-May. Her home was also sometimes a staging area where strategy meetings were held and plans were made for Indian rights actions, occupations, or marches that took place in the Bay Area and internationally.

In this household Bernice fostered a sense of collective responsibility and hospitality, which are expressions of a strongly held cultural ideal. She was also well known and respected for providing a safe haven for people who had nowhere else to go. Within the past year Bernice took in a woman of her tribe who was terminally ill, during the months she was waiting to be transferred back home to

South Dakota to a nursing facility. She also took in a young mother with two small children who was temporarily without a place to stay or a job.

Bernice herself was not residentially mobile. She clearly had a permanent and stable residence, yet those staying in Bernice's home were almost constantly coming and going. In the spring of 2000 Bernice's two-bedroom household contained a mixture of people. Her youngest daughter and her daughter's husband of a few years were there, along with their three-year-old child. Theirs had come to be a very tumultuous marriage, and for weeks or months at a time, the daughter's husband left and lived in his car or with various friends. Likewise the daughter, who abused substances, left for days on end, leaving her child in the care of his grandmother, Bernice. Also in the household at that time was a second daughter, who was in the midst of what turned out to be a nine-month visit, along with her boyfriend and her three teenage children. One of the children was attending school and stayed during the school week with an aunt in a nearby town, coming to Bernice's only on weekends. The other two children attended a local Oakland school. Usually, eight to ten people slept overnight at Bernice's: various combinations of her children and grandchildren, visitors from "back home," and local community people. This household was a demonstration of the Indian community values of extending hospitality not only to extended family members, but also to others in need in the community and to those traveling through town.

Unfortunately, Bernice became gravely ill in June and was in and out of the hospital during the summer of 2000. Her youngest daughter's husband was only intermittently there, and her daughter was also often absent. When Bernice became too ill and weak to continue to care for her grandson, he was placed in a temporary foster care home. In late August Bernice passed away, a sad and tremendous loss for the Bay Area Indian community. Without Bernice, her household disintegrated; a location vanished that had, for many years through Bernice's energies and concern, come to be an important nexus in the community network. Her youngest daughter entered a long-term residential drug treatment program; the husband was "elsewhere," and Bernice's grandson remained in foster care. Concern was expressed in the community that since the child had been placed in a non-Indian home, he might be permanently "lost" to his family and tribe. Soon after Bernice's memorial at an Indian organization, the older daughter returned with her children and boyfriend to the rural northern California community where she had lived previously, and where she felt more comfortable than in the city. The flat reverted back to the cooperative association, and a new non-Indian family moved in.

Conclusions

This article has focused on middle-aged and older women in urban Indian communities who function as Urban Clan Mothers by maintaining a home that welcomes and cares for the basic needs of many. Not only do they provide a home where people, especially those on the move, may sleep and eat, but they also often act as role models for younger men and women, serve as teachers and counselors, or carry out spiritual responsibilities. In some ways these women are fulfilling culturally based traditional roles that have been adapted to urban environments. They are activating widely shared values regarding the role of elders and women in assuring the well-being of the community overall through the sharing and circulation of resources and knowledge.

The approach here to understanding the nature of these women's crucial yet low-keyed activism has been to place their activities within the context of overall urban community structuring and to recognize the fluid nature of urban communities, as well as the mobility patterns of individuals. This descriptive analysis is yet one more illustration of the complex nature of urban American Indian communities, and the need on the part of researchers to clearly understand social organization and structural dynamics.

Notes

1 For examples of those who describe dispersed urban Indian communities see Lobo regarding the San Francisco Bay Area, Bobiwash regarding the Toronto Indian Community, Beck regarding Chicago, and Weibel-Orlando regarding Los Angeles. Susan Lobo, ed., *Urban Voices: The Bay Area American Indian Community* (Tucson: University of Arizona Press, 2002), xix–xxiii; A. Rodney Bobiwash, "Native Urban Self-Government in Toronto and the Politics of Self-Determination," in *The Meeting Place: Aboriginal Life in Toronto*, ed. Frances Sanderson and Heather Howard-Bobiwash (Toronto: Native Canadian Centre of Toronto, 1997), 85; David Beck, "The Chicago American Indian Community," in *Native Chicago*, ed. Terry Straus and Grant P. Arndt (Master of Arts Program in Social Sciences, University of Chicago; Chicago: McNaughton and Gunn, 1998), 168–70; Joan Weibel-Orlando, *Indian Country, L.A.: Maintaining Ethnic Community in Complex Society* (Urbana: University of Illinois Press, 1991), 48–52.

2 Susan Lobo, "Is Urban a Person or a Place? Characteristics of Urban Indian Country," in *American Indians and the Urban Experience*, ed. Susan Lobo and Kurt Peters (Walnut Creek CA: Altamira Press, 2001).

3 Friendship House Association, *San Francisco Bay Area American Indian Directory* (San Francisco: Friendship House Association, 2001).

4 See, for example, Joan Ablon, "Retention of Cultural Values and Differential Urban Adaptation: Samoans and American Indians in a West Coast City," *Social Forces* 49:3 (March 1971): 385–93; James H. Gundlach and Alden E. Roberts, "Native American Indian Migration and Relocation: Success or Failure," *Pacific Sociological Review* 21:1 (1978): 117–28; Billye F. Sherman Fogleman, "Adaptive Mechanism of the North American Indian to an Urban Setting" (PhD diss., Southern Methodist University, Dallas, 1972).

5 See, for example, Deborah Davis Jackson, *Our Elders Lived It: American Indian Identity in the City* (DeKalb: Northern Illinois University Press, 2003); Lobo and Peters, *American Indians*; Lobo, *Urban Voices*; Straus and Arndt, *Native Chicago*; Sanderson and Howard-Bobiwash, *Meeting Place*; and Weibel-Orlando, *Indian Country, L.A.*

6 Donald Fixico, *The Urban Indian Experience in America* (Albuquerque: University of New Mexico Press, 2000), 81, 188.

7 Susan Lobo, *American Indians in the San Francisco Bay Area and the 1990 Census* (Washington DC: Center for Survey Methods Research, Bureau of the Census, 1992); Susan Lobo, *American Indian Urban Mobility in the San Francisco Bay Area, Final Report Submitted to the Statistical Research Divi-*

sion, *U.S. Census Bureau* (Washington DC: U.S. Census Bureau, 2001). John Anner, "To the U.S. Census Bureau, Native Americans Are Practically Invisible," *Minority Trendsetter* 4:1 (1990): 15–21, has noted some of the problems at a policy level resulting from this misperception of the nature of the urban Indian communities by the U.S. Census Bureau. He says: "Census figures are used to determine, among other things, who gets what in terms of federal funding and congressional representation. If you are not counted by the census, then, in the eyes of the government agencies, you don't count. In fact, you don't exist at all. . . . For Native Americans, the last U.S. census [1990] which science writer James Gleick says 'seems certain to stand as a bleak landmark in the annals of arithmetic' —deserves the name 'statistical genocide.' It has made a lot of people vanish, for the most part people of color" (16).

8 Theodore S. Jojola, *Urban Indians in Albuquerque, New Mexico: A Study for the Department of Family and Human Services* (Albuquerque: University of New Mexico, 2000).

9 See Weibel-Orlando, *Indian Country, L.A.*; Straus and Arndt, *Native Chicago*; and Jeanne Guillemin, *Urban Renegades: The Cultural Strategy of American Indians* (New York: Columbia University Press, 1975).

10 Jojola, *Urban Indians in Albuquerque, New Mexico.*

11 Lillian Ackerman, *Residential Mobility among the Colville Indians,* (Washington DC: Center for Survey Methods Research, Bureau of the Census, 1988); Lillian Ackerman, "Residents or Visitors: Finding Motives for Movements in an Indian Population," paper read at the Society for Applied Anthropology meetings, Santa Fe NM, 1989; Nancy Bonvillain, *Residence Patterns at the St. Regis Reservation* (Washington DC: Ethnographic Exploratory Research Report no. 5, Center for Survey Methods Research, Bureau of the Census, 1989); Nancy Bonvillain, *The Census Process at St. Regis Reservation* (Washington DC: Center for Survey Methpds Research, U.S. Bureau of the Census, 1989); Matt Salo, *Findings from Focus Groups with Urban Indians of Los Angeles County, California* (Washington DC: Statistics Research Division, U.S. Bureau of the Census, 1995).

12 Martha C. Knack, *Boundaries Between: The Southern Paiutes, 1775–1995* (Lincoln: University of Nebraska Press, 2001).

13 Jojola, *Urban Indians in Albuquerque, New Mexico.*

14 Lobo, *American Indian Urban Mobility*; Terry Straus and Debra Valentino, "Retribalization in Urban Indian Communities" in Lobo and Peters, *American Indians and the Urban Experience.*

15 Renya Ramirez, "Healing through Grief," in Lobo and Peters, *American Indians and the Urban Experience*, 16.

16 Ackerman, *Residential Mobility*, 4.

17 Ramirez, "Healing through Grief," 2.

18 Salo, *Findings from Focus Groups*, 4.

19 Bonvillain, *Census Process*, 7.

20 Ramirez, "Healing through Grief," 1.

21 Paivi Hoikkala, "Feminists or Reformers? American Indian Women and Community in Phoenix, 1965–1980," in Lobo and Peters, *American Indians.*

22 Ackerman, *Residential Mobility*, 8; Ackerman, *Residents or Visitors.*

23 Jojola, *Urban Indians in Albuquerque, New Mexico*, v.

24 Census Bureau grant contract 43-YA-BC-030121.

2 Gender and Community Organization Leadership in the Chicago Indian Community

ANNE TERRY STRAUS AND DEBRA VALENTINO

This chapter concerns eight decades (1920–2000) of community organization in the American Indian community in Chicago. While the trends discussed may be particular to that community or time frame, we expect that there are parallels in other urban Indian communities. The Chicago American Indian Center was the first urban Indian center in the country; with the Oakland Intertribal Friendship House, it served as a model for later urban Indian community organizations.

In the early twentieth century, Chicago had an Indian population (188 Indians were counted in the 1910 census), but no Indian *community*. Indian people of diverse tribes passing through or settling in Chicago sought the help of Indian residents known to them through the "moccasin telegraph." Carlos Montezuma (Yavapai), for example, a medical doctor in Chicago in the early 1900s, was well known in Indian County.

[Montezuma] served as a one man social agency for Indians in Chicago. When Indian delegations passed through the city en route to Washington DC, he graciously met them and made their stay in Chicago pleasant; when Indians became stranded in the city, he interceded with their reservation agencies to help provide the opportunity for them to return home; when Indians came to the city in need of work, he helped them find it. In fact, he informally worked together with the BIA warehouse in Chicago in this latter capacity. In 1904 when a train wrecked in Maywood, Illinois, several Indian members of a travelling Wild West show were injured, some critically. Dr. Montezuma not only treated the Indians as patients, but fought (albeit unsuccessfully) through the BIA system for better compensations on their behalf.[1]

During this time there were no Indian-run or Indian-focused social services available, but generous individuals, such as Montezuma, or later Willard LaMere and Anna Harris, provided essential services to new Indian residents. Those who lived in the city, however, did not at first imagine or work toward a community of Indian people in Chicago.

An Indian Community and Men's Leadership, 1920–1960

Indian presence has been continuous in Chicago and its environs, and Indian people moved to and through the city throughout the twentieth century. However, we place the beginnings of the present-day community in the 1920s, when we have records of purposeful gatherings of Indian people of various tribes and backgrounds. At the same time, the population of Indians in the city had begun to increase as a result of employment opportunities and military experience during World War I. The celebration of Indian Day, proclaimed by the 1919 Illinois State legislature as the fourth Friday of September, recognized continued Indian presence in the city. Dr. Montezuma participated in some of these activities, as did Willard LaMere.

Indian Day celebrations were coordinated by the first Indian-focused organization in Chicago, the Indian Fellowship League. The League had a short history, in part due to tensions between its Indian and non-Indian members.[2] It provided an organizational framework for Indians to define and address their own concerns within the city and, thus, to become conscious of themselves as a group despite the diversity of their tribal backgrounds and experiences. The Indian Council Fire, formed in 1923 as the Grand Council Fire of American Indians, continued for more than half a century, providing an organizational locus for Indians and those who supported them within the city. Carlos Montezuma was the first recipient of the Indian Council Fire award, honoring an individual Indian for his or her extraordinary accomplishments. The earliest leadership in these organizations was male, although by the 1930s the Indian Council Fire included women in various capacities.

The population of Indian people in Chicago grew considerably during and after World War II. This was due in part to independent relocation for employment, war enterprise, and other personal reasons, and in part to the Federal Relocation Program. With the expanded Indian population, the desire for social contact with other Indian people and the need for basic social services expanded as well. The Indian Council Fire could not fulfill this need. In 1946 Willard LaMere (Ho-Chunk), Scott Thundercloud [Scottie Williams] (Ottawa), Ben Bearskin (Ho-Chunk / Sioux), along with a non-Indian, Russell A. Minea, formed the North American Indian Council. The initial objective of the Council was to develop a social center for Indian people, run by Indian people who "just wanted to be together."[3] Renting a hall, the Council provided a space for gathering and feasts for the growing Indian population in the city. At first they did not intend to provide social services, but the group soon became the North American Indian Mission, which served Indian veterans of World War II, many of whom had settled in Chicago. The Mission began providing a range of social services for Indians newly arrived in the city. While lack of funding soon led to the demise of the Mission, Ben Bearskin's "Intertribal Council" continued to function as a social center and location of the first Chicago powwows, in a rented hall at North and Halsted (not far from the newly yuppified Whole Foods Market, Crate and Barrel, and Aveda Salon). The Council and Mission were the first Indian-organized, Indian-run community organizations and thus represent the invention of a separate Indian community identity in the larger city. All of the people named as leaders in this effort were men.

Indian women were certainly aware of the growing need for social services for new Indian residents and of the dangers of ignoring them. Theresa Robbins (Sioux), a young Roosevelt University student who had worked in the wartime office of the Bureau of Indian Affairs (BIA) in Chicago, was one of them. Concerned about the number of Indian people "drifting to West Madison Street," she consulted various professionals and eventually made contact with the Welfare Council of Chicago about her interest in "bringing some Indian people together in an organization of their own to try to counteract some of the bad influences they are under in Chicago and also to gradually reduce the suspicion that this group holds toward 'white people' and white institutions."[4] Robbins continued to insist upon Indian control of a proposed center and never did receive Welfare Council funding. She did, however, articulate the idea and make an important funding connection with the Welfare Council. She never occupied an official position of authority in the organization that eventually developed, and her role in its foundation is frequently forgotten. But it is clear that she did not feel it was culturally or personally inappropriate to push for the welfare of Indian people in this way, using her status as a student to identify others who might support her in reaching her goal.

The Welfare Council was eventually involved in the establishment of the American Indian Center, encouraged in the effort by the BIA, which had selected Chicago as a site for relocation under the Federal Relocation Program. Actually the Center was not yet functioning at the time when the first federal relocatees began arriving in the city; the Relocation Office referred the first relocatees to the Indian Council Fire, headed at that time by Eli Powless (Oneida). It was a male community member, Al Cobe (Chippewa) who eventually succeeded in making the necessary political and funding connections to realize the dream of a center, articulated by LaMere and Robbins and others before them. At that time Cobe was already running the Indian Service League out of a church at 2413 West Jackson Boulevard, funded by individual (including his own) and church donations.

The BIA sought to settle Indian people permanently in the city and looked to the American Indian Center as a way of helping newly arrived Indians adapt to the city. When it became clear that Center leaders looked to the organization more as a place to sustain Indian culture and community, the BIA withdrew its support. Instead, the Chicago Relocation Field Office, distressed with the number of Indian people returning to their reservations after a brief sojourn in Chicago, established "Indian Clubs" in park district field houses, one on the north side and one on the south side, reflecting the two centers of Indian population in the city. In each case, the president and vice-president of the club were Indian men, consistent with government and funding expectations, while certain supporting offices were held by women. An important Halloween powwow at the northern club on October 31, 1952, attracted a surprising three hundred attendees. It was coordinated by Ben Bearskin and various other Indian men. Betty Bearskin was the one exhibition dancer who was female.

Thomas Segundo (Papago / Tohono O'odham), arriving in Chicago to attend the University of Chicago Law School, catalyzed Indian community organization in Chicago. Segundo's leadership and energy contributed significantly to the fundraising effort that underlay the establishment of the All Tribes American Indian Center in 1953, to become the first urban Indian center in the country (at just about the same time as the Oakland, California, Intertribal Friendship House was established). Thomas Segundo was the first acting director of the organization. In March 1954 he was replaced by Ted White (Sioux/Oneida), who had just completed his MA in social work from Chicago's Loyola University. The first two directors of the Indian Center, then, were impressively credentialed by outstanding local institutions and had developed both specialized knowledge and personal contacts that facilitated funding and other support for the organization. As men and especially as men accomplished and credentialed beyond most non-Indian men, they were appropriate and effective mediators, respected both within and without the

Indian community. Daily operation of Center programs, however, drew primarily on evolving community knowledge and included women as well as men. Ben Bearskin continued to organize the all important powwows and exhibition dance events, with a growing number of volunteers from the community.

Meanwhile, a mission-centered group worked to establish the Saint Augustine's Center, another early and important community organization. Saint Augustine's has persisted to the present, providing counseling and family support services as well as an Indian context for religious services. Under the leadership of Father Peter Powell, the organization included professional social workers in its leadership. At first those social workers were non-Indian men, but they were soon joined by Amy Skenadore. For the last several decades, the organization has had a preponderance of women in leadership roles. It is likely that the church and social work focus and the church funding of this other early organization in Chicago contribute to the greater presence of women in official roles. The primary organizer and intermediary, however, was Father Powell.

Consistent with the world outside the Indian community, as well as with tribal norms, the executives, those who held public positions of authority in the American Indian Center, were men. Also consistent with tribal norms, if not with the world outside the Indian community, the opinions and input of women were considered extremely important, and the public positions held by men were sanctioned by the women of the community. The men whose vision and dedication resulted in the establishment of the community organizations are understood as the founders and leaders of the present-day community. They included Willard LaMere, Bill Red Cloud, Joe White, Ben Bearskin, and Leroy Wesaw. Indian women organized community events, developed contacts with Indian people throughout the city, and provided essential support to Indian newcomers. They served on committees, went to meetings, and advised the men. They recruited members and participants in the Center's events, and they pushed for children's activities. They established clubs, including the Women's Club of the American Indian Center, where Margaret Red Cloud, Ludie Batisse, Vivian Mason, and Sandy Bird worked and socialized together. They were absolutely essential to the Center and the community in which it developed. They did so, however, "behind the scenes," through influence rather than official status.

For several decades, men continued to hold the public positions, to provide the interface with the larger Chicago community, to be the gatekeepers of community events and activities. The Indian community continued to grow, and the need for funding and for political interface with the local government and charitable organizations increased. It became important for community leaders and representatives to become knowledgeable about government and policy issues and to be certified in their positions through education. Carlos Montezuma, Thomas Segundo, and Ted White were unusual in the Indian community: most of the early community builders in Chicago had no higher education. As the importance of education to funding and other support of Indian community organizations and initiatives became ever more clear, education became a communitywide priority. The succeeding generation of community leaders benefited tremendously from this focus.

Education, Activism, and Women's Leadership, 1960–2000

Education for the new generation of leaders was a primary concern of the 1961 American Indian Chicago conference, co-sponsored by the National Congress of American Indians (NCAI) and the University of Chicago. NCAI looked toward a new future of American Indians, fueled by the enthusiasm and training of Indian World War II veterans.[5] The American Indian Chicago conference may mark the beginning of a shift in gender roles in urban community organizations. A quick survey of the more than four hundred Indian people who attended the conference reveals a preponderance of men, but also a strong representation of women. Women were sent by their tribes or communities or simply took the opportunity to participate in this first large-scale, intertribal meeting. Everyone who participated had equal say and equal vote in the decisions of the conference, and women certainly spoke out and influenced opinion and perspective. The conference steering committee, headed by D'Arcy McNickle, was predominantly male, but various aspects of the conference proceedings presaged a shift in gender roles and leadership in Indian communities. The formation of the National Indian Youth Council (NIYC) was an important outcome in this regard; its membership included many young Indian women, and its educational training for the future generations of Indian leaders attracted an increasing number of young Indian women as well as men.

The Civil Rights movement of the 1960s had its effect on the Chicago Indian community. Throughout the country, influenced in part by black activism, Red Power movements began to develop, with Alcatraz (1969) as a kind of founding moment, the "master stroke of Indian activism."[6] The American Indian Movement (AIM), beginning in the Twin Cities among young, better-educated Indian people, became the vanguard of the new generation of Indians, politically savvy, knowledgeable about federal Indian law and policy, and anxious to push their causes in the legislature and the courts as well as on the island and in the occupied BIA buildings.

Many women participated in the occupation of Alcatraz, including the now famous Wilma Mankiller. Throughout Indian Country, on reservations and in urban communities, women were much more likely to complete high school and to attend college than men. In Chicago public schools from at least the 1980s to the present, the greatest predictor of high school graduation for all races and ethnicities was gender; girls completed high school at vastly higher rates than boys.

The point, for our purposes, is that Indian women now took on a different kind of leadership in the Indian community, albeit frequently unacknowledged by themselves or others. When "activism" within the Indian community led to the establishment of new community organizations to enhance and complement the work of the Chicago Indian Center, women had a more public presence and occupied more official positions of authority than previously. The Native American Committee, which began to push for changes in the Chicago Indian community beginning in the 1970s, included women among its most outspoken leadership, women such as Phyllis Fastwolf. Indeed, as new organizations began to develop and break off from the Indian Center, the director of the Center was Faith Smith, a young woman involved in political action and in postsecondary education, and in NIYC efforts following the 1961 conference. Smith became the founder and director of Native American Educational Services College (NAES College), the purpose of which was to provide higher education and certification for adult community organization leaders and community service providers. The importance for Indian leadership of both education and certification in the greater Chicago community was clear.

Through the 1970s and early 1980s there was a balance of men and women on the boards and staffs of community organizations. New organizations developed, and a remarkable effort to coordinate organizational goals and activities emerged in the Chicago American Indian Community Organizations conference in 1981. Louis Delgado, organizer of the conference, recalls a balanced representation at the meeting; men and women participated in fairly equal numbers with fairly equal voice and influence.

The later 1980s, however, saw an interesting shift in the presence of women in Indian community organizations. By 1990 every one of the more than fifteen existing organizations, including the American Indian Center and the Saint Augustine's Center, was run by a woman. The organization that was on the strongest financial footing and that had engaged the most progressive ideas, the American Indian Economic Development Association, had not only a woman director but also an entirely female staff. The two new community organizations in the early 1990s, Chicago's Native American Urban Indian Retreat (CNAUIR) and the Native American Foster Parents

Association (NAFPA), both had women directors as well. The only exception was AIM, which had a large non-Indian membership, and which was/is not properly a community service organization.

A communitywide American Indian Women's Leadership Development (WLD) project, in which both authors of this article participated, helped to solidify and articulate the leadership roles of women in the community. Debra Valentino said about the program:

> The circle of women who came together to share, listen, and create a balance began with us. With this new circle of Indian women in leadership of all ages, our families and community members began to benefit in many different ways. We began to see our own strengths and weaknesses and work on these with the help of each other. Other Native American Indian women in and out of our community who were already in leadership roles addressed our meetings. In these meetings they shared and brought back a vision of traditional balance in understanding that our community was in need of strong voices all over the country. A growing number of women's voices were needed to bring back accountability and quality services within our organizations and close attention to the needs of our Indian community. The need for women to step into these roles of leadership became apparent and began taking place more so for the Chicago Indian community during the latter part of the 1980s, a period even before the Women's Leadership Development program started. The WLD added to this and really gave precedence to our commitment during the 1990s.

The predominance of women in community work is not unique to the Indian community. In the last two decades of the twentieth century, most community work in all communities throughout the city was done by women. Community work was family focused and child-friendly; many women become involved in it as a way to improve life for their children. Much community work is voluntary. The involvement of Chicago Indian women in unpaid, volunteer positions, on boards, in kitchens, and at registration tables, is consistent with what has been said above. However, the women who were directors of all the Indian organizations in the community were being paid salaries considerably higher than the average salary of community members in the workforce. This requires further consideration.

Beginning in the 1960s the importance of education to the success of Indian goals became clear. In Chicago, although the first college graduates were men in adult learning programs, from the late 1970s through the 1980s and into the 1990s, most Indian people entering and successfully completing college were women. It will be noticed that this period includes the time of the Tribally Controlled Community Colleges Act and the resultant availability of institutions of higher education on reservations as well as in urban areas, community-based higher education at that. Still it was the case that most students in tribal colleges, as well as in mainstream colleges, were women. Why? Indian women in Chicago, ages twenty-six to seventy, list their children and grandchildren as prime among their motivations for completing college. They realize that if they do the work to earn a degree, the young people around them will understand the value of the degree and include the idea of college in their future plans. With greater levels of educational achievement, Indian women acceded to official leadership positions and associated salaries.

At the NAES College graduation ceremony in 1985, Jesse Ben (Mississippi Choctaw) graduated with some seven or eight other students. When he took the podium to make a few remarks, he said, "I have only one question to ask. WHERE ARE ALL THE MEN?" He was the only man in the entire graduating class, a ratio repeated throughout tribal colleges around the country and in Canada.

His call has been answered. In the last few years a greater balance has developed. Indian men are in charge of the American Indian Center (Joe Podlasek), the Chicago Campus of NAES College (Ken Scott), CNAUIR (Joseph Perales), and Midwest SOARRING (Save

Our Ancestors Remains and Resources Indigenous Network Group) (Joseph Standing Bear). Again, why? In part, this normalization and balance in leadership may be due to the educational work of older women decades before. Their children are the current generation of educated community members, and many are engaged in community work and community organizations.

It is clear that leadership and community organizations are not always associated. Although women in the Chicago Indian community have been de facto leaders throughout the history of the community, and indeed, in the very establishment of the community, they have not always occupied official positions in community organizations. The balance in official positions has shifted now toward a basic balance in gender. However, if economics and adjustment to employment and income issues contribute significantly to the regularization of leadership in terms of gender today, we must predict that men will now begin to disappear again from official positions of leadership in community organizations. They will return to jobs that allow them to support their families, while women once again step in to keep things going in the community.

Notes

1 David Beck, "The Chicago American Indian Community," in *Native Chicago*, ed. Terry Straus and Grant P. Arndt (Master of Arts Program in Social Sciences, University of Chicago; Chicago: McNaughton and Gunn, 1998), 171.

2 Beck, "Chicago American Indian Community," 172.

3 Willard LaMere, "History of Indians in Chicago," October 16, 1979, transcript of audio tape recording at NAES College Tribal Research Center.

4 Grant Arndt, "'Contrary to Our Way of Thinking': The Struggle for an American Indian Center in Chicago, 1946–1953," *American Indian Culture and Research Journal* 22:4 (1998): 120.

5 Joane Nagel, *American Indian Ethnic Renewal: Red Power and the Resurgence of Identity and Culture* (New York: Oxford University Press, 1996), 118.

6 Vine Deloria, qtd. in Nagel, *American Indian Ethnic Renewal*, 132.

3 Indigenous Agendas and Activist Genders

Chicago's American Indian Center,
Social Welfare, and Native American
Women's Urban Leadership

GRANT ARNDT

In their survey of the gender dynamics of Chicago's Native American community organizations, Anne Terry Straus and Debra Valentino discovered that although Native American women made important contributions to Native American life in the city from the earliest years of the community, men tended to occupy most visible leadership positions until the 1960s. At that point, however, Native women began to take on more prominent roles in community endeavors, leading to a balanced ratio of men and women in leadership positions by the late 1970s. Then "an interesting shift" in the late 1980s led to a remarkable situation in which "every one of the more than fifteen existing organizations . . . was run by a woman."[1] Straus and Valentino argue that Native American women exercised invisible leadership throughout the community's history, and this invisible leadership was a reflection of traditional gender roles in Native societies. They suggest that Native American women rose to prominence beginning in the 1960s because of the emergence of the need for a "different kind of leadership" requiring advanced educational credentials.[2]

In this chapter I seek to expand our understanding of the gendered nature of Native American activism and institutional development in Chicago by arguing that a key development facilitating the eventual predominance of women in the leadership of Native American community organizations beginning in the 1960s was the development of a new vision of Native American activism organized around the idea of "social welfare." This chapter examines conjuncture between urban Indian activists and the structures and institutions of American urban industrial society in the early history of Chicago's American Indian Center (AIC), the city's first permanent Native-run institution and "a model for later urban Indian community organizations."[3] The Center's Native leaders and members initially rejected the introduction of social service programming at the Center but eventually modified their conception of appropriate forms of urban activism as a result of an extended dialogue with representatives of Chicago's social welfare agencies. The Center's leaders appropriated some of the conceptual framework of social welfare work as a means of obtaining the philanthropic funding necessary to the long-term survival of the Center. In the late 1950s they made the AIC into a social center much like other such centers in the city, but run by Native people for a Native clientele. I argue that these developments in the 1950s created expanded opportunities for Native women to take on leadership roles in the city in subsequent decades because social welfare work was conceived as innately connected with women's concerns and values. Indian institutions focused primarily on social welfare functions became a new arena within which Native American women could exercise community leadership and assert activist identities.

One goal of this chapter is to change the way in which we conceptualize the relationship between gender and activism. Straus and Valentino argue that Native American women's leadership roles in Chicago reflect traditional "tribal norms."[4] In this they agree with Nancy Shoemaker, who has argued, "Indian women's visibility and activism in contemporary politics and social programs can be viewed as a continuation of their traditional roles as important decision-makers within the family."[5] But ideas about gender roles are not static or timeless, and numerous studies have shown the creative ways in which Native American peoples, women and men, have adapted traditional gender roles in response to the transformation of indigenous life over the past centuries.[6] Indigenous agendas in the city and elsewhere require activist ideas about gender roles, because gender roles, whether conceived as traditional or modern, are one set of concepts used by Native people to give meaning to their engagement with present political and social projects.

Starting from this activist perspective on gender roles, my argument looks at the appropriation of a "gendered institution" drawn from the repertoire of the dominant society and examines its subsequent impact on the performance of gendered activist identities in Chicago. The concept of the gendered institution is meant to draw attention to the ways in which occupations, functions, and certain conceptual domains can be conceived as "ideologically and symbolically" reflecting the qualities associated with a particular gender.[7] This process is often (but not inevitably) accompanied by imbalances in the relative representation of gendered individuals within the institution or occupation.[8] Social welfare is a key example of such a gendered institution. As a distinctly modern approach to the problem of need, social welfare emerged in the late nineteenth century and endured in the twentieth century as an institutional framework for careers and concepts associated with women and "the feminine." In fact, as Denise Riley and others have argued, the modern concept of the "social" emerged as a gendered concept differentiated from the masculine concerns of the political and economic spheres during the same period that saw the differentiation of "separate spheres" for men and women following the decline of the earlier household economy and the rise of an industrial, wage-labor-based economy. In the realm of the social, women were understood to "exercise moral influence and insure national virtue and social order" through their roles as wives and mothers. There developed a "cult of true womanhood," in which motherhood became women's vocation, a calling "that if performed knowledgably and faithfully represented the culmination of a woman's life" and allowed women to act as "the perfect counterpoint to materialistic and competitive man, whose strength and rationality suited him for the rough and violent public world" of politics and business.[9] The social reform agenda at the foundation of the emergence of modern American social welfare institutions was originally understood to reflect the specific values of women and was described as a form of "municipal housekeeping," "a special function in developing the welfare of humanity which man cannot perform."[10] Women used this sense of their special mission and qualities to create institutions in which they could exercise power in American society. Although men often attained prestigious positions in the social sciences and social service institutions, social welfare work, whether volunteer or professional, was one of relatively few institutions in which women tended to be predominant.[11]

The rise of social welfare work at Chicago's American Indian Center offers a case study of some challenges facing Native American activists in cities. Urban life created new challenges for Native American individuals and families, calling for experimentation with new activities. Activism thus required that those who wished to be Native activists give meaning to these innovative urban activities, in part by differentiating Indian and non-Indian values, in order to determine a course of action and coordinate their collective actions. One way they gave their actions meaning was through the extension of ideas about traditional values and gender roles. Such projections of meaning helped them define an urban Indian agenda and develop their own activist identities.[12]

The Creation of the American Indian Center

Native American activists worked to create new organizations for Chicago's growing American Indian population in the years following World War II. Willard LaMere (Ho-Chunk), Scott Thundercloud (Odawa), and Benjamin Bearskin (Ho-Chunk/Dakota), founded the North American Indian Council (NAIC) in 1946, a group that existed through 1947. Al Cobe (Chippewa), an employee of the

YMCA, founded the Indians' Service League in 1949, and Meriville Powless and Cleo LaPearl organized the American Indian Lodge, which met at Hull House. Most of these groups focused mainly on social and cultural activities, although the founders of the NAIC had hoped to offer food, alcohol counseling, and job placement services. Independent Indian organizations like the NAIC faced formidable obstacles in the city. Urban organizations required adequate financial resources to allow them to rent meeting places and to provide for individual members of the community who found themselves temporarily unemployed or otherwise in need. Such resources were most readily available through the city's existing social welfare institutions. In retrospect, it seems obvious that what was needed was an organization controlled by Native people but able to draw upon the financial support of existing social welfare agencies. But American Indian residents of the city were reluctant to associate themselves with white institutions and preferred to socialize where they would be free from white interference.[13]

Indian activists in Chicago had good reason to be suspicious of social welfare institutions. Social welfare work is something more than merely a modern equivalent of traditional strategies for addressing human needs. Modern social welfare provisions have emerged alongside market-based industrial society and have been shaped by its characteristic roles and systematic conflicts. Most academic approaches to urbanization in the 1940s and 1950s tended to treat cities as quasi-natural environments to which individuals and groups needed to adapt themselves.[14] This conception of urban life and industrial production led scholars to perceive recurrent challenges facing workers in cities like Chicago as symptoms of a failure to adapt. They thus became the ideal subjects for social welfare work that often tended to conceptualize recipients of aid as in some sense deviant, assigning the blame for poverty, hunger, and unemployment to individuals conceived as ignorant, maladjusted, unhealthy, or otherwise deviant, but capable of being changed.[15] From the perspective of social welfare institutions, the problems facing Native

Americans in Chicago tended to be explained as a result of their lack of adjustment to the values and norms of urban life, leading to the enduring image of Native Americans in cities as "maladjusted Indians." Because social welfare workers generally conceived Indian identity and community as obstacles to proper adjustment to the city, they were reluctant to support independent urban organizations for Indians.[16]

Years of dialogue between Native American activists and social service institutions in Chicago were required to create a shared vision of an officially recognized (and funded) urban Indian organization. The dialogue was initiated in 1949 by a young Lakota woman named Theresa Robbins. Robbins approached representatives of the Welfare Council with the idea of creating an organization for Chicago's Native American residents. As she explained, she hoped to bring "some Indian people together in an organization *of their own* to try to counteract some of the bad influences they are under in Chicago, and also to gradually reduce the suspicion that this group holds toward 'white people' and white institutions" (emphasis in original). Robbins worked with Lucy Carner of the Welfare Council's division of education and recreation to create the American Indian Welfare Council (AIWC) for "those who desire to participate in the solution of welfare problems arising among American Indians of Chicago and nearby areas." Robbins had difficulty convincing other Native people to participate in an organization so closely aligned with non-Indian institutions, and when she proposed the creation of a small Indian center near downtown Chicago, the non-Indian members of the AIWC rejected the idea, feeling that it would obstruct Native American assimilation into urban life.[17]

The idea of an Indian center in Chicago was revived in 1952 by another group of Native activists who worked with many of the institutions and some of the same individuals who had been part of the AIWC to create Chicago's American Indian Center, which opened in the fall of 1953. While the American Indian Center was the realization of a longstanding goal for Native American activists, it was also in part a response to the needs of the Bureau of Indian Affairs (BIA) and the federal government's "Voluntary Relocation Program." A pilot Relocation Program field office opened in Chicago in November of 1951 to prepare the way for the first wave of relocatees in February of 1952.[18] By that time the relocation office staff had been convinced by discussions with Native American activists including Al Cobe that it would be necessary to encourage the creation of some sort of Native American institution that would help provide social support for relocatees to convince them to remain in the city. As they explained in a report to BIA headquarters, they felt that an Indian center would be instrumental in "helping newcomers acquire a sense of belonging [in the city and] facilitating the process of community integration."[19] The preamble to the AIC constitution, written in the fall of 1953 and adopted in October of 1953, called for the Center "to stimulate the natural integration of American Indians into the community life of Metropolitan Chicago [and] to foster the economic and educational advancement of Indian people," but also "to preserve and foster arts and crafts and Indian cultural values."[20]

There were attempts during the Center's early history to introduce social service programming. The Center's first full-time staff member, Ted White (Sioux/Oneida), had a graduate degree in social work and attempted to introduce social welfare interventions into the Center's program. The Center also offered cooking and sewing classes, and White presented educational films on topics including venereal disease and dating techniques, followed by group discussions. Yet the AIC membership resisted such programming and instead flocked to social activities held at the Center by the American Indian Club and other community groups. White left the Center in 1955 after fifteen months on the job, and those who took his place did not try to revive the failed programs. Although Center members resisted formal social welfare programming, there was much informal social work done at the Center, both by the Center's board and staff and by members as they sought to assist those in need find houses, jobs, and other forms of basic assistance.[21]

In this early period the Center's board articulated a highly politicized sense of the Center's mission as a Native-run organization.
In 1954 they issued a press release describing their vision of urban
Indian identity, the "Cosmopolitan Indian," and dedicating their
work at the Center "to the memory of our once great glory and heritage even ever more to stimulate our anticipation of new glory and
greater accomplishments through our Center." They envisioned the
Center as an instrument through which Indian people in Chicago,
"as free men and women—like any other American citizens," could
come to exercise political power, arguing that while "Chiefs count
for little nowadays," they hoped that "our Center will soon wield the
Sovereign Power to be recognized among the best."[22] Although the
idea of a pan-tribal urban organization wielding "sovereign power"
seems to conflict with the emphasis on tribal sovereignty in subsequent Native American politics, the statement demonstrates the
politicized vision of Native American activists in the period.[23]

Although the AIC offered minimal programming in this period,
and its board and members attempted to remain relatively self-
sufficient and autonomous, the Center's survival was perpetually
threatened by almost constant budget crises that made it difficult
to pay rent and basic utilities. The Center's board recognized their
need for an ongoing source of funding. Even though the Bureau of
Indian Affairs relied on the Center as a support for their relocatees,
they offered no financial support. The Center's board first sought
funding from the Welfare Council in October of 1953, only to be
informed that the Indian center was "contrary" to the Welfare Council's vision of a proper social service agency. The Center persisted,
and in September of 1954 the Welfare Council invited the board to
work toward membership in the Council, a form of official recognition that would open the way to receiving funding from the central
source of philanthropic money in the city, the Community Fund.[24]

During its early years of operation the AIC acted as a political
platform and representative body for Native people in Chicago.
While they attempted to create a space of autonomy in the city, and

even to act as a gatekeeper for the community in its dealings with researchers, the Center's leaders were most effective at providing a public platform for indigenous activists in the city.[25] These activists used their platform to challenge many of the dominant ideas about Native American culture, and the AIC became one of the key sites for critiques of the BIA's Relocation Program. At one such public meeting in 1957, the acting director of the Center, Thomas Segundo (Papago/Tohono-O'odham), argued:

> When Indians are accused of living in the past [by advocates of relocation and assimilation], it is a misunderstanding and a misstatement . . . they are simply holding on to the tribal culture. . . . It seems to me that we did fine for 10,000 years until this foreign culture entered. I thought tribal life and the things we learned had a lot to give our people and other people who came to these shores.

At the same meeting Robert Thomas (Cherokee) of the University of Chicago outlined the Center's basic critique of the ideology of the maladjusted Indian, arguing that they did not object to reading accounts of the poverty they faced and the "indignity Indians have to suffer by having their every action controlled by a federal bureau," but they did object to the implication that "there was something basically wrong with this way of life." They argued that contemporary Native people "have something to lose, a distinct way of life, and little to gain by complete integration."[26]

For several years the Center was able to make do without official recognition from the Welfare Council and Community Fund, supporting itself with the proceeds of powwows and other cultural events and with occasional small grants from local organizations. By 1956, however, the Center's militant stance had resulted in a break in its already tense relationship with the Chicago Relocation Office, as well as other social welfare agencies. Rumors were spread that the Center was "dominated by Communists," making fundraising all but impossible. In the midst of this crisis the Center made a renewed effort to appeal to the Welfare Council, writing that they had become "increasingly aware of the problems of adjustment facing American Indians living in Chicago" and drawing attention to the "problem of communication" between existing social service agencies and Chicago's Native residents. They argued that the AIC could be the site where "contact is made" and where newly relocated Indians could find initial security in the city, if only the Center was not "handicapped" by its lack of trained personnel and an adequate budget. The appeal led the Welfare Council to assign Elaine Switzer, the associate executive secretary of the division of education and recreation, to assess the Center and consult with its leaders on the changes necessary to earn the Welfare Council's approval.[27]

Switzer reported after her first visit to the Center that there was still a great deal of resistance to social welfare programming among the Center's members and leadership. She described the AIC program as mainly focusing on offering an "open house" for "the Indian who wants to just drop in and lounge around or use equipment," and that the only really organized activities were the Saturday night powwows (or "Indian ceremonial activity"), which regularly attracted 125 to 200 participants. She complained that the Center's staff did little formal programming and spent most of their time in individual consultations with "Indians who are having problems in living in the big city."[28] Switzer debated the Center's mission and program with its leadership throughout 1957. The board consistently emphasized the Center's uniqueness as "the only agency that represents American Indians or Indian viewpoints . . . we are not only a social agency, but a group of Indian people working with Indian people, Indian people making their own organization for their own purposes and for the help of their own people." They argued "in many instances those who tried to work with Indian problems, but who did not have sufficient understanding were often themselves the greatest stumbling block to the solution of those problems."[29] Such arguments, combined with the board's willingness to discuss social welfare work, led the Community Fund to allocate to the AIC just under $5,000 in 1957, with half the funding contingent on the Center's success in meeting the conditions set by the Community Fund, including the creation of a "proper" program of social services, and Elaine Switzer reported that "the agency . . . seems to be settling down to a clearly defined function" centered on social work.[30] In 1958 Switzer remarked on the apparent sea change in the Center's relationship to social welfare institutions. In a report she recalled that when she first visited the Center, "the Board . . . had great resistance to using welfare services and professional consultation," and "considerable resistance toward the acceptance of a white person, a professional and a person from a welfare agency with authority in the city," but that "during the course of two years, this attitude has changed so that [they now] "desire to become a part of the welfare pattern in Chicago."[31]

By 1958 social service work had become such a core part of the Center's mission that it led to an internal debate concerning the proper standards to be followed by the Center board and staff.[32] The Center's small staff—a director, secretary, and non-Indian caseworker—argued that the board had become involved in the operation of the Center "to the detriment of professional standards and with resultant harm to individuals and families." The board in turn accused the staff of acting unprofessionally in their management of the Center and spending too much time on casework services and not enough on recreational programming. The conflict eventually resulted in the resignation of the staff, including director Thomas Segundo. In their letter of resignation the staff called for the board to institute a "code of personal practices in accordance with the standards recommended by the National Federation of Settlement and Neighborhood Centers and by the National Association of Social workers." Switzer reported that afterward the board had told her that the conflict had convinced them of the need to create a more professional relationship with the staff in the future.[33]

The Center weathered the controversy and in June of 1959 was finally accepted for membership in the Welfare Council. The board announced the acceptance of their application for membership in the Welfare Council with an editorial in the *Warrior*, explaining that the Center

> is like a great many other social agencies in many ways. We have a program of recreation which we try to match to the interests and needs of our membership and of all Indians in Chicagoland that we can serve. We have an educational part of our program to try and provide opportunities for those who have an interest in learning about some particular activity or in getting some special skill. We have a welfare program in which we try our best to provide emergency assistance when this is needed, to aid those who need help of any kind to get to the best place in Chicago to get it. In all these things our program is much like many others. But in one very important way, our Center is different. Although we do provide programs, we are the ones who take part in the program that we provide! Our Center is operated by its membership. And this is our "big" program and our Center is an agency of dignity and importance, taking its place with other agencies in its Chicagoland community.[34]

In the years that followed, the American Indian Center began to offer counseling services for individuals and families in need, tutoring programs, and also job placement. It continued to host regular powwows and cultural activities and developed an array of social programs for children and youth.[35]

Through the Center's dialogue with the Welfare Council, Native activists in Chicago had appropriated social welfare work as a means of ensuring indigenous agency in the city. They also convinced the social welfare community (as represented by Elaine Switzer) that Native American identities and cultural activities were not incompatible with life in the city.[36] The American Indian Center had created an institutional framework in which it was possible to simultaneously work for American Indian welfare and for Native American community.

From the Appropriation of Social Welfare to the Expansion of Opportunities for Native American Women

The appropriation of social welfare work as an acceptable form of Native American activism at the American Indian Center created new institutional opportunities for women's leadership in Chicago. When new community organizations were created "to enhance and complement the work of the Chicago Indian Center," Straus and Valentino found that "women had a more public presence and occupied more official positions of authority than previously."[37] A new generation of Native American activists came to Chicago following their experience in other forms of Native American activism, and they often possessed advanced educational credentials that allowed them to excel in the new era of increased funding and institutional diversification. But the acceptance of social welfare work as a mode of Native American urban activism also created opportunities for women with no previous activist experience or prior advanced education. Amy Leicher Skenandore, the first Native American director of Chicago's St. Augustine Center, was one such woman. She arrived in Chicago in 1958 with her construction worker husband. At the American Indian Center she met Episcopalian priest Father Peter J. Powell, who founded the St. Augustine Center in 1962. Skenandore started to volunteer at St. Augustine's as soon as it opened, eventually becoming a staff member and running the Center's food and clothing distribution program. She trained to be a social service caseworker, and in 1972, when Powell stepped down to allow for Native American leadership, Skenandore assumed the directorship. At the time the St. Augustine Center was the "largest Native American run casework agency in the nation" and served 1,200 families. Under her leadership St. Augustine's programming expanded to include a new alcohol treatment center, new cultural programs, and a food program based on Native American food preferences. She described "St. Augustine's counseling work as rooted in a Native American emphasis on the sharing of talents and skills as well as on material aid," and she made sure that all of St. Augustine's caseworkers were Native Americans, explaining that "our people relate better to Indian counselors . . . with a white counselor they are likely to clam up." Skenandore also described her leadership at St. Augustine's as an expression of her identity as a Native American woman, explaining that she had learned "what it meant to be an Indian" through her involvement with the Center.[38]

The American Indian Women's Leadership Development Project, a community initiative from the 1980s described by Straus and Valentino, provides another example of the way Native American women in Chicago developed an empowering sense of urban activism as an expression of their indigenous identities. At the Leadership Development Project, Native women in Chicago "shared and brought back a vision of traditional balance in understanding that . . . [a] growing number of women's voices were needed to bring back accountability and quality services within our organizations." The idea that urban activism was consistent with women's traditional roles and responsibilities allowed the women involved with the project to call for "women to step into these roles of leadership," providing powerful support for the increase in women's leadership in Chicago during in the 1990s.[39] This is an active use of ideas about gender roles and shows how ideas about gender can be activist even when gender roles are conceived as "traditional."

Additional support for the idea that the gendered character of social welfare work empowered Native American women as activists and leaders comes from the history of Native American organizations prior to the American Indian Center. During the period from 1949 to 1953 the groups discussing Native life in the city were all gender balanced or had more women than men as participants. The Citizen's Committee assembled by the Welfare Council in 1953 to assist in the planning of the Center was also gender balanced. Even the early leadership of the American Indian Club, the organization that formed the foundation for the American Indian Center community, was gender balanced, although men held the key leadership positions. Only with the creation of the first American Indian Center Board, which had only one female officer (as secretary) and a single female board member, did women seem to disappear from leadership positions.[40]

When I initially began to examine the role of gender in the early history of the AIC, the contrast between the absence of women on the AIC Board and the fact that a woman (Elaine Switzer) represented the Welfare Council seemed to me to be the product of divergent understandings of the nature of the American Indian Center in the context of broadly shared ideas about gender roles. My initial hypothesis was that if Switzer's role as the Center's interlocutor with the Welfare Council reflected the feminine nature of social welfare work as a gendered institution, the predominance of men in the leadership of the Center during this period could be seen as a reflection of the political nature of the AIC as conceived by its Native leaders and their acceptance of the conventional coding of the political as a masculine domain. I have found, however, no evidence that the form of activism conducted by the leaders of the AIC was ever explicitly conceived as masculine even when it was at its most political. Key documents produced by the Center during the period are deliberately gender inclusive in their language, referring to "American Indian men and women."[41] In its role as a political platform for Native people in Chicago, the AIC allowed both men and women to voice their concerns and opinions.[42] And when most of the indigenous members of the Center board were unable to attend meetings at the Welfare Council in 1956, they sent a number of women to represent the Center.[43] Although there are reports from the period of domestic tensions over women's autonomous participation in community activities, the Center's leaders never (to my knowledge) argued that either activism or leadership were male prerogatives.[44] It would be most accurate to describe activism and leadership in the early history of the American Indian Center (and in Chicago's Native community more generally) as tending to reflect contemporary ideas about gender roles within the local

Native community that seem to have been generally similar to those of the rest of American society. Gender roles do not seem to have been an overt ideological concern of Native activists in the 1950s. Both women and men engaged in urban activism, and there is little evidence of indigenous arguments for distinct forms of Native American women's and men's activism.

Conclusion

The development of Chicago's American Indian Center as a social welfare agency in the 1950s created new ways of thinking about activism that shaped the development of Native American institutions in Chicago in subsequent decades. David Beck's recent overview of the development of Native American community organizations in Chicago identifies the creation of the American Indian Center as a milestone in "the development of self-determination for the Chicago Indian community in the twentieth century." The American Indian Center provided "a platform for community members to develop a voice to speak out on behalf of community needs and became the social and social service center of the community."[45] It was not inevitable that social welfare work would become accepted and valorized within Chicago's Native American community, although it was perhaps an overdetermined option given the challenges of life in the city. The acceptance of social welfare work as an appropriate form of Indian activism provided the foundation for the extension of ideas about the gendered division of labor traditional to Native American societies to such work.

The traditional association of women with care for families, communities, and social welfare has long been both a source of pride and frustration for feminist scholars and activists. The study of Native American urban life would benefit from engaging with existing discussions of the complex and often contradictory impact of social welfare work on women in order to better understand the political implications of various practical decisions about the nature of urban Indian activism. I close, however, by simply reiterating the more basic historical argument of this chapter: just as middle-class white American women transformed their separate sphere into a platform for activism in the late nineteenth and early twentieth centuries, Native women have used Native social welfare institutions as arenas within which they can exercise community leadership. Thus, despite their absence from formal leadership roles during the process, the development of Chicago's American Indian Center into a social welfare agency in the 1950s constituted a key moment in the history of Native American women's activism in Chicago because it helped create a framework within which Native women could seek to expand their leadership in subsequent decades. They did so through the active use of ideas about the meaning of their identities as Native American women.

Notes

1 Anne Terry Straus and Debra Valentino, "Gender and Community Organization Leadership in the Chicago Indian Community," *American Indian Quarterly* 27:3 (Summer 2003): 523–32, 529. The article is reprinted as chapter 2 of this book.

2 Straus and Valentino, "Gender and Community Organization," (this volume) 29.

3 Straus and Valentino, "Gender and Community Organization," (this volume) 22.

4 Straus and Valentino, "Gender and Community Organization," (this volume) 27.

5 Nancy Shoemaker, ed., *Negotiators of Change: Historical Perspectives on Native American Women* (New York: Routledge, 1995), 12.

6 See, for example, Patricia Albers, "Sioux Women in Transition: A Study of Their Changing Status in Domestic and Capitalist Sectors of Production," in *The Hidden Half: Studies of Plains Indian Woman,* ed. Patricia Albers and Beatrice Medicine (Boston: University Press of America, 1983), 175–236; Lucy Murphy, "Autonomy and the Economic Roles of Indian Women of the Fox-Wisconsin Riverway Region, 1763–1832," in Shoemaker, *Negotiators of Change.*

7 Dana M. Britton, "The Epistemology of the Gendered Organization," *Gender and Society* 14:3 (June 2000): 418–34, quote on 426; Joan Acker, "From

Sex Roles to Gendered Institutions," *Contemporary Sociology* 21:5 (September 1992): 565–69.

8 Britton, "Epistemology of the Gendered Organization," 424.

9 Denise Riley, *Am I That Name? Feminism and the Category of "Women" in History* (Minneapolis: University of Minnesota Press, 1988); Paula Baker, "The Domestication of Politics: Women and American Political Society, 1780–1920," *American Historical Review* 89:3 (June 1984): 620–47, reprinted in *Women, the State, and Welfare*, ed. Linda Gordon (Madison: University of Wisconsin Press, 1990), 55–91. On true womanhood, see Barbara Welter, "The Cult of True Womanhood: 1820–1860," *American Quarterly* 18:2, pt. 1 (Summer 1966): 151–74. For recent discussion of the concept, see Mary Louise Roberts, "True Womanhood Revisited," *Journal of Women's History* 14:1 (Spring 2002): 150–55. There is a large critical literature on the rise of separate gender spheres. See, for example, the readings collected in Joan B. Landes, ed., *Feminism, the Public and the Private* (New York: Oxford University Press, 1998); Joan B. Landes, "Further Thoughts on the Public/Private Distinction" *Journal of Women's History* 15:2 (Summer 2003): 28–39. For early critiques of the idea that separate gender spheres are a reflection of biology or tradition rather than history and power, see Mona Etienne and Eleanor Leacock, eds., *Women and Colonization: Anthropological Perspectives* (New York: Bergin and Garvey, 1980).

10 Theda Skocpol, *Protecting Soldiers and Mothers: The Political Origins of Social Policy in the United States* (Cambridge MA: Harvard University Press, 1992) 331–32; Gwendolyn Mink, "The Lady and The Tramp: Gender, Race, and the Origins of the American Welfare State," in Gordon, *Women, the State, and Welfare*, 102. See also Linda Gordon, *Pitied but Not Entitled: Single Mothers and the History of Welfare* (New York: Free Press, 1994), and the articles collected in Gordon, *Women, the State, and Welfare*.

11 Robin Muncy, *Creating a Woman's Dominion in American Reform, 1890–1935* (Oxford: Oxford University Press, 1991). See also Gordon, *Women, the State, and Welfare*.

12 In invoking the idea of differentiation, I have in mind work by Susan Gal, Judith Irvine, and others: for a recent discussion, see Susan Gal, "A Semiotics of the Public/Private Distinction," *Differences: A Journal of Feminist Cultural Studies* 13:1 (Spring 2002): 77–95. On the extension of meaning to novel activities as a basis for understanding the historical life of cultural structures, see Marshall Sahlins, *Islands of History* (Chicago: University of Chicago Press, 1985), vii–xvii.

13 On the NAIC, see "War Drums on Halsted Street," *Chicago Sun Times*, November 18, 1947. See also Janusz Mucha, "From Prairie to the City: Transformation of Chicago's American Indian Community," *Urban Anthropology* 12 (Fall/Winter 1982): 345.

14 For discussions and critiques of theories representing the city as a natural environment, see Ira Katznelson, *Marxism and the City* (Oxford: Oxford University Press, 1992); Mark Gottdeiner, *The Social Production of Urban Space*, 2nd ed. (Austin: University of Texas Press, 1994).

15 For a sophisticated discussion of this mode of "liberal governance," see Barbara Cruikshank, *The Will to Empower: Democratic Citizens and Other Subjects* (Ithaca NY: Cornell University Press, 1999), 39–54. For the idea of social welfare as a mode of social control and regulation, see Francis Fox Piven and Richard Cloward, *Regulating the Poor: The Functions of Public Welfare* (New York: Vintage Books, 1971).

16 When the Chicago Field Office reported that only 205 of the 556 individuals they had relocated were still in the city at the end of the program's first year, they listed "maladjustment" as the main reason for relocatees leaving the city (Chicago Relocation Office, Bureau of Indian Affairs, National Archives, Chicago, RG 75). See Wade B. Arends, "A Socio-Cultural Study of the Relocated American Indians in Chicago" (MA thesis, Division of the Social Sciences, University of Chicago, 1958), for a study of relocated persons in Chicago that documents the many non-"adjustment"-related challenges facing Native people.

17 "Letter to Files from Lucy Carner. Re: Conference on American Indians in Chicago with Teresa Robbins," December 8, 1949, Chicago Historical Society, Archives and Manuscripts, Papers of the Metropolitan Welfare Council, Box 146, Folder 1.

18 James LaGrand, *Indian Metropolis: Native Americans in Chicago, 1945–75* (Urbana: University of Illinois Press, 2002), 53.

19 March 1953 Narrative Report; in Files, Chicago Relocation Office, Bureau of Indian Affairs, RG 75, National Archives, Great Lakes Branch, Chicago.

20 Constitution of the American Indian Center; in Files, Chicago Relocation Office, Bureau of Indian Affairs, RG 75, National Archives, Great Lakes Branch, Chicago.

21 April Narrative Report; in Files, Chicago Relocation Office, Bureau of Indian Affairs, RG 75, April 1954, National Archives, Great Lakes Branch, Chicago.

22 "Cosmopolitan Indian Not Cigar Store"; in Files, Chicago Relocation Office,

Bureau of Indian Affairs, RG 75, March 1954, National Archives, Great Lakes Branch, Chicago.

23 Heather Howard pointed out the problems with the use of sovereignty in the "Cosmopolitan Indian" (personal communication, 1997). There is much work to be done on the impact on urban forms of politics of the subsequent rise of the "treaty ideology" as the central articulating concern of Native American politics. See Nancy Oestreich Lurie, "The Contemporary American Indian Scene," in *North American Indians in Historical Perspective*, ed. Eleanor Burke Leacock and Nancy Oestreich Lurie (New York: Random House, 1971).

24 Grant Arndt, "Contrary to Our Way of Thinking: The Struggle for an American Indian Center in Chicago, 1946–1953," *American Indian Culture and Research Journal* 22:4 (1998): 117–34.

25 Arends, "Socio-Cultural Study."

26 Fletcher Martin, "Indian Protest Portrait of Misery," *Chicago Sun-Times*, May 19, 1957.

27 Arends, "Socio-Cultural Study," 95, n. 16; American Indian Center (AIC), "Letter to Frank Keller," April 23, 1956, Community Fund Papers, Special Collections, University of Illinois at Chicago, Box 53, Folder 5.

28 Elaine Switzer, Service Report on the American Indian Center, April 30, 1956, Community Fund Papers, Special Collections, University of Illinois at Chicago, Box 76, Folder 9.

29 Minutes of the Meeting of the Board of Directors, AIC, 30 November 1956, Community Fund Papers, Special Collections, University of Illinois at Chicago, Box 53, Folder 5.

30 "Minutes of the Meeting of the Specialized Services Reviewing Committee," December 5, 1956, Community Fund Papers, Special Collections, University of Illinois at Chicago, Box 53, Folder 5; Elaine Switzer, "Conditions for Follow-up by the Welfare Council and Community Fund for 1957," Specialized Services reviewing committee, April 2, 1957, Welfare Council Papers, Chicago Historical Society, Box 246, Folder 13.

31 Elaine Switzer. Log entry for September 10, 1958, Welfare Council Papers, Chicago Historical Society, Box 246, Folder 13.

32 Switzer log for September 27, 1957, Welfare Council Papers, Chicago Historical Society, Box 246, Folder 13.

33 Thomas Segundo et al. to Benjamin Bearskin, Chairman, September 4, 1958, Welfare Council Papers, Chicago Historical Society, Attachment to Elaine Switzer log for September 10, 1958.

34 *Chicago Warrior*, March 25, 1959.

35 David R. M. Beck. "Developing a Voice: The Evolution of Self-Determination in an Urban Indian Community," *Wicazo Sa Review* 17:2 (Autumn 2002): 117–41.

36 In June 1958 Switzer attended a party at the American Indian Center and noted in her log that "the party was lovely with Indian dancing which . . . interests me because of the almost trance-like expression as the dance progresses . . . .I ate fry bread and Indian corn soup for the first time." Elaine Switzer, Log Entry for June 16–20, 1958, Welfare Council Papers, Chicago Historical Society, Box 246, Folder 13.

37 Straus and Valentino, "Gender and Community Organization," (this volume) 29–30.

38 The information in this paragraph is from Grant Arndt, "Amy Leicher Skenandore," in *Women Building Chicago, 1790–1990: A Biographical Dictionary*, ed. Rima Lunin Schultz and Adele Hast (Bloomington: Indiana University Press, 2001).

39 Straus and Valentino, "Gender and Community Organization," (this volume) 31.

40 For early groups, I am thinking in particular of the AIWC: see Lucy Carner, "Minutes of a meeting regarding American Indians in Chicago," December 28, 1949, Welfare Council Papers, Chicago Historical Society, Box 146, Folder 1. See also Welfare Council meetings organized in response to relocation, such as that described in "Minutes of the Meeting with Mr. Ken Fitzgerald, Arena Placement Officer," Lucy Carner, Welfare Council Papers, Chicago Historical Society, Box 146, Folder 1. For the 1953 Citizen's Committee, see Lucy Carner, "Minutes of meeting of citizen's committee for the establishment of an All-Tribes American Indian Center," July 7, 1953, Welfare Council Papers, Chicago Historical Society, Box 146, Folder 1. On the American Indian Club, see the programs for the 1952 Halloween and Christmas Powwows, in the October and December files of the Chicago Relocation Office, Bureau of Indian Affairs, RG 75, National Archives, Great Lakes Branch, Chicago. Information on American Indian Center board membership in 1956–59 is found throughout the Welfare Council and Community Fund files cited above.

41 One example is the use of this phrase in "Cosmopolitan Indian, Not Cigar Store."

42 For example, Susan Kelly's contribution to the Center's public meeting to protest press representations of urban issues, as documented in Fletcher

Martin, "Indian Protest Portrait of Misery," *Chicago Sun-Times*, May 19, 1957.

43 The specific example I have in mind here is the December 5, 1956, meeting of the Specialized Services Reviewing Committee of the Community Fund, Community Fund papers, Box 53, Folder 5.

44 I have in mind issues at the Kenmore-Uptown Center, a relocation office created as an alternative to the American Indian Center that existed for about a year beginning in 1956. See Arends, "Socio-Cultural Study," 102.

45 Beck, "Developing a Voice," 140.

4 "Assisting Our Own"

Urban Migration, Self-Governance,
and Native Women's Organizing in
Thunder Bay, Ontario, 1972–1989

NANCY JANOVICEK

In the 1960s, settlement patterns of First Nations peoples in
Canada began to change dramatically.[1] In 1966, 80 percent of
the Aboriginal population still lived on reserve. By 1991, 49.5
percent of the Aboriginal population lived in towns and cities.[2]
Migration patterns of women and men differed; 16.4 percent
of status Indian women lived off reserve in 1966, compared
to 15.4 percent of status Indian men, a disparity that grew over
time. Twenty years later, 32.8 percent of status Indian women
lived off reserve, and only 26.4 percent of status Indian men
did so.[3] While most scholars agree that Aboriginal people have
been more likely to leave the reserve because they were pushed
away, there is a consensus that more men than women chose to
leave the reserve seeking employment or educational opportunities. Many women who left the reserve were compelled to do so
because they were fleeing violence, or because they had lost their
status and housing.[4] Despite the disparity between women's and
men's migration patterns, gender has not been central to the
analysis of the urban experience of First Nations people.

This chapter discusses how Native women in Thunder Bay,
Ontario, organized services and programs to help women adapt
to urban life in the 1970s and 1980s. It investigates the founding of Beendigen, an emergency hostel for Native women and
their children. In 1978 Thunder Bay Anishinabequek,[5] a chap-

ter of the Ontario Native Women's Association (ONWA), opened Beendigen because they believed Native women in crisis and their children, most of whom were fleeing violent families, should not be further isolated in non-Native environments. Beendigen, Ojibwa for "welcome," offered emergency shelter for women whose connection to their home reserve had been severed, and who subsequently faced hostility in the city. Anishinabequek insisted on Aboriginal control over services for Aboriginal people, and their programs emphasized cultural retention and promoted pride in indigenous culture. Thus, Beendigen organizers contested the assumption that deciding to move to the city indicated a choice to assimilate into Canadian society. Anishinabequek was part of an emerging movement that was struggling to define an urban Native identity that retained indigenous nationhood. Working in an urban context, Anishinabequek engendered a conception of Aboriginal identity that opposed the view that it could not exist off reserve. By taking control of services for Aboriginal people and basing them on Aboriginal values, and by using these services to protect indigenous identity in the city, Beendigen organizers began to develop discourses that would become the foundation of urban self-governance.

Native women's organizing in Thunder Bay developed during a dynamic period in the broader histories of the Aboriginal rights movement and the women's movement. The debates that shaped these histories simultaneously opened up spaces for Native women's organizing and constrained their political goals. To provide a context for Anishinabequek's local initiatives, I begin with a brief overview of the Indian rights movement and Native women's organizing in Canada in the late 1960s and 1970s. I then discuss the general activities of ONWA to explain why women organized independently of the Native movement. The examination of the founding of Beendigen demonstrates how Thunder Bay Anishinabequek and ONWA countered the negative impact of government policies that tried to assimilate Aboriginal peoples by organizing services that drew on Aboriginal knowledge, cultures, and values.

This research is based on the records of Beendigen and ONWA. Few documents remain from the founding years of the shelter, and there were not many direct references to family violence in the ONWA documents in the 1970s and 1980s. Thus, my interpretation of the evidence relies on oral histories with two women who were active in the founding years of ONWA and Beendigen.[6]

Citizens Plus, Citizens Minus

Pressure from Native leaders and a greater awareness of poverty on reserves had put "the Indian problem" on the national agenda in the 1960s.[7] Native leaders demanded resources from the federal government that would help them to govern their communities and preserve their special status in Canadian society. The Department of Indian Affairs (DIA) developed adult education and community mobilization programs that emphasized community empowerment, but the goal was to teach Native people skills and practices that would expedite their assimilation into Canadian society.[8] This agenda became clear in 1969 when the federal government released the *Statement of the Government of Canada on Indian Policy*, commonly known as the White Paper. Its most controversial recommendation was the termination of the Indian Act, arguing that the eradication of special rights would foster improved social, economic, and political participation in Canadian society.[9] In its response to the White Paper, entitled *Citizens Plus* and referred to as "The Red Paper," the Indian Chiefs of Alberta insisted that termination of the Indian Act would foster cultural annihilation by eroding indigenous peoples' connection to their territories.[10] Indian leaders successfully impeded the implementation of the White Paper, and the federal government agreed that no part of the Indian Act would be amended without full consultation.[11]

The defeat of the White Paper was a catalyst for the revival of Native activism in the 1970s, but Indian leaders' defense of the Indian Act curtailed women's efforts to protect their rights. The central goal of Native women's organizing was the removal of Section 12(1)(b) from the Indian Act. Under Section 12(1)(b), a woman's status was determined by marriage, not by familial association or blood. Between 1958 and 1968, 4,605 women who had married men who did not have Indian status were removed from the Indian registry.[12] Thus, Native women's claim to treaty rights was weaker than men's. Instead of women holding special status, Kathleen Jamieson asserted, the Indian Act constructed non-status Native women as "citizens minus."[13] Forceful removal from their ancestral territories mobilized Native women to lobby for the repeal of Section 12(1)(b) and the reinstatement of Native women and their children who had lost their status.[14] Between 1971 and 1981, individual Native women initiated national and international court actions to amend the Indian Act.[15] Indian Rights for Indian Women (IRIW), founded in 1971, mobilized support for legal action.[16] These cases raised public awareness but failed to repeal Section 12(1)(b).[17]

The campaign to amend the Indian Act divided Native communities. Indian leaders dismissed it as a feminist plot, arguing that a few women, influenced by the women's movement, were putting their individual needs before the collective rights of Native peoples.[18] The support of the National Action Committee on the Status of Women, a national lobby group for the Canadian women's movement, created new political opportunities for IRIW. But it must be stressed that non-status women's defense of their rights was grounded in an articulation of their identity and citizenship claims that was significantly different from the mainstream women's movement's focus on gender-based discrimination. Non-status women grounded their demand for improved rights in the injustice they had suffered as Native people and struggled for their individual rights in order to strengthen their role in the movement to restore the collective rights and pride of Aboriginal peoples.[19]

These national political battles influenced Anishinabequek's organizing in Thunder Bay. At the local level, activists drew from the broader Native women's movement to help women understand the implications of the federal legislation on their lives and to develop services that did not perpetuate the deep divisions the Indian Act had created. This was particularly important in urban contexts where the indigenous population comprised status and non-status Indians, Métis, and people of indigenous heritage who had never lived on reserve. The Native movement's insistence that services and programs for Native peoples should be based on indigenous culture and traditions also informed Thunder Bay Anishinabequek's services.

Anishinabequek, the Traditional Movement, and Urban Indigenous Identity

As the largest city in Northwestern Ontario, Thunder Bay is the regional hub and the home of branches of provincial and federal government departments. People from remote communities and smaller towns have customarily traveled to Thunder Bay for specialized medical treatment and postsecondary education. It was also the destination point for many Native people who moved there from northern reserves hoping to find employment and better living conditions. The Native population of Thunder Bay grew in the 1960s and 1970s. By 1978 an estimated seven thousand Native people lived in Thunder Bay, comprising 6.3 percent of the city's population; in 1979, 36.3 percent of Aboriginal people in the Lakehead District lived off-reserve.[20]

In response to the increasing numbers of Native people living in the city, activists founded the Thunder Bay Indian Friendship Centre as an ad hoc organization in 1964. The organization incorporated in 1968 and acquired the resources to find a permanent home in 1972. The political career of Bernice Dubec, a founding member of ONWA and Anishinabequek, began at the Friendship Centre. She remembered that the most important services the center provided were advocacy to protect Aboriginal families from being exploited by landlords and helping families who had recently arrived from the reserve adjust to urban life. Through this work Friendship Centre organizers hoped to revitalize indigenous traditions in the city's Native community. Dubec recalled:

I remember in the 1970s largely through the Friendship Centre, and different gatherings, they'd bring in elders to come and talk to the community. . . . It really hit me in my own spirit, in my own heart. This is the way we should be living. This is how we should be doing our services and our programs. We need to go back to the culture.[21]

Holistic approaches would address the colonizing practices that perpetuated poverty and social problems so that Aboriginal families could thrive in contemporary society.

In the 1970s the Native movement embraced indigenous cultures in defiance of the DIA's policy of assimilation. The movement, which focused on traditional practices that were being rapidly eroded, sustained Aboriginal cultures by organizing ceremonies, seeking out guidance from elders, and learning their languages. The traditional movement was salient particularly in urban settings where Aboriginal people were removed from elders and ceremonies. These activists created services that followed indigenous knowledge and were critical of charitable initiatives that cast white people as authorities on Native problems.[22] Returning to traditional teachings afforded expertise to Aboriginal people. Anishinabequek took up the traditional movement's emphasis on culture and control over services.

Women learned that they had specific needs that were not being addressed by the Friendship Centre, and they decided to organize autonomously because their voices were not respected. Audrey Gilbeau, raised at the Longlac 15th First Nation, became political by volunteering at the Friendship Centre where "the ladies took [her] under their wings." She recalled how watching her elders struggle to be heard in meetings taught her that Native women needed their own organizations to develop a political voice. She explained:

When I became involved with Anishinabequek and started to see, particularly the power of the women, and the strength of individual women. . . . And then listening, and also observing—I guess the struggles they had in gaining that recognition. . . . You see things that you think are part of the natural order, and even though it doesn't feel right, you just assume that this is the way it's supposed to be done. It was a great deal of education that took place for me at the time.[23]

Dubec remembered defending the need for Native women's rights to men who were skeptical about women's autonomous organizing:

They would kid you, saying you're just a bunch of women's lib-bers. . . . It was ribbing and that kind of thing. Or sometimes they would debate you. I didn't mind. I enjoyed it. I could debate with any of them. . . . But again we must have caused some fear I guess. . . . Because we were asking questions. Because we were able to debate and talk about our rights as Aboriginal people.[24]

For Dubec, defending Aboriginal rights was linked inextricably to her advocacy for Native women's rights.

Native women who had been organizing independently of each other in reserve and off-reserve communities across Ontario met in Thunder Bay in May 1972 to found the Ontario Native Women's Association. Agendas were set locally, but all chapters agreed with ONWA's principal tenet to "honour the belief of supporting the unity of all Native women, regardless of legal categories."[25] Respecting the heritage of status and non-status women was the foundation of promoting self-worth among Native women, thus enabling them to take an active role in developing programs for all women claiming indigenous heritage. In their words, these services were "status-blind." The motto, based on the organization's acronym, expressed succinctly the organization's priorities: "Our home is first; Native women speak; Working together; Assisting our own."[26] Cultural events helped Native women develop social and political networks. At these gatherings, organized by local chapters, ONWA promoted more explicitly political goals. For International Women's Year in 1975, Thunder Bay Anishinabequek organized a Native women's festival to give women the opportunity to "display their talents as homemakers and craft people" and to "get some new blood and new leadership for the local chapter."[27] Organizing combined fellowship and service provision. At social gatherings organizers learned what services women needed.

Family violence was among the issues raised at these gatherings. Gilbeau recalled that some women on reserves tried to organize alternatives for abused women, but usually women who left abusive relationships could not remain in their communities because of the lack of services on reserves. Thunder Bay offered little more. The Friendship Centre referred people to the city's services, and the Native People of Thunder Bay Development Corporation was beginning to provide subsidized housing for Native families. Despite the prevalence of violence in Aboriginal families, neither of these organizations had developed a policy for women who were abused. Gilbeau explained that apathy prevented action:

> That issue was always there. People talked about it like that was just the way it was. "Violence, oh yeah well what about this. Women are getting beaten up. Oh well." There was no passion, no sympathy. . . . Not that people were oblivious to what was going on. It was just so prevalent. It was all around you so people just chose not to get involved.[28]

Non-Aboriginal people considered violence an insurmountable problem in Native society. Sympathetic policymakers may have attributed violence to poverty and discrimination, but underlying this analysis was the belief that Native communities had resigned themselves to a violent lifestyle. This indifference to the predicaments women in abusive relationships faced was not specific to Aboriginal women. Spousal abuse was not recognized as a political issue until the women's movement began to organize shelters for battered women in the 1970s.

Founding Beendigen

Anishinabequek founded Beendigen in 1978 to provide culturally sensitive emergency shelter for Native women and their children.

They argued it was necessary because the services available in Thunder Bay were not sensitive to the specific needs of women who had just left the reserve. Some Native women from Thunder Bay stayed at Community Residences, a shelter the city opened in 1975.[29] A study on the efficacy of the service attested that Native women were quiet and withdrawn in the homes.[30] Beendigen accommodated any Native woman and her children who were in crisis but gave priority to abused women. Programs were grounded in Aboriginal values and proposed a family-centered approach to help violent families. ONWA's subsequent analysis of family violence, released in 1989, concentrated on the impact of colonization on Aboriginal families and argued that leaders could not ignore abused women because families were the foundation of traditional forms of governance and strong indigenous nations.

In February 1978 Anishinabequek received a Canada Works grant to pay for the development of a Native Women's Crisis Centre. It established a board, comprising thirteen members, and incorporated as Beendigen, Inc.[31] The Native People of Thunder Bay Development Corporation purchased a home to rent to Beendigen for a shelter and office space. The house could accommodate only one family at a time and did not meet the demand for the service. Staffing the shelter was difficult because the grant was designed to move the employees of the shelter from welfare to work and allowed for only minimum wage salaries. Because wages were low, it was difficult to recruit and retain capable staff to counsel women and to maintain the home.[32] Beendigen had also attained a substantially smaller grant to hire a fundraiser. The fundraiser took on the responsibility of running the house when the Canada Works funds were exhausted and Beendigen could no longer pay staff.[33] As was too often the case in the histories of transition houses, Beendigen was, from the beginning, in a funding crisis that threatened its future.

In their endeavor to stabilize funding, the Beendigen board members gained political experience and articulated the importance of self-governance. Dubec remembered that they lobbied many members of Parliament and government bureaucrats until they "finally hit the right one." The DIA official in Thunder Bay was not receptive to the shelter, but an official who worked at the provincial Ministry of Social Services and who had worked closely with other Native programs did support Beendigen's goals. He advised the board that if they reworked their proposal to emphasize how the shelter would prevent juvenile delinquency, they would be eligible for funding through the Ministry's Children's Services Department.[34]

The proposal, submitted to the Ministry of Social Services in 1978, focused on the impact of urbanization and colonization on Aboriginal families. It included an extensive discussion about children, explaining that many Aboriginal children's problems were linked to the increasing pace of urban migration. Families who left the reserve for a better life often adjusted to urban life with difficulty. Economic hardship exacerbated lifestyle changes. Few Native people had adequate education or job-training skills to find employment, and subsequently many lived in overcrowded housing. Poor living conditions and shattered expectations induced alcoholism, "leading to a general breakdown of family relations."[35] In cities, families lost the support network of their extended families. For abused women there were usually no family members to turn to if their relationship became violent. Isolation was not restricted to women who had recently arrived in the city. Some Thunder Bay residents moved away to escape from violent spouses, but most women wanted to stay in Thunder Bay and needed some place to go.[36]

Beendigen organizers had to defend culturally sensitive services because the provincial government was reluctant to support services that targeted particular social groups.[37] Organizers insisted that their shelter would not duplicate existing services because none of these addressed the difficulties Native families faced when they moved from the reserve to the city. Though often well intentioned, services staffed by white employees did not know how to serve Native women. At Beendigen, women did not have to explain their circumstances. Gilbeau explained,

You don't have to explain the challenges. You don't have to explain the geography. You don't have to explain the roles. You don't have to educate people as to what you're suffering. Often times, they've experienced it themselves. [White] people give you that, "poor dear." What are you gonna do with that? But they don't know any better. They just don't know.[38]

Many women from remote reserves did not speak English. Beendigen employees were able to overcome this basic barrier by providing counseling and advocacy in Cree or Ojibwa.

For Aboriginal women, an advocate who understood their cultural background was important because mainstream service intervention had broken up many Aboriginal families. Andrew Armitage submits that the transfer of responsibility of services for Aboriginal children to the provinces in the 1960s was more disruptive than the residential school system because child welfare practices terminated the relationship between First Nations children and their parents and, more often than not, separated siblings.[39] Keeping mothers and their children together was a cornerstone of Beendigen's programs. By providing shelter for single mothers who could not cope with urban life, the founders hoped to keep Native children out of the child welfare system and to protect women from the devastating impact of losing their children.[40]

Although the decision to emphasize the negative impact of child apprehension was strategic to some extent, their proposal drew on Aboriginal child-rearing practices. The proposal explained that Children's Aid policies for Native communities were the result of clashing worldviews that were based in different physical realities. Once Native people were the only people living in North America, but they now found themselves a minority who were "trying to survive intact, preserving the values and traditions of their past."[41] Indigenous lifestyles and social structures derived from the harsh realities of living in harmony with the land. Children, who were integral to the family, were expected to be independent. The materialism of

Canadian society conflicted with traditional values and encouraged continuing dependency. Children who moved from the reserve with their families lost their connection with their extended family and cultural education. The proposal acknowledged that alcoholism and violence were serious problems but added that breaking up families was also harmful because children who were placed in white homes could not develop pride in their ancestry. The shelter would "offer a kind of extended family situation, in keeping with Native culture."[42] Beendigen would provide counseling for the entire family in order to alleviate cultural dislocation and preserve Aboriginal children's sense of identity. The proposal was approved, providing Beendigen with money to open a shelter with seven beds. However, funding remained precarious throughout the 1980s.

Beendigen's catchment area was vast because it was the only shelter in Northwestern Ontario expressly for Native women. Other shelters in the region accepted Native women, but most preferred to go to Beendigen, where they received cultural support as well as safety.[43] Getting the message out to the reserves was part of Beendigen's mandate. Gilbeau remembered that convincing band councils that family violence was an important issue was difficult. Nonetheless, women learned that Beendigen would help pay for transportation costs in extremely dangerous situations. In 1982 the average occupancy rate at the shelter was 87.8 percent, and it was full in the months of March, April, and July. That year 187 families stayed at the shelter.[44]

Despite their awareness of abuse in their communities, the few documents the organizers of Beendigen kept about their founding years were relatively silent on the issue of violence. They mention family violence, but the primary rationale for the shelter was that women migrating to the city needed culturally specific services. Dubec and Gilbeau acknowledged that although they knew that abused women needed services, neither of them deemed it to be a political issue then. This had parallels in the women's movement. It was not until the 1980 publication of Linda MacLeod's national study, *Wife Battering in Canada: The Vicious Circle*, that many feminists realized the extent of spousal assault. MacLeod adopted the feminist critique of the family as an institution that perpetuated women's inequality. The report established spousal assault as an equality issue for all women.[45]

Strategies for change developed by the battered women's shelter movement influenced Native women to conceptualize family violence as a political issue, but there were significant differences between the goals of Native-run and feminist transition houses. Aboriginal women did not agree that wife abuse was fundamentally an issue of gender inequality. They also differed with the feminist criticism of the family because the family had historically offered protection from racism. Because of the importance of family in indigenous culture and governance, Native-run shelters offered programs that sought to heal all family members as well as to protect women in abusive relationships. Feminists were most concerned with protecting abused women and their children and endorsed the criminal prosecution of abusive men. In the 1980s feminists convinced governments to adopt policies that recommended the mandatory prosecution of abusers. Native women activists did not agree with this strategy because of the disproportionately high representation of Aboriginal men in the prison system.[46] By the end of the decade these differences deepened the rift between Aboriginal women and the mainstream women's movement. Patricia Monture-Okanee, a Mohawk lawyer and ONWA activist, challenged the women's movement to incorporate an analysis of race in the theorization of violence against women. Strategies to end violence against women, she argued, would not be successful in Aboriginal communities unless white women relinquished their power over the definition of violence against women.[47]

Aboriginal women were also silenced in their communities when they tried to raise the issue of family violence because Aboriginal leaders had set the entrenchment of constitutional rights and self-government as priorities. Family violence, like the campaign of

Native women against Section 12(1)(b), was deemed to be about individual rights. Leaders argued that the collective rights of Aboriginal peoples had to be secured before communities could effectively address social problems.[48] Dian Million proposes that residential school students' revelations about sexual assault created a space in which to talk about abuse in Aboriginal communities as a public issue. These discussions allowed Native women to position themselves as the foundation of healthy families and, subsequently, their nations. First Nations analysis of abuse involved both genders and explained that state and church interventions had destroyed the Aboriginal family, an institution that was the foundation of indigenous governance.[49]

Statistical evidence of the pervasiveness of violence in Native families was not available until 1989, when ONWA released *Breaking Free: A Proposal for Change to Aboriginal Family Violence*. It was the first Canadian study that focused exclusively on family violence in Aboriginal communities.[50] ONWA founded the Aboriginal Family Violence Project in 1987 to examine family violence from the perspective of Aboriginal women. The research was necessary because previous studies on family violence had subsumed Aboriginal women within the broader context of "ethnic minorities" and had presented their needs in a manner ONWA deemed to be misleading.[51] The report's frequently cited statistic that eight out of ten Aboriginal women had been abused or assaulted was shocking even to those who wrote the report. The report forced leaders to acknowledge that family violence was an issue that could no longer be ignored.

Breaking Free analyzed the issue in the context of colonizing relations. It explained that in Native communities family violence was "a reaction against an entire system of domination, lack of respect, and bureaucratic control" over every aspect of Aboriginal life and argued that family violence would not end without self-government.[52] In the short-term, it called for more Native-run shelters and second-stage housing for battered women and children and counseling services for abusive men. The report underscored the importance of restoring and strengthening the family. Protection for women and children was important but had to be part of a broader program that did not "sacrifice" abusive men's healing. These services would be effective only if they were organized according to traditional healing methods. It called for a grassroots approach in which each community would define the problem and create solutions. In urban areas women needed more culturally specific services, and ONWA demanded that the provincial and federal governments provide Aboriginal organizations funds to organize healing lodges and shelters.

Without adequate services and support systems on reserve, many women had to choose between personal safety and their home. Beendigen provided services to mitigate racism and hostility these women and children faced when they moved to Thunder Bay. Insisting on control over services for Aboriginal peoples and providing status-blind services challenged the destructive impact of federal legislation and policies on First Nations communities and families. Beendigen organizers drew on indigenous values and knowledge to preserve Aboriginal identity and helped to lay the groundwork for urban self-governance in Thunder Bay.

Conclusion

In the 1970s and 1980s Native women used the discourses of the Aboriginal rights movement and the women's movement to defend their rights as Aboriginal people. Native women played an important role in the movement through cultural retention, education, and community work. Yet Aboriginal leaders' insistence that Native women's political goals threatened the collective rights of Aboriginal peoples precluded the advancement of Native women's rights within the Aboriginal movement. This chapter has examined Native women's organizing in Thunder Bay to shed light on the important role that women played in developing discourses and practices that would become fundamental principles of urban self-governance. Gender and aboriginality produced a unique political identity that struggled to balance indigenous tradition with the new realities

Aboriginal women faced in an urban context. The central premise of Anishinabequek's services for abused women and their children and its analysis of family violence was that strengthening and restoring Aboriginal families was integral to self-government. ONWA developed a unique analysis of family violence that resisted the claim that violence against women was an individual problem that must be secondary to the collective goal of self-government.

Notes

I thank Bernice Dubec and Audrey Gilbeau for sharing their memories with me, and the Ontario Native Women's Association (ONWA) and Beendigen for granting me access to their records. This chapter is based on my doctoral research, which was supported by graduate fellowships from Simon Fraser University, the William and Ada Isabelle Steel Memorial Graduate Scholarship, and the Canadian Research Institute for the Advancement of Women Marta Danylewycz Award. Joy Parr and Marjorie Griffin Cohen supervised the dissertation and were astute critics. Hugh Shewell provided constructive commentary at the eighty-first meeting of the Canadian Historical Association. Margaret Conrad and Corrina Clement offered cogent criticisms of earlier drafts of this article.

1 The terms *First Nations* and *Aboriginal* refer to all people of indigenous ancestry and include Métis and status and non-status Indians. *Status Indian* is a legal classification determined by the Indian Act (1876) and refers to a person of indigenous ancestry who is registered with his or her band office. *Non-status Indians* are people of indigenous ancestry who were divested of their legal status by federal legislation and government policies.

2 Royal Commission on Aboriginal Peoples, *Aboriginal Peoples in Urban Centres: Report on the National Round Table on Aboriginal Issues* (Ottawa: Minister of Supply and Services, 1993); 1991 statistics from the Aboriginal Peoples Survey are cited in Evelyn Peters, "Demographics of Aboriginal People in Urban Areas," in *Aboriginal Self-Government in Urban Areas: Proceedings of a Workshop May 25 and 26, 1994*, ed. Evelyn J. Peters (Kingston ON: Institute of Intergovernmental Relations, 1995), 4.

3 Lilianne Ernestine Krosenbingk-Gelissen, "The Native Women's Association of Canada," in *Native Peoples in Canada: Contemporary Conflicts*, 5th ed., ed. James S. Frideres (Toronto: Prentice Hall, 1998), 302.

4 Peters, "Demographics of Aboriginal People," 15; Carol LaPrairie, *Seen but Not Heard: Native People in the Inner City* (Ottawa: Department of Justice, 1994), 16, 57; Allison M. Williams, "Canadian Urban Aboriginals: A Focus on Aboriginal Women in Toronto," *Canadian Journal of Native Studies* 17:1 (1997): 75–101; Anne McGillivray and Brenda Comaskey, *Black Eyes All of the Time: Intimate Violence, Aboriginal Women, and the Justice System* (Toronto: University of Toronto Press, 1999).

5 *Anishinabequek* means "woman" in Ojibwa and was a common name for ONWA locals.

6 I conducted this research in the autumn of 1999 and the summer of 2000.

7 Noel Dyck, *What Is the Indian "Problem"? Tutelage and Resistance in Canadian Indian Administration* (St. John's NF: Institute of Social and Economic Research, 1991); J. R. Miller, *Skyscrapers Hide the Heavens: A History of Indian-White Relations in Canada*, rev. ed. (Toronto: University of Toronto Press, 1991), 222–29.

8 Hugh Shewell, "'Bitterness behind Every Smiling Face': Community Development and Canada's First Nations, 1954–1968," *Canadian Historical Review* 83:1 (March 2002): 58–84.

9 Dyck, *What Is the Indian "Problem"?*, esp. chapter 7.

10 Indian Chiefs of Alberta, *Citizens Plus* (Edmonton: Indian Association of Alberta, 1970).

11 Sally M. Weaver, *Making Canadian Indian Policy: The Hidden Agenda, 1968–1970* (Toronto: University of Toronto Press, 1981).

12 *Report of the Royal Commission on the Status of Women in Canada* (Ottawa: Information Canada, 1970), 238.

13 Kathleen Jamieson, *Indian Women and the Law in Canada: Citizens Minus* (Ottawa: Canadian Advisory Council on the Status of Women, April 1978).

14 Mary Two-Axe Early, "'The Least Members of Our Society': The Mohawk Women of Caughnawaga," *Canadian Woman Studies/Les cahiers de la femme* 11:2 (1980): 64–66; Janet Silman, *Enough Is Enough: Aboriginal Women Speak Out* (Toronto: Women's Press, 1987).

15 In 1973 the Supreme Court of Canada ruled against Jeannette Corbière Lavell and Yvonne Bedard, from the Wikwemikong Reserve and Six Nations Reserve, respectively, who argued that Section 12(1)(b) was discriminatory according to the Canadian Bill of Rights (1960). Four years later, Sandra Lovelace, a Maliseet woman, filed a complaint against the Canadian government with the United Nations Human Rights Committee (UNHRC).

On July 30, 1981, the UNHRC ruled that the Canadian government was in breach of the International Covenant on Civil and Political Rights, but the government, fearing reprisal from male leaders, did not amend the Indian Act. Shirley Bear, with the Tobique Women's Collective, "'You Can't Change the Indian Act?'" in *Women and Social Change: Feminist Activism in Canada*, ed. Jeri Dawn Wine and Janice L. Ristock (Toronto: James Lorimer, 1991): 198–220.

16 Non-status Native women in Alberta founded IRIW in 1971 because the Voice of Alberta Native Women would not support legal action to amend the Indian Act. Kathleen Jamieson, "Multiple Jeopardy: The Evolution of a Native Women's Movement," *Atlantis* 4:2 (Spring 1979): 157–78.

17 The federal government finally repealed Section 12(1)(b) in 1985 when it passed Bill C-31. Though the legislation reinstated 12(1)(b) women and recognized band control over band membership, it did not meet Native women's demand for the full and equal restoration of the rights of all persons of Native heritage. For a detailed discussion of the constitutional debates, see Sally Weaver, "First Nations Women and Government Policy, 1970–1992: Discrimination and Conflict," in *Changing Patterns: Women in Canada*, ed. Sandra Burt, Lorraine Code, and Lindsay Dorney (Toronto: McClelland and Steward, 1993): 92–150. For analysis of the impact of Bill C-31 on women, see Joan Holmes, *Bill C-31: Equality or Disparity? The Effects of the New Indian Act on Native Women* (Ottawa: Canadian Advisory Council on the Status of Women, March 1987). For a discussion of the implications of Bill C-31, see Audrey Huntley and Fay Blaney, *Bill C-31: Its Impact, Implications and Recommendations for Change in British Columbia — Final Report* (Vancouver: Aboriginal Women's Action Network, December 1999).

18 Harold Cardinal, *The Revival of Canada's Indians* (Edmonton: Hurtig, 1977), 107–15. The tension between women's individual rights and Aboriginal people's collective rights remains a divisive issue. Sharon Donna McIvor, "Self-Government and Aboriginal Women," in *Scratching the Surface: Canadian Anti-Racist Feminist Thought*, ed. Enaksi Dua and Angela Robertson (Toronto: Women's Press, 1999): 167–86.

19 Barbara Freeman argues that the media played an important role in reshaping Native women's arguments in the equality of opportunity model. Barbara M. Freeman, *The Satellite Sex: The Media and Women's Issues in English Canada, 1966-1971* (Waterloo ON: Wilfrid Laurier University Press, 2001), chapter 8.

20 AO, RG 68, Series 6, box 5, file 7151-1, "Native People in Northern Ontario:

A Demographic Profile, Ministry of Northern Affairs," December 1981.

21 Author's interview with Bernice Dubec, Thunder Bay ON, July 26, 2000.

22 Harold Cardinal, *The Unjust Society: The Tragedy of Canada's Indians* (Edmonton: M. G. Hurtig, 1969), chapter 6.

23 Author's interview with Audrey Gilbeau, Thunder Bay ON, July 28, 2000.

24 Interview with Dubec.

25 ONWA Records, file: By-Laws #3 and #4, "ONWA By-Law #4, Article XXXI, Code of Ethics."

26 ONWA *Resource Manual* (Thunder Bay ON, 1981).

27 University of Ottawa Special Collections, Lisa Bengtsson Fonds, box 276, file: Thunder Bay Anishinabequek, 1975, "Evaluation of Native Women's Festival."

28 Interview with Gilbeau.

29 For a discussion of other initiatives in Thunder Bay and Northwestern Ontario, see Nancy Janovicek, "No Place to Go: Family Violence, Women's Activism and the Mixed Social Economy, Northwestern Ontario and the Kootenays, BC, 1965–1989" (PhD diss., Simon Fraser University, 2002).

30 Northern Studies Research Centre, Lakehead University, *Breaking Point: An Evaluation of Community Residences of the Thunder Bay City Social Services* (Thunder Bay ON, May 1979).

31 Beendigen Records, Fort William Reserve (hereinafter BR), file: Supplementary Letter of Patent, "Application for Incorporation," May 1978; "Beendigen Proposal for Funding," 1978.

32 Interview with Dubec; BR, file: Incorporation History, Colborne and Tomlinson to Department of National Revenue, June 27, 1978; Beendigen Board to Registrar Charitable Organizations, January 5, 1979.

33 BR, file: Incorporation History, "Final Report to Secretary of State," December 4, 1978, to January 26, 1979; "Secretary of State Project Income and Expenses," May 1, 1978, to December 1, 1978.

34 Faye Peterson Transition House Records, box: General Correspondence 1, file: Interviews, "Interview—Dori Pellitier."

35 BR, "Beendigen funding proposal," 1978.

36 Interview with Dubec.

37 Both Gilbeau and Dubec remembered opposition to Beendigen on the ground that it was Aboriginal specific.

38 Interview with Gilbeau.

39 Andrew Armitage, *Comparing the Policy of Aboriginal Assimilation: Australia, Canada, and New Zealand* (Vancouver: UBC Press, 1995), 120–21; Patri-

cia A. Monture, "A Vicious Circle: Child Welfare and the First Nations," *Canadian Journal of Women and the Law* 3 (1989): 1–17.

40 BR, file Beendigen Inc. History, "Crisis Home," n.d.

41 BR, "Beendigen funding proposal," 1978, 5.

42 BR, "Beendigen funding proposal," 1978, 14.

43 Interview with Gilbeau.

44 Northwestern Ontario Women's Centre, Margaret Phillips, "Transition House Services in Northwestern Ontario" (Thunder Bay: Northwestern Ontario Women's Decade Council, July 1984), 9.

45 Linda MacLeod, *Wife Battering in Canada: The Vicious Circle* (Ottawa: Canadian Advisory Council on the Status of Women, 1980).

46 For an overview of Aboriginal opposition to laying charges against abusers and a discussion of the potential dangers of restorative justice measures for First Nations women, see McGillivray and Comaskey, *Black Eyes*.

47 Patricia A. Monture-Okanee, "The Violence We Women Do: A First Nations View," in *Challenging Times: The Women's Movement in Canada and the United States*, ed. Constance Backhouse and David H. Flaherty (Montreal and Kingston: McGill-Queen's University Press, 1992): 193–204.

48 Jo-Anne Fiske, "The Womb Is to the Nation as the Heart Is to the Body: Ethnopolitical Discourses of the Canadian Indigenous Women's Movement," *Studies in Political Economy* 51 (Fall 1996): 84.

49 Dian Million, "Telling Secrets: Sex, Power and Narratives in the Social Construction of Indian Residential School Histories" (unpublished paper presented at "What Difference Does Nation Make?" Canadian/American Cultures of Sexuality and Consumption, Weatherhead Centre for International Affairs, and Department of Women's Studies, Harvard University, March 10, 1999). A revised version of this paper is published in *Canadian Woman Studies/Les cahiers de la femme* 20:2 (Summer 2000): 92–104. See also Jo-Anne Fiske, "Child of the State, Mother of the Nation: Aboriginal Women and the Ideology of Motherhood," *Culture* 13:1 (1993): 17–35.

50 ONWA, *Breaking Free: A Proposal for Change to Aboriginal Family Violence* (Thunder Bay: ONWA, 1989).

51 ONWA, *Breaking Free*, 6.

52 ONWA, *Breaking Free*, 9.

5 Their Spirits Live within Us

Aboriginal Women in Downtown Eastside
Vancouver Emerging into Visibility

DARA CULHANE

> WE ARE ABORIGINAL WOMEN. GIVERS OF LIFE. WE
> ARE MOTHERS, SISTERS, DAUGHTERS, AUNTIES AND
> GRANDMOTHERS. NOT JUST PROSTITUTES AND DRUG
> ADDICTS. NOT WELFARE CHEATS. WE STAND ON OUR
> MOTHER EARTH AND WE DEMAND RESPECT. WE ARE NOT
> HERE TO BE BEATEN, ABUSED, MURDERED, IGNORED.
>
> From a flyer distributed at Downtown Eastside Women's Memorial
> March, February 14, 2001, Vancouver, British Columbia, Canada

Anyone passing through inner-city Vancouver on foot, on a
bus, and or in a car cannot help but *see*, in a literal sense,
the concentration of Aboriginal people here. For most urban
Canadians, and visitors from elsewhere, this is an unusual and
often surprising visual experience on which they feel compelled
to remark. Even so, many representations of this and other
inner-city neighborhoods in Western Canada are characterized by a marked *invisibility* of Aboriginal people, and women
in particular.[1] This essay describes both the construction of
this invisibility in public culture and an event that symbolizes
Aboriginal women's active resistance to these acts of erasure.

While academic, professional, public, and popular discourses
deploy a plethora of identifying labels and categorizations that
obscure and depoliticize the embodied nature of colonialism
that evidences itself, the annual Valentine's Day Women's

Memorial March gives political expression to a complex process through which inner-city Aboriginal women in Vancouver, British Columbia, are struggling to change the language, metaphors, and images through which they come to be (re)known as they emerge into public visibility. The demand for recognition and respect articulated in the flyer quoted from above encompasses a critique and redefinition of dominant representations of Aboriginal women that are deeply embedded in Canadian colonial history and culture, as well as a claim for inclusion in the larger Aboriginal struggle for rights in place and to health, dignity, and justice.

The intersection of Main and Hastings Streets—known locally as "Pain and Wastings"—marks the heart of Vancouver's inner-city neighborhood: the Downtown Eastside. Since 1997, when the City of Vancouver Health Department declared a public health emergency in response to reports that HIV infection rates among residents exceeded those anywhere else in the "developed" world, Downtown Eastside Vancouver has become a focal point in emerging local, national, and international debates about the causes of, and solutions to, widespread practices of intravenous injection of illicit drugs and the spread of HIV/AIDS. Public health and law enforcement authorities, in an effort to respond to these "twin epidemics," have treated the Downtown Eastside as a containment zone, rather than as an enforcement zone: few if any arrests are made for simple possession or trafficking of small quantities of illegal drugs, or for soliciting for the purposes of prostitution.[2] An open, publicly visible street market in illicit drugs and commercial sex has mushroomed.

Predictably, national and international media as well as a surfeit of both well-intentioned and brashly self-promoting artists, writers, and researchers have been drawn as moths to flames to document, analyze, represent, treat, and market the dramatic and photogenic spectacle of social suffering in this neighborhood. A favorite focus of the cameras and interviewers is the southwest corner of Main and Hastings Streets: the entranceway to the Carnegie Community Centre. Television and video crews offer the virtual voyeur disturbing—or titillating—images of emaciated heroin, crack cocaine, and prescription drug users buying, selling, injecting, and smoking. Young women hurry back and forth between this corner and others, in and out of alleyways, cars, and parking lots. The money that women make selling sexual services passes quickly through their fingers from "johns" to drug dealers.

On one day of the year, though, for at least a few hours, the scene at Main and Hastings is dramatically altered. In 1991 Aboriginal and non-Aboriginal women's organizations in inner-city Vancouver declared February 14th a day of remembrance to honor neighborhood women who have been murdered or who have disappeared. In the Downtown Eastside, Valentine's Day has been transformed into an occasion to protest against racism, poverty, and violence against women, and to celebrate resistance, solidarity, and survival. In this struggle visibility and recognition are inseparable from the goals of material survival: these women are engaged in a struggle to stay alive, and to change the material and symbolic conditions of existence for women who come after them.

Media spectacles of sex, drugs, crime, violence, murder, and disease have brought Downtown Eastside Vancouver into living rooms around the world.[3] Yet this overexposure is at the same time constitutive of a "regime of disappearance." I borrow this term from Goode and Maskovsky, who have coined it to describe a neo-liberal mode of governance that selectively marginalizes or erases categories of people through strategies of representation that include silences, blind spots, and displacements that have both material and symbolic effects.[4]

In this densely woven veil—or regime of disappearance—behind and through which Aboriginal women in Downtown Eastside Vancouver wage their struggle for visibility, for self representation in public culture, several key themes emerge. The first is a preference for exotic and spectacular representation of drugs, sex, violence, and crime rather than the ordinary and mundane brutality of everyday poverty. The second is the medicalization or pathologizing of poverty. The third is a relative lack of interest in resistance practiced and visions of change articulated by subjects of these discourses. The thread that ties these themes together in the specific context of Downtown Eastside Vancouver is a particular form of "race blindness." Recognition of the burden of social suffering carried by Aboriginal people in this neighborhood—and in Canada as a whole—elicits profound discomfort within a liberal, democratic nation-state like Canada, evidencing as it does the *continuing* effects of settler colonialism, its ideological and material foundations, and its ongoing reproduction.

The City of Vancouver is built on land owned and occupied by the Coast Salish peoples for at least 10,000 years. In 1923 the last Aboriginal village was relocated across Burrard Inlet to a reserve north of the new city. Aboriginal people from Coast Salish and many other First Nations have maintained a continual presence in what is now called the Downtown Eastside, and in recent years the numbers of Aboriginal people living here have increased significantly to current estimates of around 5,000, representing about one-third of the total population of the neighborhood.[5] It is important to note that not all Aboriginal people in the City of Vancouver live in the Downtown Eastside.[6] However, while about 10 percent of the Canadian population as a whole is Aboriginal, they are disproportionately located in the poorest neighborhoods of Canadian cities, at the bottom of the socioeconomic hierarchy.[7]

In the Downtown Eastside, as elsewhere, while much *public* space has been taken over by police, drug dealers and users, sex workers and pimps, pawn shops and street fences, the majority of residents of the neighborhood are none of the above.[8] The Downtown Eastside is one of the poorest neighborhoods in Canada, where average annual incomes hover far below the national poverty line at around C$12,000.[9] Approximately 16,000 people now live in the Downtown Eastside, and estimates are that around 6,000 are active drug users.[10] Some are people suffering from mental illness who have been "deinstitutionalized," but the majority are people too poor to live anywhere else in Canada's highest-rent city.[11] While poverty is frequently noted as a characteristic of the inner city, it is most often presented in the form of a naturalized, inevitable backdrop against which exoticized practices of drug addiction and commercial sex are played out. Dominant explanatory discourses tend toward pathologizing or medicalizing poverty. That is, poverty is identified as the *outcome* of drug addiction, which itself is increasingly explained as a "chronic relapsing mental illness." Poverty is rarely analyzed as a causal condition that gives illicit drug use and sex work their particular public character and devastating consequences in this place, at this time. Illicit drug use and the exchange of sex for material benefit are, after all, not limited to the Downtown Eastside and other impoverished inner-city locales. Rather, denizens of wealthier neighborhoods engage in these practices as well. They do so in private homes, brothels, and escort agencies. There, wealth serves to conceal and privatize what, here, poverty reveals to the public gaze.

A less publicized aspect of Vancouver's HIV/AIDS crisis is that infection rates are significantly higher among women than among men, and about twice as high among both male and female Aboriginal intravenous drug users than among non-Aboriginals.[12] Aboriginal women are seroconverting at higher rates than any other designated population in Canada in general, and in Vancouver in particular. Epidemiologists studying the epidemic represent research subjects as IDUS (intravenous drug users) and carriers of HIV/AIDS, for whom "Aboriginality" is one of many "risk factors" along with age, education, marital status, and others.[13] While neither HIV/AIDS nor IV drug use are restricted to impoverished and marginalized communities, it is the case, across the globe, that the burden of these epidemics is disproportionately borne by those with the least economic and political power.[14]

In the case of Aboriginal peoples, debates about social/political versus biological etiologies of poverty, alcoholism, and despair have raged for decades. Current scholarly thinking on these questions is best represented by work such as that of Kirmayer, Brass, and

Tait, who analyze the effects of colonial policies and practices on individual and community well-being:

> The collective trauma, loss and grief caused by . . . short-sighted and self-serving policies are reflected in the endemic mental health problems of many communities and populations across Canada.

> However, framing the problem purely in terms of mental health issues may deflect attention from the large scale, and, to some extent, continuing assault on the identity and continuity of whole peoples. To these organized efforts to destroy Aboriginal cultures are added the corrosive effects of poverty and economic marginalization.[15]

Social workers describe clients as "marginal," "poor," "socially excluded." Identifying "multi-generational poverty" as a unique characteristic of this neighborhood that is not as prevalent in adjacent communities, they avoid acknowledging both the kinship networks that characterize urban Aboriginal life and a long history of colonial displacement. Youth workers identify their clientele as "street entrenched youth," while the province of British Columbia Ministry of Child and Family Services statistics record that 70 percent of "children in care" in the City of Vancouver are of Aboriginal descent.[16] Health care professionals speak of individual "patients" and "cases." The police pursue "criminals", "perpetrators," and "offenders." Advocates talk about "sex workers," "the poor," "the homeless," and "the missing women."

A study conducted in 2000 estimated that 70 percent of street prostitutes working in the most dangerous and lowest-paying "tracks" in the Downtown Eastside were Aboriginal women under the age of twenty-six, and most are mothers.[17] In the racialized hierarchy of Vancouver's sex trade, non-Aboriginal women who work on the street have access to the somewhat safer and higher earning areas of Downtown Centre, Downtown South, and the West End. Others work through escort agencies and massage parlors. Researchers, sex workers, and advocates alike agree that men who seek out women working the "low track," in Vancouver and elsewhere, are buying license to commit violence, to degrade and to demean women considered disposable by johns and by society as a whole. Few non-Aboriginal analysts or advocates, however, acknowledge the *specific* vulnerability and overexposure of Aboriginal women to sexual exploitation, violence, and murder that has historically been, and continues contemporarily to be, a fact of Canadian life.

The most dramatic example of both the material and symbolic location of Aboriginal women in Downtown Eastside Vancouver and their representation in public culture is the story of the "Missing and Murdered Women." Since 1983 at least sixty-one women from Downtown Eastside Vancouver have been officially listed as "missing persons." When the women's relatives and friends began trying to alert police and other authorities to this, they were ignored. Then-mayor of Vancouver Philip Owen responded to the families' appeals to the police to investigate these disappearances by saying that public monies would not be spent running a "location service for prostitutes." As the numbers of missing women grew, and as academics, advocates, and journalists became involved and joined forces with women's families, "Vancouver's missing women" became a public issue, and the possibility that a serial killer was preying on the neighborhood captured widespread attention. On July 31, 1999, the reality television show *America's Most Wanted* aired a segment on Vancouver's missing women. Over half of the Downtown Eastside's missing women are Aboriginal women. Yet, when *America's Most Wanted* aired its segment on Vancouver's missing women, in the dramatic reenactment of a street sex worker climbing into a car driven by a possible serial killer, a blond white woman was chosen for the part.[18]

In February 2002 Robert William Pickton, a pig farmer from suburban Port Coquitlam, was arrested. He has since been charged with fifteen counts of first degree murder, making this the largest serial killer investigation in Canadian history. International media has flocked to Vancouver to film court proceedings, and the massive multi-million dollar search for evidence currently being conducted utilizing state-of-the-art technology at the Pickton farm. It has become a reality-based version of the popular television dramatic series *csi: Crime Scene Investigation*. Families of the missing and murdered women and their supporters maintain a vigil at the Pickton farm, standing as witnesses. Aboriginal women conduct healing ceremonies, insisting on inclusive—*not exclusive*—recognition that so many of the women whose body parts or DNA might be found are or were Aboriginal.[19]

In comparison to depictions of illness and hopelessness, less attention is paid by media, politicians, and the public to the strength and courage of many people in the Downtown Eastside who struggle daily to maintain and create community, to initiate and support change, to survive. The Downtown Eastside is an active and activist neighborhood with a long tradition of labor and anti-poverty organizing. In the 1970s and 1980s there was an increase in the number and influence of feminist organizations whose work has focused on developing spaces for women such as drop-in centers, social housing, shelters, and transition houses that are safe from public and private violence. Aboriginal women have long been a part of leftist anti-poverty and feminist anti-violence political movements, but beginning in the early 1990s they began to take significant leadership as organized Aboriginal voices per se in the Downtown Eastside. Their numbers had increased locally, and the Aboriginal movement—and the Aboriginal women's movement specifically—gained more prominence nationally and provincially.[20] Urban Aboriginal political recognition also advanced at this time in the form of inclusion of Aboriginal individuals and representatives on citizens' advisory and community participation panels. Aboriginal women, particularly older women no longer using drugs or alcohol, have emerged as community organizers, ritual specialists, spiritual icons, and political leaders in the neighborhood.

The feeling that the issues particular to women in the Downtown

Eastside—specifically poverty, racism, violence against sex workers, HIV/AIDS, and addiction—are given insufficient attention by other Aboriginal and non-Aboriginal organizations is cited as a reason for holding the annual Valentine's Day marches. By organizing their own events on a specific day, Downtown Eastside women activists mark their difference from other feminist anti-violence groups, and from mainstream Aboriginal organizations.[21] The main social/political movements in the neighborhood—Aboriginal, women's, anti-poverty, and community development movements for the most part, each including several highly politicized factions—co-exist in uneasy coalitions fraught by conflict but moved to collective action such as the Valentine's Day March by shared though diverse visions of social justice. I return now to Valentine's Day, turning the focus away from the regimes of disappearance to resistance, survival, and possibility.

The Valentine's Day March changes somewhat each year. The particular event I am describing is the 2001 March. The day began at noon with a gathering in the auditorium of the Carnegie Community Centre. The people gathered were mostly, but not exclusively, women of a variety of ages, dressed in fashions ranging from trendy to punk to understated but very expensive leather to pickings from donations from free clothing bins. Many, but not all, were Aboriginal. Gathered too were young Asian women, white women of all ages, a few African Canadian women, and a handful of men of different ages and races. Most of the dignitaries on stage and all of the singers, drummers, and speakers to come were Aboriginal women. The program at the Carnegie Centre began, as community gatherings usually do now, with an offer of thanks to the Coast Salish First Nations upon whose unceded land the ceremonies were about to take place. This was followed by prayers, drumming, and smudging led by elderly Aboriginal women. A round of speeches ensued. Most of the speakers were middle-aged or elderly Aboriginal women, many of whom were leading community activists. Some were employed in social service agencies, but most were self-described "Volunteer

Queens" and women called "Street Moms" who simply live in the community. They talk. They help. They cook. They run AA and NA meetings. They look after children and old people. They conduct healing circles. They try to keep young people off the street.

A representative from an Aboriginal women's organization narrated how European patriarchal values and structures were superimposed on indigenous societies, displacing women from the positions of respect they held traditionally. Another talked about the Indian Act and how registered Indian women who married non-Indian men were denied legal status and prohibited from living on reserves. Since 1985 most of these women and their children have been eligible for reinstatement, but conditions on reserves that include competition over distribution of scarce resources, and sometimes long-standing conflicts within and between families, have made returning to reserves more a disappointment than a reality for many. Homophobia, fear of HIV and those who are infected and lack of services for them, and high rates of domestic violence and abuse in some First Nations communities, as well as employment and education opportunities and more possibilities for diverse lifestyles in the city, also play a role in creating an urban population made up predominantly of women and youth. Not all the women who live in the Downtown Eastside are from reserves, though. There are Métis women, non-status women, people whose families have lived off reserve for more than a generation or two, and many young people who grew up in the foster care system or were "adopted out" and have more questions than assumptions about their Aboriginal identity and their relationships to reserve-based communities.

Another speaker criticized the existing Aboriginal health and social services and accused them of paying insufficient attention to the needs of Aboriginal people in the Downtown Eastside. As evidence of the inadequacy of existing services she cited lack of treatment facilities for drug and alcohol recovery, absence of follow up care or resources for people coming out of treatment, lack of safe and secure housing, discriminatory child apprehension practices, and slow police responses to calls about domestic or street violence. She blamed the lack of jobs and below-subsistence welfare rates for driving young women into the sex trade and young men into the drug trade. She concluded with a critique of those people she calls "poverty pimps" and demanded that staffing of neighborhood social services be culturally proportionate to clientele: "If half your clients are Native people," she said, "Then I want to see half your staff Native too!"[22] Her speech was angry, emotional, and at times hard to follow. Reading the transcript carefully, however, revealed an anti-colonial analysis, indigenous explanations of addiction in Aboriginal women's lives, and a list of policy and treatment recommendations that have been repeated in more professional and restricted language in well-financed study after well-financed study.

The speeches continued. Multigenerational kinship groups stood together behind their speakers. Mothers, grandmothers, great-grand-mothers, and aunties related their own histories, lamented the loss of children to drugs and alcohol, and pointed proudly to those who have survived.

Daughters, granddaughters, sisters, and nieces mourned their predecessors who had died on the street, and described their own struggles. A middle-aged woman cried when she talked about how disappointed she was that her daughter did not meet her here today as she had promised. "We mothers have to remember," she told the crowd, "That it isn't that our daughters don't love us. It is just that they love their drugs more. Drugs take our children away from us."[23]

A young man, holding his toddler-aged daughter, talked about how he never knew his parents or his grandparents, had never even seen pictures of them. He grew up in foster homes and became a street kid and drug user in Victoria. Then he cleaned up and began a search for his roots. This is what brought him to the Downtown Eastside, where he discovered that his mother and his grandmother had both died, violently. He promised that his generation would mark the change. His children would not grow up in foster homes and would not know the street. Some speakers made a point of saying that they worried not only about their own children, but also about the children of all nations who are dying.

For the last few years the Valentine's Day Memorial March has focused on the "Missing and Murdered Women," now the subject of international media attention. The Carnegie Centre Auditorium was decorated with red hearts, each one bearing the name of a disappeared woman. Individuals, adopting a tactic made famous by the Madres of the Plaza de Mayo in Argentina, carried pictures of their missing relatives.

The gathering in the auditorium drew to a close with a prayer and a two-minute silence in honor of the dead, and the crowd filed out of the Carnegie Centre led by Aboriginal women in button blankets and shawls singing songs and beating drums. Joining hands and linking arms they formed a circle anchored on each of the four corners of Main and Hastings, stopped traffic of all kinds, disrupted popular images, and demanded recognition.[24] Contingents assembled around their various banners, and the annual Valentine's Day Women's Memorial March began.

The marchers wound their way down Hastings Street, detouring through alleys and parks. Women stopped to smudge outside notorious bars and strip clubs, in alleyways and parking lots, and beside dumpsters where women's bodies have been found.[25] They read the names of women who had died, told how they died, and listed their relations: mother of ———, sister of ———, daughter of ———, friend of ———. In this way they inscribed these women's lives on land and in place. It is appropriate that there is so much focus on mourning and death. Perpetual, repetitive, relentless experiences of tragic loss permeate the lives of individuals and families in this community. The representational politics surrounding the missing women mark an important moment for Aboriginal and non-Aboriginal women. The strongest criticism of the police—and, by proxy, of the public—has been that they ignored early reports because the women were prostitutes, addicts, Aboriginal. And that this is wrong, that these women have equality rights of some sort, that they are as human as anyone else, and that *their* families' grief is as important as any other families' grief. "These women are MOTHERS, SISTERS, AUNTS. They are HUMAN BEINGS," a speaker proclaimed.

By politicizing the issue of the Missing and Murdered Women in particular, and rallying considerable support across class, gender, racial, and neighborhood divides, the families of the missing women and their supporters have claimed a space of dignity for the poorest and most marginalized women in Canada and have achieved some degree of victory in setting the terms and conditions under which a previously invisible population has entered into public discourse. The sad irony is, of course, that the recognition and respect now accorded the Missing and Murdered Women in death was often denied them in life.

The march proceeded through "historic Gastown" with its high-end tourist shops and galleries displaying Northwest Coast and Inuit art in every window from exclusive galleries to tacky T-shirt and trinket carts. The march concluded with a feast at Oppenheimer Park where a totem pole was built five years ago: the most significant marker of the historical and continuous presence of Aboriginal people in the Downtown Eastside. At this feast elders were served first. In keeping with life expectancy levels in this neighborhood, anyone over forty-five is designated as an elder. The feast closed with a prayer led by an elder Aboriginal woman, and the marchers dispersed to carry on their lives, one way and another. Some stayed behind and joined—in various ways—drug dealers, users, shelterless people, and sex workers who take over the park after dark. Others returned to other homes, families, and jobs located elsewhere.

Material conditions for Aboriginal women in Downtown Eastside Vancouver have worsened considerably during 2001 to 2003 as a result of an aggressive program of cutbacks in government services and support for unemployed and disabled people initiated by a provincial government elected in 2003. British Columbians elected an extreme right-wing party—ironically named the Liberals—to form the provincial government. Welfare reform policies adopted from the United States have been implemented that have reduced benefits and services to single mothers, unemployed youth, and disabled people. HIV infection rates continue to increase, with Aboriginal youth between the ages of seventeen and twenty-five constituting the "highest risk group." Homelessness is increasing, and anecdotal reports, observations, and research data demonstrate that the numbers of young Aboriginal women arriving in the inner city is on the rise.

Nevertheless, Aboriginal women continue to resist and to envision change. A group called "Breaking the Silence" advocates for safe housing and for health and social services for neighborhood women. They organize a weekly gathering at the totem pole in Oppenheimer Park. A community service organization donates space to a woman named Grace, who has initiated a drop-in center for Downtown Eastside women and children a few nights a month following the day welfare checks are issued. "The Place of Grace" provides shelter from violence that sometimes erupts during this period, protection from theft, and companionship and nonjudgmental support for women in recovery who find the temptation to "slip" or "binge" harder to resist during this week than others. The Valentine's Day Women's Memorial March in 2003 was large, well-attended, sorrowful, and celebratory.[26] A woman speaking on behalf of the Aboriginal Women's Action Network addressed the gathering, saying: "We've shown the world that we won't stand by while our women are murdered and disappeared. We demand justice for the missing and murdered women of all nations. And we won't tolerate it that our young women are still pushed onto the street by poverty and racism. This is our land and we belong here. We have a right to justice and a decent life. We are not going anywhere."[27]

Notes

1   For statistical overview of Aboriginal populations in Canadian inner cities see Carol LaPrairie, *Aboriginal Over-Representation in the Criminal Justice System: A Tale of Nine Cities* (Ottawa: Department of Justice, 2001). For

discussion of "invisibility" of urban Aboriginal people in mainstream Canadian culture, see Evelyn J. Peters, "Subversive Spaces: First Nations Women and the City," *Environment and Planning D: Society and Space* 16 (1998): 665–85. For analysis of routinized violence against inner-city Aboriginal women in Canada see Sherene Razack, "Gendered Racial Violence and Spatialized Justice: The Murder of Pamela George," *Canadian Journal of Law and Society* 15:2 (2000): 91–130. For a case study of mental health and substance abuse issues among inner-city Aboriginal populations in Canada see Kahá:wi Jacobs and Kathryn Gill, "Substance Abuse in an Urban Aboriginal Population: Social, Legal and Psychological Consequences," *Journal of Ethnicity in Substance Abuse* 1:1 (2002): 7–25.

2 In Canada, prostitution—that is, the exchange of sexual services for money—is not illegal. However, soliciting for the purposes of prostitution is illegal.

3 Beverley A. Pitman, "Re-mediating the Spaces of Reality Television: *America's Most Wanted* and the Case of Vancouver's Missing Women," *Environment and Planning A* 334 (2002): 167–84.

4 Judith Goode and Jeff Maskovsky, eds., *The New Poverty Studies: The Ethnography of Power, Politics, and Impoverished People in the United States* (New York: New York University Press, 2001).

5 For a discussion of current census and other demographic data, and for a recently published article that signals the beginnings of a movement into academic visibility of Aboriginal women in Downtown Eastside Vancouver, see Celia Benoit et al., "In Search of a Healing Place: Aboriginal Women in Vancouver's Downtown Eastside," *Social Science and Medicine* 56:6: (2003): 821–33.

6 Reliable demographic data is hard to establish in this milieu, but estimates can provide an overview. In 1998–99 the Vancouver/Richmond Health Board, hoping to obtain a more accurate estimate of the Aboriginal population of the City of Vancouver, commissioned a "Capture/Recapture Study" based on Census Canada 1996 figures. This study, entitled "Healing Ways," estimated a total population of 28,000 Aboriginal people living in the City of Vancouver. Of these, approximately 5,000 (17 percent) reside in the Downtown Eastside; 14,000 (50 percent) live in the adjacent neighborhoods of Northeast, East, and Southeast Vancouver, with the remaining 9,000 (33 percent) scattered throughout other neighborhoods. Over 50 percent of urban Aboriginal households in Vancouver are headed by women, and these are concentrated in the sectors of East Vancouver where

the majority of Aboriginal people live. *Healing Ways: Aboriginal Health and Service Review* (Vancouver: Vancouver/Richmond Health Board, 1999).

7 For analysis of the systemic nature of current poverty and economic marginalization among Aboriginal people in Canada, see Joan Kendall, "Circles of Disadvantage: Aboriginal Poverty and Underdevelopment in Canada," *American Review of Canadian Studies* 31:1/2 (2001): 43–59.

8 Phillipe Bourgois, "Understanding Inner-City Poverty: Resistance and Self-Destruction under U.S. Apartheid," in *Exotic No More: Anthropology on the Front Lines*, ed. Jeremy MacClancy (Chicago: University of Chicago Press, 2002), 15–32.

9 *Downtown Eastside Community Monitoring Report*, Population Statistics, Census Canada 1996 (City of Vancouver, 2000).

10 *Downtown Eastside Community Monitoring Report*.

11 Vancouver/Richmond Health Board, *Healing Ways*.

12 Patricia Spittal et al., "Risk Factors for Elevated HIV Incidence Rates among Female Injection Drug Users in Vancouver," *Canadian Medical Association Journal* 166:7 (2002): 894–99. See also Susan Ship and Laurel Norton, "'It's Hard to Be a Woman': First Nations Women Living with HIV/AIDS." *Native Social Work Journal* 3:1 (2000): 69–85.

13 Spittal, "Risk Factors."

14 Sally Zierler and Nancy Krieger, "Reframing Women's Risk: Social Inequalities and HIV Infection," *Annual Review of Public Health* 18 (1997): 401–36.

15 L. J. Kirmayer, G. M. Brass, and C. L. Tait, "The Mental Health of Aboriginal Peoples: Transformations of identity and Community," *Canadian Journal of Psychiatry* 45:7 (2000): 607–16. See also Theresa D. O'Nell, *Disciplined Hearts: History, Identity and Depression in an American Indian Community* (Berkeley: University of California Press, 1996).

16 Vancouver/Richmond Health Board, *Healing Ways*.

17 Sue Currie, "Assessing the Violence against Street Involved Women in the Downtown Eastside/Strathcona Community," Report for the Ministry of Women's Equality (Province of British Columbia, 2000).

18 Pitman, "Re-mediating the Spaces."

19 On December 9, 2007, Robert William Pickton was convicted of second-degree murder in the deaths of six women, and he remains a suspect in an additional twenty deaths. He appealed the murder convictions in January 2008. Both the appeal and prosecution on remaining charges remain pending as of November 2008.

20 For analyses of the Aboriginal women's movement in Canada see Jo-Ann

Fiske, "The Womb Is to the Nation as the Heart Is to the Body: Ethnopolitical Discourses of the Canadian Indigenous Women's Movement," *Studies in Political Economy* 51 (1996): 65–96; Native Women's Association of Canada, *Hear Their Stories: 40 Aboriginal Women Speak* (Ottawa: Native Women's Association, 1997); Winona Stevenson, "Colonialism and First Nations Women in Canada," in *Scratching the Surface: Canadian Anti-Racist Feminist Thought,* ed. Enakshi Dua and Angela Robertson (Toronto: Women's Press, 1999).

21 Since the "Montreal Massacre" of December 6, 1989, when a man burst into an engineering class at L'École Polytechnique at the Université de Montréal yelling that he "hated feminists" and gunned down fourteen female students, activists in the movement against violence against women mobilize on December 6 every year. The anti-rape movement holds "Take Back the Night" marches in October each year. Trade union and left-wing-affiliated women focus on International Women's Day on March 8.

22 Dara Culhane, Fieldnotes, February 14, 2001.

23 Culhane, Fieldnotes.

24 The intersection of Main and Hastings streets has become an icon in popular discourse and media imagery evoked to symbolize degradation, squalor, and degeneration. Photographs, films, news clips, and articles depicting emaciated drug addicts and sex workers characterize the most common representations of the corner. Hundreds of women standing shoulder to shoulder, carrying banners and picket signs, circling the intersection, chanting and drumming, offer an alternative image that subverts and challenges.

25 Smudging is an Aboriginal ceremony in which sweetgrass or sage is burned, and the smoke is used to purify and cleanse bodies and spaces.

26 For discussion and examples of Aboriginal women's activities surrounding health and health care, see Connie Deiter and Linda Otway, "Sharing Our Stories on Promoting Health and Community Healing: An Aboriginal Women's Health Project," *Prairie Women's Health Centre of Excellence* (Winnipeg MB, 2001).

27 Culhane, Fieldnotes.

6 "How Will I Sew My Baskets?"

Women Vendors, Market Art, and Incipient Political Activism in Anchorage, Alaska

MOLLY LEE

When the alarm goes off at six o'clock on a late October morning, the Anchorage sky is sullen with clouds that have already dumped a foot of early snow on the city. As I splash water on my face, I hear Flora Mark (a pseudonym), my Yup'ik Eskimo collaborator on a long-term research project, in the kitchen brewing coffee: "It's Starbucks!" she told me proudly last night when I arrived from Fairbanks.[1] We are hurrying to make the 7 a.m. deadline for setting up Flora's table at the annual Alaska Federation of Natives craft fair, which opens today in downtown Anchorage. We gulp down the coffee, and as we pack up to leave, Flora struggles into her best flowered *qaspeq*, the Mother Hubbard–like garment part way between shirt and dress that is regulation wear in every Eskimo village. In the city *qaspeq* wearing is not taken for granted, however, so as Flora pokes her head out through the opening, she feels compelled to explain: "They [the crafts fair organizers] want us to wear these."

In this chapter I examine the multifaceted role of the Alaska Federation of Natives crafts fair in the lives of Alaska Native women who have left their home villages and moved to Anchorage, Alaska's largest city. At the same time, this discussion raises broader issues such as the evolving politicization of women traders and the growing role of market art in the articulation of political concepts. These themes link Alaska Natives to Native Americans generally as they move from formerly isolated small-scale groups to multiethnic entities that participate in the globalized economies and emergent political institutions characterizing Fourth World peoples of the twenty-first century.[2] I argue that across Alaska institutions such as the Alaska Native Federation crafts fairs help the increasing number of urban-based Native women in a variety of ways to adjust to city life while maintaining their connection to their home villages and to the land and animals from which they obtain the raw materials for craft production.

AFN and the Urban Experience

Founded in 1966, as an oversight organization to support Alaska Natives' ongoing land claim issues, the Alaska Federation of Natives (AFN, as it is familiarly known) holds its annual convention each October. For three days the city of Anchorage plays host to 5,000 to 10,000 of Alaska's 65,000 indigenous people. At AFN time Tlingit and Athabascan Indians, Inupiaq, Yup'ik and Siberian Yupik Eskimos, Aleut and Alutiiqs flock into town to renew friendships, participate in debates about current land claim issues, do their Christmas shopping, and escape for a few days from the inevitable social pressures of life in small, rural communities.

At the same time that politics are being argued on the ground level of Anchorage's Egan Conference Center, the AFN craft fair, a second dimension of the conference, is going ahead full tilt on the floor below. Begun in the 1980s as an add-on activity to help generate cash for in-town shopping, the AFN crafts fair is by now such an established institution that securing selling space at its tables is highly competitive. Formerly, Native people made the rounds of downtown gift shops with their wares tucked under one arm or traveled across town to the Alaska Native Medical Center and set up shop in the reception area, but today the AFN fair has mushroomed into the largest arts and crafts sale in the North, anticipated across Alaska by Natives and non-Natives alike.

The craft fair may originally have been organized to benefit rural residents in town for AFN, but in 2003 it also serves the growing number of Alaska Native vendors who have relocated to Anchorage mainly to take advantage of the economic opportunities in urban areas.³ For women like Flora, the AFN fair serves several purposes: it is a marketplace, social club, and, increasingly, political forum for her group of urban friends whose homes are widely scattered across the city rather than in the close proximity of the village.

Elbowing our way through the crowd in the main floor lobby, Flora and I inch toward our destination. Balancing an assortment of purses, backpacks, plastic tubs and grocery bags, we shove our way onto the down escalator. Below, another form of hubbub reigns; several hundred vendors mill around, locating their tables, embracing old friends, or gossiping with someone from home. On the tables the usual amalgam of goods has materialized from all manner of bundles and boxes. For *kassaqs* (white people) and the so-called Brooks Bros. Natives with well-paying jobs in industry or Native organizations, there are high-end items. Grass baskets from the Yup'ik area join beaded moccasins and folded birch bark containers from Interior Alaska. From Nunivak Island come hats and scarves knitted of musk ox wool as light and as soft as thistledown. Walrus ivory and whalebone carvings from Bering Strait are arrayed alongside caribou-skin masks from the North Slope. Dolls with the Siberian Yupik style bead-wrapped hair braids and the ubiquitous Pan-Indian thread and bead dreamcatchers are also in evidence. Among these are scattered the occasional item intended for Native use. The artisans admire bundled stalks of the rare, purplish basket grass from Goodnews Bay, rolls of translucent sea mammal intestine for doll and parka making, *ugruk* (bearded seal) boot soles for mukluks, and sealskin for Eskimo yo-yos.⁴ Settling in at her table, Flora spots a St. Lawrence Islander hawking ribbon seal pelts, a variety unavailable in her home area. She rushes over, consults with him *sotto voce*, and returns triumphantly bearing one of the pelts. The hide is only partially cured, so later that day we will leave her table in the hands of a friend and make a mad dash across town to drop off the pelt at the tannery.

Flora's day at the AFN crafts fair is probably typical of those of her urban-based vendor friends. She is one of some 7,500 Alaska Native women who have left rural villages and moved to Anchorage during the past decade. The history of her relocation is not unlike the stories of others. In the early 1990s, as her three children grew up and entered high school, Flora saw that with wage labor jobs declining in rural Alaska and subsistence salmon fishing curtailed by dwindling stocks, the children's prospects in the village would be limited. So in 1994 she and her husband, who works construction in Bethel, the regional hub of southwest Alaska and joins her when he can, moved into the first of several efficiency apartments they have occupied in Anchorage since then. Like many other relocated ruralites, the Marks maintain their house in the village, return there several times a year for subsistence activities, and continue to think of it as home. Flora regards Anchorage as her work site; since the move, she has put her basket- and doll-making talents to good use, selling at AFN and the other less profitable fairs scheduled regularly in urban Alaska four or five times a year. Largely due to her efforts, all her children have received college educations.

Back at AFN I see just how fierce the competition for tables has become. I count only 160 of the cafeteria-size selling tables but at least three times that many vendors. Clearly the time-honored Alaska Native value of sharing is in effect here. Those who have been lucky enough to score a table are dividing the space (and rent) with one or two others. This year Flora has teamed up with a relative, but other years she has shared with new friends from town. Part of the appeal of AFN is the occasion it provides for socializing. Thanks to her years of craft fair attendance, Flora has met Native women from all over Alaska. Most in her close circle are Yup'ik, though, for she welcomes every chance to speak her native language. Her circle exchanges visits and shares food from home. For urban Native women, such sharing networks, as Fogel-Chance has called them, are an important factor in easing the adjustment to city life.[5]

Rural In-Migration and the Subsistence Debate

Flora's move into town is by no means unique, nor is urban in-migration a recent trend in Alaska. Rather, it is the escalating rate over the past few decades that is startling. A look at the census statistics from the past three decades is revealing: in 1970, 7.7 percent of the Alaska Natives lived in Anchorage; by 1980, that figure had doubled. By 1990, it had risen to 18 percent, and by 2000, with 34 percent of Alaska's Native population living in Anchorage, it had almost doubled again. If the 2000 percentage is added to the 30 percent of Natives living in Fairbanks and Juneau, Alaska's other urban centers, 64 percent of Alaska's Native people—well over half—are now city dwellers.[6] As Fienup-Riordan points out, Anchorage is now the largest Native American village in the world.[7]

Well over half the urban-dwelling vendors at AFN are female. This demographic reflects the gender breakdown of Anchorage-based Alaska Natives as a whole. In 2000 there were slightly over 7,000 Alaska Native women eighteen years and above residing in Anchorage, but only some 5,500 men.[8] The reasons are complicated, but paramount among them is the longstanding division of labor between the sexes. As a general rule Alaska Native men are the hunters and Alaska Native women are the gatherers, and gathering is more easily adapted to new terrains than hunting. Women can forage for berries near the roadsides outside Anchorage or gather clams along the shoreline of the Kenai Peninsula, but when a man moves from the village to the city he forfeits access to, and specialized knowledge of, the hunting and fishing areas he has known all his life.

Urban-based Native women confront political issues arising from the struggle over land claims on a daily basis and perhaps more intensively than they would have if they were living full-time in their home communities. Though the women vendors at AFN are kept too busy to attend the political sessions on the floor above, they are by no means unaware of the issues under discussion or of the need to resolve them. The topic dominating this and all recent annual conventions has been guaranteed access to the millions of acres of public land in rural areas, the issue known throughout Alaska as the subsistence debate. Because of its centrality in the lives of Alaska Native urbanites, it will be helpful to summarize the main points here.

After Alaska became a state in 1959, with the North Slope oil boom fast becoming a reality, it became expedient for the federal and state governments to settle the Aboriginal land claims of Alaska's Native peoples. In 1971 passage of the Alaska Native Claims Settlement Act (ANCSA) was intended to have this effect. Under ANCSA Alaska Natives ceded their claims on public lands for a cash settlement and assurance that the secretary of the interior and the state of Alaska would "take any action necessary to protect the subsistence needs of the Natives."[9] In 1978 the Alaska Legislature passed the State Subsistence Law. It identified subsistence as the highest priority use on public lands but failed to grant to Alaska Natives priority over these resources in times of shortage. In 1980 Congress passed the Alaska National Interest Lands Conservation Act (ANILCA). Like the State Subsistence Law, ANILCA also begged the question of Native priority, but did so by granting priority to all residents of rural Alaska regardless of ethnic affiliation. In 1986 the state of Alaska amended its 1978 Subsistence Law with a rural residence (though not an Alaska Native) clause, but in 1982 the law was overturned on the grounds that it violated the equal protection clause of the Alaska State Constitution. At present, then, all Alaskans, regardless of ethnicity or residence, have equal access to state lands for hunting, fishing, and gathering, and all rural residents have priority over federal lands for the same purpose. As the political body representing Alaska Natives on such matters, AFN, deciding that half a loaf was better than none, has supported the rural residence solution.[10] However the Alaska Legislature, undoubtedly spurred on by powerful non-Native hunting and guiding interests, refuses to bring state law into alignment by passing a rural-priority amendment to the state constitution. With the recent depletion of salmon stocks in the rivers, the matter has become increasingly critical, but year after year, despite AFN's best efforts, the question remained unresolved.

Urban Native Women and Political Activism

By 1998 AFN, its collective patience worn thin by delay, and with funding from the Native American Rights Fund, decided to take action. That spring AFN president Julie Kitka and the board of directors called for a public protest, summoning rural and urban Natives to a march and rally in downtown Anchorage, the first of its kind. To appreciate the momentousness of this decision, it is necessary to understand that by custom most Alaska Natives prefer to avoid direct confrontation and to settle disputes by negotiation.[11] This is even truer of Native women, who are encouraged not to call attention to themselves. Therefore, the upcoming march was a subject of intense debate among Flora's sharing network, so much so that when I went to pick her up that day, I had given it less than fifty-fifty odds that she would decide to march. But there she was on the doorstep. "It's for my grandkids," she explained as she climbed into the car, "And anyway, if I can't go home to pick grass, how will I sew my baskets?"[12] And march she did, along with many of her friends. The assembled multitude—estimated at 4,000, and certainly the largest political protest ever held in Alaska—snaked through the streets of downtown Anchorage. Marching to the beat of Indian and Eskimo drums, the protesters, many in Native dress, brought traffic to a halt as they streamed toward the Delaney Park Strip for the rally. A notable percentage were women, mothers with babies on their backs, aunts, and even grandmothers in wheelchairs, exercising their citizens' rights for the first time. Many bore signs such as "Standing our Ground." Some, just as eloquently, carried placards marked with only the name of their rural communities, making explicit the bedrock fundamentality of place in their personhood.[13]

The intersection of women traders, urbanism, market art, and incipient political activism at the AFN craft fair is by no means unique. In fact, the circumstances replicate those of Native American women across North America in a number of interesting ways. First, Flora, like many of her friends and co-vendors, has come into to the city because access to the world's goods is limited in rural areas. Inevitably, along with such a significant demographic shift, comes the need for economic, social, and political readjustments. As Seligman has made clear, participation in grassroots political movements is a common byproduct of in-migration, particularly as women enter informal markets as traders.[14] Many factors including the globalized economy and the greater intrusion of state policy on urban lives appears to explain it. In the AFN case, and perhaps in other cases elsewhere, there is an irony attached. Urban though the Alaska Native vendors have become, the arts and crafts they sell still depend for their appeal on exotic raw materials such as seal hide, walrus stomach, and basket grass, and these are only obtainable in rural areas. So, guaranteed access to these lands in the future is critical to their continuing livelihood, and it is this concern that has led to their incipient political mobilization.

What is more, the AFN craft vendors are no longer alone in their need to organize. Elsewhere in the state Northwest Coast Indian women basketmakers on Alaska's southeastern Panhandle, who have watched access to their spruce-root gathering sites shrink in the face of burgeoning urbanization, are in the process of forming a basket organization for the express purpose of bringing their concerns into a wider public forum.[15]

In both cases, though, participating in the political process does not come easily; it requires the transgression of the strong cultural taboo against calling attention to oneself. From this perspective the AFN crafts market can be viewed as a site of power production, linking the women vendors to local and national politics and to women elsewhere in Native America who are experiencing similar conflicts.

Second, there is in the AFN case another area in which Native women and the objects they sell are linked to the political sphere, and that is the increasingly common appropriation of market art for political purposes. I have only anecdotal information to support this claim, but I would guess this trend is not limited to Alaska. In the AFN case Yup'ik Eskimo grass baskets, by far the most popular art commodity sold at the fair, appear with some degree of frequency in newspapers, on the covers of telephone books, and on posters where a symbol of the Alaska Native stand on subsistence is called for. In November 2000, for example, a photograph published in the *Anchorage Daily News* showed Julie Kitka, president of the Alaska Federation of Natives, addressing an audience of federal and state legislators in Juneau, Alaska's capital, on the subsistence issue. Beside Kitka, prominently displayed on the podium, stands a small, coiled grass Yup'ik Eskimo basket of the sort sold at AFN. The photograph is striking for several reasons. For one, this art form has, until recently, been regarded as a relatively insignificant art form despite its popularity with tourists. For an example to be elevated to this stature signals a shift in its valuation. For another, Kitka is an Alaska Native of mixed Athabascan Indian and Alutiiq—but not Yup'ik Eskimo—ancestry. This suggests that the basket, rather than some more traditional and highly regarded object such as a mask, was selected to stand for Alaska Native subsistence and Alaska Native cultures more generally.

Non-Natives' use of Native art as a basis for collective political action has long been documented, but the extent to which Native people have adopted the practice for their own ends has as yet to receive the attention it deserves.[16] Edelman points out that "contrary to the usual assumption—which sees art as ancillary to the social scene . . . [it] should be recognized as an integral part of the transaction that engenders political behavior."[17] In an age when Walter Benjamin's mechanical reproduction has become electronic and global, art is now more than ever in a position to serve as a source of imagery for promoting politically motivated actions. And in the present-day struggles of subordinate groups involving land claims, social service access, artifact repatriation, and other inequities, the use of Native artifacts as symbols of resistance and dissent can be expected to proliferate.

Finally, not only are the art forms sold at AFN commoditized and politicized, but so are the vendors who sell them. As Flora pointed out that morning when she pulled on her *qaspeq*, the organizers of the event expect them to wear Native dress even though it is not customary for them to do so in the city. Complying is an intelligent marketing strategy, but as Bourdieu has shown, it also has political implications.[18] Forms of dress are symbolic codes that reproduce the social status quo, and the status quo in this case is one of unequal class structures with Native vendor at the bottom and non-Native customer at the top. Though the women may wear the *qaspeq* with pride, the implication is nonetheless present.

Through the agency of the AFN crafts fair, then, Alaska Native women are smoothing off some of the sharp edges of adjustment to urban living. For them the fair, in addition to its function as an economic venue and a place where social bonds are created and strengthened, is also a site of political empowerment advancing them toward taking their place as full participants in the modern world.

Notes

I am grateful to my collaborator, known here as Flora Mark, for permission to write about her life. Margaret B. Blackman, Nelson Graburn, Chase Hensel, and Tom Kizzia also provided useful comments and information.

1 In Alaska, unlike Canada, the term *Eskimo* is still the preferred ethnonym. For a full discussion of the topic see the Alaska Native Language Center Web site, www.uaf.edu/anlc.

2 Nelson Graburn, *Ethnic and Tourist Arts: Cultural Expressions from the Fourth World* (Berkeley: University of California Press, 1976), 1–2. According to Graburn, Fourth World peoples are those whose territories are now encapsulated by industrialized nations of the First, Second, or Third Worlds.

3 Nobuhiro Kishigami, "Why Do Inuit Move to Montreal? A Research Note on Urban Inuit," *Études/Inuit/Studies* 23:1/2 (1999): 221–27. According to Kishigami, economic opportunity is only one attraction of metropolitan areas. Inuit women also list problems stemming from the growing social problems found across the rural North, e.g., flight from abusive relationships and the attraction of increased access to drugs and alcohol in urban

areas. See Nobuhiro Kishigami, "Life Problems of Urban Inuit in Montreal: Report of 1997 Research," *Jinbun-Ronkyu* [Journal of Liberal Arts] 58 (1999): 81–109.

4 Molly Lee, "Strands of Gold," *Anchorage Daily News (We Alaskans)*, October 17, 1999, E8–13. The Eskimo yo-yo is a toy popular with Alaskans and tourists alike that involves rotating two sealskin balls suspended on sinew strings in opposite directions. It probably evolved on St. Lawrence Island from the similarly constructed sinew and rock bolas used in bird hunting.

5 Nancy Fogel-Chance, "Living in Both Worlds: 'Modernity' and 'Tradition' among North Slope Inupiaq Women," *Arctic Anthropology* 30:1 (1993): 94–108.

6 Molly Lee, "The Cooler Ring: Urban Alaska Native Women and the Subsistence Debate," *Arctic Anthropology* 39:1/2 (2002): 3–9.

7 Ann Fienup-Riordan, *Hunting Tradition in a Changing World: Yup'ik Lives in Alaska Today* (New Brunswick NJ: Rutgers University Press, 2000), 151.

8 Lee, "Cooler Ring," 5.

9 Mary Kancewick and Eric Smith, "Subsistence in Alaska: Towards a Native Priority," *University of Missouri–Kansas City Law Review* 59:3 (1991): 645.

10 Many if not most urban Natives maintain homes in their villages, which they use regularly for subsistence-related activities. They also participate in sharing networks of friends and relatives there and expect to continue subsistence practices with them.

11 This is less true of the Tlingit, Haida, and Tsimshian Indians, who participated in the ranked societies of the Northwest Coast Indians.

12 *Mingqaaq* (plural *mingqaat*) means "sewn" in the Central Yup'ik language. It refers to the baskets' construction technique in which a grass bundle is oversewn with a grass-threaded needle.

13 Tom Kizzia, "March Organizers Predict Record Crowd," *Anchorage Daily News*, May 7, 1998, A12; Tom Kizzia, "4,000 Rally for Rights of Natives," *Anchorage Daily News*, May 8, 1998, A1; Chase Hensel, personal communication, February 25, 2003.

14 Linda J. Seligman, *Women Traders in Cross-Cultural Perspective* (Stanford: Stanford University Press, 2001), 11.

15 Leila Kheiry, "Alaska Basket Makers Gather," *Ketchikan Daily News*, February 28–March 2, 2003.

16 Nelson Graburn, "Inuit Art and Canadian Nationalism: Why Eskimos? Why Canada?" *Inuit Art Quarterly* 1:3 (1985): 5–7.

17 Murray Edelman, *From Art to Politics: How Artistic Creations Shape Political Conceptions* (Chicago: University of Chicago Press, 1995), 2.

18 Pierre Bourdieu, *Language and Symbolic Action*, ed. John B. Thompson, trans. Gino Raymond and Matthew Adamson (Cambridge MA: Harvard University Press, 1991), 12.

7 Women's Class Strategies as Activism in Native Community Building in Toronto, 1950–1975

HEATHER A. HOWARD

> Another important decision was to come to Toronto
> and live with my grand-daughters. I was very concerned
> for them. They had finished High School and wanted
> to go to Business College. So I decided to come with
> them just for a year. That's all I intended. But then
> I became involved in the Indian community here in
> Toronto, and realized the bad image Indians have
> . . . and so I felt I just couldn't leave. . . . It never
> occurred to me that I would run a boarding house for
> other students. I was only thinking of my relatives.
>
> Rosamund Vanderburgh, *I Am Nokomis, Too: The Biography of*
> *Verna Patronella Johnston*

This was the response Verna Patronella Johnston (Anishinaabe, 1910–1995) gave anthropologist Rosamund Vanderburgh when asked why she came to Toronto in the 1960s from her home on the Cape Croker Reserve located about one hundred miles northwest of the city. Vanderburgh documented Johnston's life in the book *I Am Nokomis, Too,* published in 1977. Her words "I was only thinking of my relatives" embody a common transition for Native women in rural-urban migration, from their roles as providers of shelter, food, and cultural knowledge transmission to kin to new roles as activists and strategists for building community for Native people in the city.

Like Johnston's granddaughters, between the end of World War II and the early 1970s, many Native women in Ontario came to Toronto in the hopes of accessing higher education, jobs, and freedom denied them on reserves under the oppression of federal government tutelage. However, much of the literature on Native rural-urban migration in Canada concentrates on an association between urbanization and social problems, or on Native peoples' "failure" to assimilate into urban society.[1] Conversely, I contend that attention to women's experiences in the history of Native community building in Toronto illustrates diversity and complexity in the socioeconomic life of Native urban migrants. For some, their personal journeys to Toronto positioned them as members of an emergent Native "middle class," itself characterized by the particularities of Native historical and cultural experiences, which I discuss in the first section of this chapter.

In particular, many Native women in this position did not equate their relative economic success with assimilation. Rather, they utilized their class mobility to support the structural development of Native community organizations and promote positive pride in Native cultural identity in the city. In the second section, I sketch some of the intersections between Native women's lives and the development of community for thousands of Native people in Toronto between 1950 and 1975. I describe the involvement of Native women in the North American Indian Club (1950–78), from which emerged the Native Canadian Centre of Toronto (founded 1962), the city's oldest Native community center, and the women's participation in the Native Centre's Ladies' Auxiliary. Their experiences also highlight the specificity of emerging Native "middle-class" identity in Toronto. This is further explored in the third part of this chapter, examining the engagement of Native women in socioeconomic class mobility, Native image making, and networking with women members of the Toronto white elite. Their work here served as a means to generate positive forms of Native identity grounded in notions of cultural pride and authenticity, while also securing resources to empower Native community self-determination.

Work in the City and the Emergence
of Urban Native "Middle Class"

"So You Are Coming to Toronto" was the title of a pamphlet issued by the Canadian government for Native people who, by the late 1930s, had begun migrating in large numbers to the city. The pamphlet (circa 1957) featured on the cover three attractive young Native women in nurse's uniforms. Inside, practical paternalistic suggestions were given, such as "pay your rent, be on time for work, and spend your money wisely." In a further attempt to de-emphasize stereotypical "Indianness," it also warned young Native people that "consumption of alcoholic beverages has led to the ruin of many people," and they should "follow all the rules of personal hygiene, cut your hair, and refrain from questionable entertainment." On the other hand, the pamphlet also advised that Native people should not be "alarmed if many foolish questions are asked of you. Many people have not had the benefit of your experience and who is better prepared to advise them about Indians than yourself? Always be courteous in your reply, even if the question appears silly."[2]

This pamphlet was addressed specifically to young Native people attending a particular technical school in Toronto, but it is a rare concrete example of federal attempts to control the behavior of urbanizing Native people in Canada. Unlike in the United States, Native urban migration in Canada in the last century was in many instances more a form of resistance to the assimilative oppression of government control and surveillance on reserves than it was a strategically implemented plan concocted by federal authorities to assimilate Native people into mainstream.[3] It was responded and reacted to, more than it was instigated. In Canada, it was believed that the intense suppression of Native languages, ceremonial life, and subsistence practices, along with re-education in the ways of dominant society (the purpose of the residential school system), would be enough to ensure a smooth transition of Native people into mainstream society. While much damage was accomplished, Native people also utilized and maximized the "tools of the oppressors" to resist assimilation and to organize their struggles to strengthen and assert Native cultural identity, self-determination, and inherent rights within the urban context.[4]

Various pathways led individual Native women to come together as "middle-class" activists. Some found their way to the city and to higher education through work as nannies in the homes of wealthy Toronto families. In interviews I conducted for the Toronto Native Community History Project in connection with my dissertation research, a number of women told me how working as nannies opened new doors for them. Many had good domestic skills, but little English language competency. Time spent with a white elite family gave them the chance to improve their English, and some were allowed to attend classes in secretarial school, nursing, or teaching in their time off. Several also strategically engaged the "benevolence" of their wealthy white employers and other new contacts in mobilizing the funds and political will necessary to establish and develop Native-based community organizations and services, beginning with the North American Indian Club in 1950, and the Native Canadian Centre of Toronto, incorporated in 1962.[5]

These Native women, along with men who gained skills in the armed forces or trained as teachers and in technical trades, began to form a professional middle class in the burgeoning Native community in the city. They actively sought to integrate into the cosmopolitan and consumer lifestyle of mainstream society in the city, while valuing and promoting their Native heritage. They also tended to hold relatively conservative political views, in contrast to their peers who were involved in the Red Power movement, one of whom described the Toronto Native community in 1974 as "the biggest number of middle-class Native people in Canada [who] liked the benefits they were receiving from the system, or were afraid of the system. They wanted to prove they were not trouble-makers."[6]

This urban Native middle class needs to be understood within the parameters of specific historical, cultural, and socioeconomic contexts for Native and non-Native relations in Canada. Wotherspoon and Satzewich note that no serious examination of the complexities of socioeconomic class among Canadian Native people has been undertaken with the exception of discussions of their position as an "underclass" in relation to the larger class structure of Canadian society. This has given rise to an impression of Native people as homogeneously constituent of this underclass and to a silence "on the theoretical and political significance of class and gender divisions within the aboriginal population."[7]

The legacy of imperialism and colonialism, the specific and enduring nature of Native poverty, and practical and symbolic gendered divisions of labor are also contributing factors to understanding how class is conceptualized from a Native perspective. Socioeconomic relations emerging from imperialism and colonialism contributed a particular blend of occupational, ethnic, and gendered characteristics of Native Canadian identity. There is an association between Native identity and particular rural, "bush," and reserve occupations, such as fur trade, guiding, and lumber work. These "traditional" jobs correspond to the symbolic opposition between Native and urban identities. They likewise contribute to a gender division in urban Native identity. "Traditional" jobs are mostly associated with men, and this has perhaps added to the limitations on the types (general labor) and duration of work (short-term and transient) for Native men during the early days of mass urban migration in the post–World War II period. Native women, on the other hand, had come to occupy jobs in the colonial economy that were relatively transferable to the urban context, such as working in domestic jobs. Women also accessed opportunities made available to them through Christian conversion efforts, becoming involved in church activities and organizing.[8] Canadian Indian policy since the mid-1800s also actively instituted a virtually irreversible state of extreme poverty among Native people. Just as *urban* and *Native* have been constructed as impossible contradictions, *poor* and *Native* have correlated as an inseparable basis of Native identity.[9]

In the ethnographic literature Edgar Dosman's 1972 study of Saskatoon and Mark Nagler's research in Toronto in the 1960s offer some further insights on the socioeconomic diversity among Native people in these cities. Dosman describes a Native "aristocracy" or "affluent" group, which is defined not strictly by wealth, but by such factors as living in stable families and comfortable, well-located homes with infrequent address changes. They also tend to have job stability, which is essentially defined as an "absence of dependence on public welfare."[10] Interestingly, Dosman notes that while these characteristics seem to indicate assimilation, in fact the "affluent" Native people are least likely to suffer from Native identity crisis, shame, or disorientation. It is they who advocate pride in Native identity and promote urban pan-Indian culture.[11]

Nagler's 1970 ethnography of Native urbanization in Toronto did not offer an analysis of occupational differences between the eighty-five men and sixty-five women he interviewed. However, scrutiny of the jobs he listed as "Characteristics of Indians Interviewed" reveals that Native women in the study could be categorized in higher numbers in occupations considered professional, middle-class, or "white collar," as Nagler terms them, and men were statistically more present among working-class or blue-collar sectors. Forty-five percent of the women were found to be in "professional" or "middle class" occupations, such as health professions, office work, and teaching, compared with 19 percent of the men.[12]

Native middle class is thus constituted from particular historical, gendered, and cultural contexts and is therefore distinctive from the notion of class for the general Canadian population. Class is not merely determined by salary, but by the perceived prestige associated with jobs such as secretarial or office work. Sherry Ortner provides a model for how classes are relationally constituted, in that "they define themselves always in implicit reference to the other(s)." She further argues that "it appears overwhelmingly the case in working-class culture that women are symbolically aligned, from both the male point of view and, apparently, their own, with the 'respectable,' 'middle class' side of those oppositions and choices."[13] When this approach is applied to understanding the urban Native middle class, it is clear that some Native people moving to the city are not simply becoming assimilated because they adopt the wider North American cultural goals of aspiring to middle-class lifestyles. Rather than a linear movement toward assimilation, there is a processual production of urban Native culture that is relational to "class." For Native people the definitions of lower-, middle-, working-, or professional-class categories are constructed through the ongoing interactions within and between Native and non-Native communities.

Women's Lives and Organizational Development: The North American Indian Club, the Native Canadian Centre of Toronto, and the Ladies' Auxiliary

I found the "So You Are Coming to Toronto" pamphlet among the personal papers donated to the Toronto Native Community History Project by a founding member of the Native Canadian Centre of Toronto, Ella Rush. She had attached a note to the back of it that read, "Rules the Indian Affairs gave to all the newcomers (mostly girls) who came down to Toronto." Rush came from the nearby Six Nations of the Grand River reserve in the 1930s to train to be a nurse. Through school and work, she came to meet many other young Native people who, like herself, were in the city to make better lives for themselves than could be had on the increasingly economically and culturally depressed reserves. They formed a social network, which quickly came to include people from a wide diversity of Native cultures. Many pursued higher education (which meant beyond the limit of grade eight available on reserves) through military training and in technical schools, where they became nurses, teachers, and secretaries.

Verna Johnston first came to Toronto in 1945. In 1965, she opened a boarding home for young Native women while they attended technical schools — so they could become "career women" as she put it — more independent and not confined to what she felt was the limited option of marriage. In the environment of "Indian consciousness-raising" of the 1960s and 1970s, Johnston became acutely aware that the younger generations of urbanizing Native people needed the help of "Nokomis," meaning "grandmother" or a knowledgeable respected elder. Within her home for girls and eventually at many public venues she taught crafts and spoke on Native culture and language, with the goals of defeating stereotypes and promoting pride among urban Native people. In 1970 she published the book *Tales of Nokomis*, a collection of stories she learned from her "Grandma Jones."[14] Johnston recalled the sense of "Indian awakening" during these times and articulated how the experience of coming to the city and needing to establish a sense of Native identity and community stimulated both the collective and her own individual consciousness:

> I grew as a person in those years, and I don't mean just running the house for Indian students. I came into contact with Indians from other parts of Ontario, and other provinces. I found out that there were a lot of Indians working to help their own people. That is Indians helping Indians—it's not the same as white do-gooders! Indians who have lived in the city know what it's all about, they are the best ones to help people. City Indians had really good ideas about how to help their people adjust to city life.[15]

The first known gathering place for the burgeoning Toronto Native community in the twentieth century was at the house of a family named Jamieson who were from the Six Nations of the Grand River reserve. As early as the mid-1920s, they welcomed all young Native people into their home, primarily to provide an opportunity for them to meet and socialize with each other. After World War II, Ella Rush and several others (mostly women) who had met regularly at the Jamiesons' home felt they should try to form a club. They approached the YMCA and founded the North American Indian Club there in 1950. Under the auspices of the YMCA a minimum number of members were required to form a new club. Patricia Turner, also of Six Nations, who was a founding member along with her mother, remembered that a few Native men took out several memberships to meet the male numbers requirement.

At that time it was estimated that only two or three hundred Native people lived in the city. In retrospect the numbers may have been much higher. In light of the racism Native people faced in the city, the tendency of many was to respond with invisibility, attempting to pass for white if possible. Many were made to feel ashamed of their heritage or were cut off from their roots through removal to residential schools, like Hettie Sylvester, an Anishnaabekwe from the Beausoleil First Nation who stated: "Being at residential school for twelve years took away a lot of my culture. I thought I was like everyone else. It wasn't until I left that I realized I was Indian. And it wasn't until the last few years that I began to understand what being Indian means."[16]

Sylvester came to Toronto in 1940, when she was nineteen. She got her first job housekeeping and working as a nanny through the YWCA and was an early member of the Indian Club. She was later a founder of the Native Canadian Centre's craft shop, which still provides an important source of income for the Centre. She was president of the Centre's Ladies' Auxiliary for fifteen years. Her residential school experience highlighted her inequality in racial terms when she came to the city, not realizing she was Indian until she left. However, the city was also a place where she could meet other Native people and utilize resources to organize a cultural community, in which her own identity as an Aboriginal person could be cultivated.

Another early member of the Indian Club, Lillian McGregor, came to the city as a teenager during World War II and worked as a nanny. McGregor pursued her education to become a nurse. She was born on Whitefish Reserve on Birch Island in 1924 and spent her childhood there. During the summers in 1938 and 1939 she worked at a tourist lodge in the area. In 1939, when she had completed the eighth grade, she worked as a waitress at the lodge. This, she says, helped her to learn more English and to gain more confidence in herself. This was also where McGregor had the opportunity to become the nanny for a family from Toronto. Not wanting to jeopardize her chance of getting a higher education, she, her family, and the Toronto family worked it out so she could complete high school while looking after the children and doing her housework duties in the evenings and on weekends. McGregor is still very active in the community, serving until 2008 as elder in residence at the University of Toronto, where she received an honorary doctorate in 2002, and on the Native Canadian Centre's Taam Kadinikiijiik (Elders Council). Her opportunities in the city rested upon her own ambitions, but they were fostered also within a context of cross-cultural class negotiations between her own family, who were prominent on the reserve, and the Toronto elite family, who had the power to assist her.[17]

The differentiation Verna Johnston made between Native people helping each other and the work of "white do-gooders" underlines a duality carefully managed by Native women involved in community organizing in Toronto in the 1950s and 1960s. In addition to their involvement in establishing the North American Indian Club and the Native Canadian Centre of Toronto, Native women formed the Native Centre's Ladies' Auxiliary in 1963. These women were particularly instrumental in the continuity and development of Native cultural pride, through education, social support, and the institution of an urban market for Native art and crafts, which supplied both financial and cultural support to the Native Centre and the community in Toronto.

Native women who organized community activity also shared the experience of being on the front line of the immediate social, health, employment, and educational needs of Native people in the city. Therefore, in addition to social events, early North American Indian Club activities also included hospital visiting and clothing and food drives. Later, the Ladies' Auxiliary provided counseling and inmate visiting at the Kingston Prison for Women. The *Toronto*

Native Times reported several times on the Ladies' Auxiliary's trips to Kingston, and the social conditions that put the women in jail in the first place became a central concern for the Auxiliary.[18] The Auxiliary's first president, Millie Redmond, a Potawatomi from Walpole Island First Nation, became interested in trying to help women in penal institutions set up their own clubs, on one occasion saying: "Perhaps a club could be formed to coordinate programs which would help the women's stay behind bars be a more pleasant and meaningful experience. Perhaps our visit will help create the kind of interest necessary for such a club to be formed."[19]

Redmond, who passed away in the early 1990s, is often credited in the Native community with being the main founder of the North American Indian Club. She was also behind numerous other Native programs and organizations in the city. In the 1930s she was a frequent visitor to the home of the Jamieson family mentioned earlier, who welcomed young Native people into their home. She reflected on how that experience led her to think about forming a community organization for Native people in the city:

> I wanted to do something—meet other Native people. And that's how I got the Native Indian Club started in my home, where I'd start to meet Native people. We wanted to get a club going, just like the Scottish and the Irish, and the German clubs. And we didn't have any so we called the Y and asked them to help—and sure enough they did. I helped form the Ladies' Auxiliary with Ella Rush. . . . Helping to form the Indian Club was one of the real good things because we got to know each other.[20]

Other Ladies' Auxiliary women like Josephine Beaucage also made the trips to Kingston penitentiary to demonstrate and teach craft making. She saw teaching as part of her mission to bring traditional practices and elements of Native culture to spaces where they might re-affirm Native identity and forge links of cultural solidarity, whether in the city or the penitentiary.[21] Beaucage was born on the Nipissing Reserve in 1904. She worked for Northland Boatlines as well as in tourist camps during the summer; in the winter she and her husband worked on their traplines. In 1960 her husband suffered brain damage from nearly drowning in a boating accident, and their daughter, who lived in Toronto, convinced Beaucage to bring him to the city, where he might receive better health care. Unfortunately, he never recovered, and he died in 1970.

Beaucage pursued higher education in secretarial school and then taught herself how to do beadwork, a craft for which she soon learned she had a natural talent. She was responsible for starting beadwork classes at the Native Centre and in a number of other locations, many of them sponsored by the Toronto Board of Education. Eventually she was busy teaching traditional crafts throughout the province of Ontario. Beaucage's work life and her commitment to sharing her beadwork skills with others illustrate not only the contributions of women to cultural continuity and community, but also to the wider economy. About her career as a beadworker and Native crafts instructor, she recalled:

> I started to go out teaching in different places. I went to reserves [all] around. And when I used to go to these reserves, I ordered all my leather through B. B. Smith here in Toronto. I used to order by thousands, hundreds and thousands of square feet of leather for each course that I give. And the same with the bead company. I got my beads from a big bead company here in Toronto and that was the only bead company I would deal with. When [the owner] saw me he would say, "Boy, thank you for your advertisement—for advertising us."[22]

These women were particularly instrumental in the development of the urban market for Native arts and crafts, which supplied structural, financial, and cultural support to the Native Canadian Centre and to the wider Native community in Toronto. For example, between 1963 and 1968 Ladies' Auxiliary member Dorothy Jones of Six Nations was responsible for obtaining crafts from local reserves to sell to raise money for the Centre. An outspoken advocate for Native people representing themselves, Jones placed a high emphasis on the authenticity of the crafts. In 1966 in the first edition of Centre's newsletter, later called *Beaver Tales*, it was reported:

> Mrs. Dorothy Jones personally selects all the articles in the display in an effort to be sure that the handicraft is a true representation of high quality Indian handicraft, indicative of the ability of the old-time craft workers. . . . Here you may find lovely hand-loomed necklaces of beads, (made by Indians long before the Japanese made replicas for the tourist trade), fur-trimmed moccasins, beautiful woven baskets for various purposes, birchbark and horn rattles, drums and quill boxes. . . . At the present time, Mrs. Jones could use more birchbark and sweetgrass items, but remember—of careful workmanship![23]

Hettie Sylvester's recollections of how the Native Centre's craft shop was started during her service as president of the Ladies' Auxiliary illustrates how the Ladies' Auxiliary's work combined cultural, social, and economic concerns in their volunteer service to community development. They were not only generating economic development through the organization of craft production and sales, but they also emphasized and articulated the value of positive Native identity, pride, and strength within the urban context. They also ensured the availability of some form of traditional social structures, particularly in terms of the roles of women as advisers and cultural transmitters.[24] Sylvester recalled fondly:

> I said, "Let's get Indian Crafts." I always had in my mind that I was an organizer. When I got to be president I was the busiest person, there was a project going on every month, fundraising or something. I enjoy working there, and not only as a salesperson. A lot of people come in and talk to me as their mother, I think. They come talk to me and tell me their problems. It is really interesting to listen to them and what they go through. I don't know why, there was a counselling room back there, but maybe

they see me as motherly, I don't know. I liked it. I enjoy talking to these people.[25]

The variety of experiences of these Native women are departures from the stereotypical molds to which Native people are generally expected to conform, grounded in the deeply entrenched view that there is some fundamental contradiction between Native identity and the cosmopolitanism of the city. Social geographer Evelyn Peters questions the assumption that being urban and Aboriginal necessarily constitutes an impossible and contradictory schism of identity. She describes how, conventionally, city living has been most often presented as the antithesis of Native culture. The imagery of "Aboriginality" in dominant European thought has equated "authentic" Native culture with the natural, mystical, and "non-civilized" world.[26] The conditions of urban living subvert the possibilities of generating and sustaining authentic Native cultural communities in cities. However, Native people in Toronto challenge the urban-Indian oxymoron, not by assimilating but by generating a rich and diverse Native community. The achievement of this richness and diversity has been the result of a range of dynamic struggles mediated by race, gender, and class relations with both non-Natives and within the Native community.

Native Urban Class Mobility, Community Building, and Networking with Elites

As part of the emergent Native middle class, many of the Ladies' Auxiliary women were also key in a strategic collaboration with wealthy white women, which helped to provide much of the funding needed to establish the Centre. In particular they nurtured relationships between the Native Canadian Centre and the Imperial Order of the Daughters of the Empire (IODE).[27] The IODE, founded in 1900, is an international organization devoted to Commonwealth citizenship. It was made up primarily of women from the urban industrial upper class, who engaged in a variety of benevolent works. In the 1960s

IODE women turned their attention to concerns of Canadian national identity and citizenship. They focused their energies and resources on the integration of immigrants and Native people into Canadian society. IODE members were mobilized by a combination of ideological, gender, and class motivations that included their sense of duty to act benevolently and charitably toward the less fortunate in society and to contribute to the project of nation-building, patriotism, and citizenship. In the 1960s they were instrumental in establishment of at least five urban Native Friendship Centres across Canada, including the Toronto Centre.

The IODE's relationship with the Toronto Native Centre, and with Native people across the country, manifested itself most in the person of Peggy Jennings, who served as the first president of the Native Canadian Centre of Toronto's board of directors. She used her influence with her wealthy acquaintances and vocalized the concerns of urban Native people in the media. For instance, Mrs. John D. Eaton (of the Canadian chain of Eaton's department stores) was also recruited as a member of the Native Centre's board of directors. She donated $25,000 of the $45,000 price tag for their second building, purchased in 1966.

Between 1963 and 1967, Jennings appeared frequently in the print media across the country, reprimanding her fellow non-Native citizens for their lack of sensitivity to Native people and praising Aboriginal people coming to the cities for their great potential to become good Canadian citizens. She also lauded their emphasis on pride in their national and cultural heritage. Jennings led the IODE pressure on the federal minister of immigration and citizenship, then overseeing Indian Affairs, for an in-depth study of "all aspects of the life of our Indian citizens to help them achieve equality of opportunity so they may become full participating members of Canadian society."[28]

The middle-class status of some of the Native women involved in the Indian Club and the Ladies' Auxiliary afforded them a degree of "leisure," which allowed them to commit time and effort to community service. They pursued the dual goals of ensuring and maintaining the integrity of Native cultural identity in the city and building financial support for the establishment and delivery of services to Native people. This initially captured the attention of organizations like the IODE. The women of the Native Centre's Ladies' Auxiliary and the IODE held in common a rejection of mainstream feminist perspectives that were perceived to present the home and family as oppressive institutions that imprisoned women. They also shared a desire to see improvements in the social conditions and recognition of Native people in Canada. Where they differed was in the underlying culturally based motivations behind these perspectives. The culture of the dominant class deployed an ideology that constructed gender roles in terms of a "calling" to carry out the bidding of the empire and citizenship. Native women's actions were based in their common experiences of politicized identity, cultural appropriation and devaluation, and their sense of duty to affirm Native cultural identity and build strong self-determined communities.

Conclusion

Native women's volunteer work in the early years of community building in Toronto did not represent a uniform platform for action, but rather was composed of diverse perspectives that changed over time and depended much on the concerns and directions taken by those in leadership positions. Under the guidance of Millie Redmond, for instance, the activities of the North American Indian Club and the Ladies' Auxiliary led to the establishment of social services for Native people in the city. Verna Johnston, Dorothy Jones, and Ella Rush were significant in affirming a positive image for Native people in the urban environment, as well as the development of a discourse around the authenticity of Native identity emergent from the common experiences of people from diverse Native cultural backgrounds. Women like Hettie Sylvester and Josephine Beaucage were instrumental in the development of the urban market for Native art and crafts and also contributed to the transference and adaptation of traditional Native women's roles of leadership and cultural transmission in the urban context. The types of Native women's activism described in this chapter highlight the links between gender and class mobility for urban Native people and the shaping of identity and community. They illustrate the dynamics of Native urbanization in the post–World War II era, particularly in terms of the gendered character of volunteer service and of educational and employment opportunities in the city for Native people. Native women's work and volunteer service has impacted the struggle for social equality and community development. Native women have also rejected the restrictions of reserve life, maximized opportunities in the urban context, and cultivated a space for the revitalization and growth of Native culture and identity, while striving for social justice.

Notes

I am very grateful to the Native Canadian Centre of Toronto and the many people there, including past members of the Ladies' Auxiliary for their confidence in me and their insights into this research. I am also most thankful to my co-editor of this volume and a tremendous mentor, Dr. Susan Applegate Krouse. I also acknowledge the financial support of the Fonds FCAR (Formation des chercheurs et aide a la recherche-Quebec) doctoral scholarship, the Social Science and Humanities Research Council of Canada, and the Department of Anthropology, University of Toronto.

1   For example, Hugh Brody, *Indians on Skid Row* (Ottawa: Northern Science Research Group, Dept. of Indian Affairs and Northern Development, 1971); Trevor Denton, "Strangers in Their Land: A Study of Migration from a Canadian Indian Reserve" (PhD thesis, University of Toronto, 1970); Edgar Dosman, *Indians: The Urban Dilemma* (Toronto: McClelland & Stewart, 1972); Larry Krotz, *Urban Indians: The Strangers in Canada's Cities* (Edmonton AL: Hurtig, 1980); Mark Nagler, *Indians in the City: A Study of the Urbanization of Indians in Toronto* (Ottawa: Canadian Research Centre for Anthropology, Saint Paul University, 1970); Joan Ryan, *Wall of Words: The Betrayal of the Urban Indian* (Toronto: PMA Books, 1978); William Stanbury, *Success and Failure: Indians in Urban Society* (Vancouver: University of British Columbia Press, 1975).

2   Canadian Indian Affairs Branch, "So You Are Coming to Toronto," circa 1957, Ella Rush Collection (pamphlets, flyers, and posters), Toronto Native Community History Project, Native Canadian Centre of Toronto.

3   For an overview of U.S. urban relocation policy see Donald L. Fixico, *Termination and Relocation: Federal Indian Policy, 1945–1960* (Albuquerque: University of New Mexico Press, 1986).

4   Heather Howard-Bobiwash, "Dreamcatchers in the City: An Ethnohistory of Social Action, Gender and Class in Native Community Production in Toronto" (PhD diss., Dept. of Anthropology, University of Toronto, 2005).

5   The Native Canadian Centre of Toronto is the oldest existing Native organization in Toronto and was the third Friendship Centre established in Canada, following one in Winnipeg (1958) and Vancouver (1960). For a detailed history of the Native Canadian Centre of Toronto see Roger Obonsawin and Heather Howard-Bobiwash, "The Native Canadian Centre of Toronto: The Meeting Place for the Toronto Native Community for 35 Years," in *The Meeting Place: Aboriginal Life in Toronto*, ed. Frances Sanderson and Heather Howard-Bobiwash (Toronto: Native Canadian Centre of Toronto, 1997), 25–59.

6   Vern Harper, *Following the Red Path, the Native People's Caravan, 1974.* (Toronto: NC Press, 1974), 44.

7   Terry Wotherspoon and Vic Satzewich, *First Nations Race, Class, and Gender Relations* (Regina SK: Canadian Plains Research Center, 2000).

8   For more on Native women in imperial/mission/colonial history see Karen Anderson, *Chain Her by One Foot: The Subjugation of Women in Seventeenth Century New France* (New York: Routledge, 1991); Carol Devens, *Countering Colonization: Native American Women and Great Lakes Women, 1630–1900* (Berkeley: University of California Press, 1992); Eleanor Leacock, "Montaignais Women and the Jesuit Program for Colonization," in *Myths of Male Dominance: Collected Articles on Women Cross Culturally* (New York: Monthly Review Press, 1981); Nancy Shoemaker, ed., *Negotiators of Change* (New York: Routledge, 1995); Susan Sleeper Smith, *Indian Women and French Men: Rethinking Cultural Encounter in the Western Great Lakes* (Amherst: University of Massachusetts Press, 2001); Sylvia Van Kirk, *Many Tender Ties: Women in Fur Trade Society, 1670–1870* (Winnipeg: Watson & Dwyer, 1980).

9   Evelyn Peters, "'Urban and Aboriginal': An Impossible Contradiction?" in *City Lives and City Forms: Critical Research and Canadian Urbanism*, ed. Jon Caulfield and Linda Peake (Toronto: University of Toronto Press, 1996).

10 Edgar Dosman, *Indians: The Urban Dilemma* (Toronto: McClelland & Stewart, 1972), 48.

11 Dosman, *Indians*, 56.

12 Nagler, *Indians in the City*, 95–103.

13 Sherry Ortner, "Reading America: Preliminary Notes on Class and Culture," in *Recapturing Anthropology: Working in the Present*, ed. Richard G. Fox (Santa Fe NM: School of American Research Press, 1991), 172.

14 Heather Howard-Bobiwash, "'Like Her Lips to My Ear': Reading Anish-naabekweg Lives and Aboriginal Cultural Continuity in the City," in *Feminist Fields: Ethnographic Insights*, ed. Rae Bridgman, Sally Cole, and Heather Howard-Bobiwash (Peterborough ON: Broadview Press, 1999), 119–20; Patronella Johnston, *Tales of Nokomis* (Don Mills ON: Musson, 1975).

15 Rosamund Vanderburgh, *I Am Nokomis, Too: The Biography of Verna Patronella Johnston* (Don Mills ON: General, 1977), 122, 141.

16 Edna Manitowabi, "Hedy Sylvester: The Founder of the Centre's Craft Shop," *Boozhoo, Newsmagazine of the Native Canadian Centre of Toronto*, 1:4 (1987): 35–37.

17 "'There's So Much to Learn Each Day': A Profile of Lillian McGregor," *Native Canadian Newsletter* (Native Canadian Centre of Toronto), 10:1 (October 1996): 1, 3.

18 The *Toronto Native Times* was a community-based monthly newspaper published by the Native Canadian Centre of Toronto between 1968 and 1981. Including this publication, the Centre has always produced some form of regularly appearing serial during its forty-plus year history.

19 Irene Lee, "Ladies' Auxiliary Visits KP," *Toronto Native Times* (Native Canadian Centre of Toronto), 2:4 (April 1971): 8.

20 Millie Redmond, interview by Evelyn Sit, Toronto Public Library Indian History Project, OHT 83030, 1983, 27–29.

21 Josephine Beaucage, interview by Cyndy Baskin, Toronto Public Library Indian History Project, OHT 83037, 1983.

22 Beaucage, interview by Cyndy Baskin, 13.

23 *Canadian Indian Centre of Toronto Newsletter*, February–March 1966, 4.

24 See Susan Lobo, chapter 1 of this volume.

25 Hettie Sylvester, interview by Jaime Lee, Toronto Public Library Indian History Project, OHT 82020, 1982, 9–10.

26 Evelyn Peters, "'Urban and Aboriginal': An Impossible Contradiction?" in Caulfield and Peake, *City Lives and City Forms*, 48.

27 For a more detailed account of the relationship between the IODE, the Native Canadian Centre of Toronto, and other national action on behalf of urban Aboriginal people in the 1960s, see Heather A. Howard, "How Did Native Women Employ Strategic Alliances with Non-Native Reformists

to Organize Community in Post-WWII Toronto?" forthcoming in "'See ing the Same World through Different Eyes': Canadian Women's Activism since 1945," special Canadian issue of *Women and Social Movements*, ed. Lara Campbell, Nancy Janovicek, Tamara Myers, and Joan Sangster (Alexandria VA: Alexander Street Press; online document project, http://alex anderstreetpress.com/).

28 "IODE Asks for Study of Indians" (Ottawa—CP), Unidentified Toronto Native Community History Project News-clipping file, c. 1963. The history project has an extensive collection of news clippings, which are believed to have been collected by members of the Native Canadian Centre of Toronto's Ladies' Auxiliary between 1962 and 1968. Many are undated and the sources unidentified. This particular clipping was determined to date during or prior to 1963, as "Minister Bell" is mentioned. His term as citizenship minister was from 1957 to 1963 under Prime Minister John Diefenbaker. It is interesting that IODE women were advocating this in-depth study sometime before the pivotal "Hawthorne Report" was commissioned by the government in 1964 (*A Survey of the Contemporary Indians of Canada Economic, Political, Educational Needs and Policies*, 1966). In 1969 Prime Minister Pierre Trudeau cited this report to propose the elimination of Indian Status and assimilate Native people completely into Canadian society. This prompted nationwide protest from Native people, often said to mark the official beginning of the Red Power movement in Canada.

8 Creating Change, Reclaiming Indian Space in Post–World War II Seattle

The American Indian Women's Service League
and the Seattle Indian Center, 1958–1978

MARY C. WRIGHT

The March 2, 2004, memorial service marked the passing and celebrated the life of Adeline Hannah Skultka Garcia (Haida) as the last founding member of Seattle's American Indian Women's Service League. The themes that Garcia "always made a place for people" and "made everyone feel at home" ran through the eulogy.[1] Indeed, Garcia and other American Indian women reclaimed Native space first by establishing the American Indian Women's Service League in 1958 and then by founding the Seattle Indian Center in the 1960s.[2] Here, by utilizing Native gender roles, they created social space, community space, and eventually political space for the post–World War II Seattle Indian community.

The founding women of the American Indian Women's Service League (hereafter the Service League), led by Pearl Warren (Makah), met for their informal and often social activities in the personal space of their homes and in borrowed church space. From this initial toehold they began helping Indians new to the area with information, assistance, and advocacy to navigate the city and its services. The group went on to establish the Seattle Indian Center, one of the earlier multipurpose urban Indian centers in the country, housed in a sequence of better-suited spaces.

The growth trajectory of the Service League's Seattle Indian

Center began in a small downtown storefront. Opening in 1960 at 1st and Vine, it soon hummed with activities. Expanding programs and increasing popularity motivated the Center's move in 1963 to a converted church at 1900 Boren. Even using every inch of that building's space, it too eventually became insufficient. The Seattle Indian Center made a final move in 1973 to the so-called 2nd and Cherry Building (a better moniker was never awarded), sharing this downtown facility with other Indian agencies.

The Service League and their Indian Center launched many of the city's Indian-focused social services as well as many Natives' public service careers. The space claimed and created throughout the 1960s and 1970s by the Service League served as a base camp for Seattle's Red Power movement and contributed to the growth of a new urban Indian identity. As this study delineates, the women knew that to create change, Native place and space must first be reclaimed.

Native Place and the Seattle Indian Center

Colonialism impacted America's Native people in a number of ways — population loss due to epidemic disease, cultural loss from U.S. assimilation policies — but the loss of lands through the five centuries of contact are of particular interest to this study. Scholars consider geographies of encounter and contested terrain as central to Indigenous and European historic interaction.[3] Native loss is more than simply a matter of the distant past. The post–World War II years saw efforts to terminate federal treaty obligations with tribes that ceded lands and to deny Indians residing in urban areas federally funded services available on the reservations. The realities of such contested terrain in twentieth-century Indian and non-Indian encounter roused modern Indian activism.

If consideration of the contested places and the geographies of encounter are expanded to include abandoned federal property and space in the city, especially for the 1960s and 1970s, our understanding of the era and the Red Power movement becomes clearer. Since "geography is centrally implicated in the construction of difference," by reclaiming urban and federal spaces, Indians gained a place from which to shift power relations, taking on bigger battles of cultural identity, treaty rights, self-determination, and Indigenous sovereignty.[4]

The varied locations of the American Indian Women's Service League's Seattle Indian Center filled many empty spaces in Seattle's downtown—vacant due to post-WWII population losses due to suburban growth and the snaking of Interstate 5 through neighborhoods near downtown. The urban renewal movement increased Seattle's tourism allure. For instance, the Service League's craft shop was a suggested stop while sight-seeing in "restored" Seattle. *Century 21*, Seattle's 1962 World's Fair, made the filling of empty city space desirable. The *Argus*, a Seattle news weekly, applauded the Service League's efforts and urged the city to support the Center since the Fair highlighted Native motifs and "atmosphere."[5] In Seattle the Native women of the Service League seized opportunities to fill and reclaim that newly available space, however marginalized. By doing so they helped to reassert (and return to) previous spatial arrangements for Indigenous peoples.

As the storefront Indian Center opened, President Pearl Warren emphasized the importance of *place* to its purposes. The women meant the Center to be "a friendly Indian meeting place" where those new to the city could go for help and medical, educational, or other needed advice or referrals.[6] The Center was a "place that would help preserve Pacific Northwest Indian culture" and bolster Indian identity.[7] As Pearl Warren expressed in an early newsletter, "We hope to bring together as many Indians as we can, regardless of where they come from, or the degree of Indian blood." Participation suggests the group succeeded. For instance, young hostesses for the first open house came from many tribal groups. In a representative year with approximately 145 members, officers and the executive board included women from the lower Northwest Coast/Puget Sound (8), Alaskan Indians (2), and Plains and Plateau Indians (2).[8]

From the very first the Service League women cast a wide net, going door to door, visiting the bus station for new arrivals, and giving out aid to an increasing number of Indian families who flocked to cities.[9] Discrimination in housing and jobs kept many in dire economic straits, and images of the drunken skid row Indian abounded. "Back then there were still signs on the doors that said 'No Dogs or Indians Allowed.' These women really had the courage to step out of the stereotypes and stand up for their people and themselves," remembers activist Ramona Bennett (Puyallup) on the Service League's importance.[10]

They established the first Indian Center some blocks from the city's skid row. But by keeping a constant supply of hot coffee available in a comfortable setting, they welcomed the most downtrodden of Seattle's Indian residents. Enforcing a "no drinking allowed" policy also established the Center as a place of healing.[11]

Advocacy for Indians released from area hospitals, a special Service League blood bank account, and support for an Alcoholics Anonymous group spurred the early Service League, according to Adeline Garcia.[12] Volunteer doctors (and later dentists) worked for an Indian Health Clinic that developed into the successful Seattle Indian Health Board (SIHB).[13] The history of this nationally renowned medical organization, reaching thirty-five years of service in 2006, is beyond the scope of this limited study. Its emergence is closely tied to the Service League, the Seattle Indian Center, and the United Indians, and it expanded under the able leadership of Luana Reyes (Colville).[14] The SIHB's services and offices would later find space away from other Indian agencies to be closer to Seattle medical facilities and the Public Health Hospital.[15]

Indian culture was celebrated at the Indian Center with popular art and craft classes, dance instruction, and the recounting of traditional legends and with the sponsorship of art and craft exhibits and sales.[16] Indian art proved so popular that the women's gift counter grew into a gift shop and gallery selling Native works. The shop "Traditions and Beyond," later located in the 2nd and Cherry Building, provided revenue for scholarships and offered Native craftspeople a more profitable outlet.[17]

Reclaiming the care, education, and guidance of Indian children and youth from the American establishment became another early priority of the Service League's Indian Center. They offered tutors, study halls, referrals to vocational training, help with locating scholarships and financial aid for Native students, and GRE classes and testing.[18]

In 1963, when the Service League's Indian Center expanded to the larger quarters, their educational programs included Upward Bound, National Endowment for the Humanities (NEH) grants for legal and heritage education, tutoring, and scholarship assistance. The Indian Center's cultural programs offered an annual powwow, Indian dancing family nights, youth activities, and Indian art and craft displays and sales.[19] Potluck dinners, emergency aid, a clothes bank, referrals, and advocacy also continued.

In 1967 the Service League hoped to gain a facility near south Lake Union built to their specifications and needs. Stressing historic land loss, Warren adamantly argued, "We feel the city should *give us back some land* and we won't settle for some haphazard deal. We want an Indian-style longhouse—a place with a meeting room, craft workshop and display center. A site in Denny Park would be ideal."[20] Such a purpose resonated since Arthur Denny, one of Seattle's founders, bequeathed land for the park from his holdings claimed before 1855 when local tribes ceded Indigenous title to the U.S. in treaties.[21]

The City of Seattle (and the wider Puget Sound and Western Washington region) was, of course, Native space from the beginning. Seattle was built on Duwamish territory and takes its name from Sealth, a local Duwamish-Suquamish leader friendly to the American settlers. Native contributions to the economic and social relations of the nineteenth-century period facilitated the city's successful establishment and growth, even as Seattle came to displace Indigenous people from (and pave over) their original geography.[22]

The hoped-for use of Denny Park land made a nice complement to the Service League's annual Salmon Bake on the opposite side of town. By using Alki Beach, where the Denny party and a number of Seattle's other Euro-American founders came ashore in 1851, the Service League women symbolically reclaimed that colonized space. The women sold salmon dinners during the city's summer Sea Fair festival over more than twenty years, raising funds for a permanent Seattle Indian Center building, hopefully a longhouse. For example, at the 1965 Salmon Bake they sold 1,000 dinners and had widespread community support. At the 1966 event they served over 1,500 meals. In 1980 they held the twenty-second annual salmon bake.[23]

Others also demanded the return of Native lands but went further than Warren. In 1970 an Alcatraz-style invasion of Fort Lawton, federal surplus property in Seattle, brought local and national media and government attention to the issue of urban Indian needs. While Bernie (Reyes) Whitebear (Colville) is credited with planning and executing the takeover of Fort Lawton, many others in Seattle's Indian community also contributed. For instance, Service League leaders and members participated in the demonstration to reclaim Native land. Ella Aquino (Lummi, Yakama) related how she, and others she identified as "old ladies," scaled the fences at Fort Lawton with sandwiches and thermoses of coffee in hand for the demonstrators. The support of elders validated the demands of the invaders, who primarily were young people.[24]

Service League volunteers also stepped in "to cook, donate food, write letters of support and man the phones," remembers Julie Johnson (Makah), a Service League employee at the time and later its president. Press releases were written and news conferences held at the Seattle Indian Center.[25]

Bernie Whitebear led the negotiators and won a ninety-nine-year lease for twenty acres near Seattle's Magnolia neighborhood.[26] However, without the Service League as part of the negotiating team, the efforts to secure the Fort Lawton lands may have failed. The Service League refused the city's tempting offer of its own facility free of charge and supported Whitebear.[27] Cooperation thus ensured an urban Indian cultural center.

A new group formed around Whitebear, the United Indians of All Tribes Foundation (hereafter United Indians), which gained government, tribal, and private foundation funding for construction. The resulting Daybreak Star Cultural Center opened in 1977 to great fanfare on the Fort Lawton property.[28] With Whitebear's leadership it became a permanent asset for Seattle's Indian community, with its focus on culture, art, powwows, and other community events.[29]

The Native space reclaimed by the Service League women for their Seattle Indian Center provided a place from which Northwest Indian political activism could grow. Ironically several emerging Native organizations and competing leaders challenged the Service League on issues ranging from its leadership style and community role to its fundraising approach and provision of services. These new political forces would displace Service League leadership as too complacent.

Whitebear and his allies were instrumental in wresting power away from the venerable Service League organization. Whitebear got his start, like many others, with cultural activities tied to the Seattle Indian Center run by the Service League. He participated in the All-American Indian Dancers group and led a troupe through Europe on a celebrated tour.[30] Afterward he headed a series of successful Seattle powwows. He also served as the first Native director of the Seattle Indian Health Board.[31] Having led the invasion of Fort Lawton, Whitebear enjoyed the support of a loyal following and exerted considerable political influence.[32]

When Indian Center Director Pearl Warren "could not be persuaded to change her mind and support Bernie and the UIATF [United Indians], it became obvious she would have to be replaced," reported Whitebear's brother Lawney Reyes (Colville). "At a UIATF meeting it was decided to run Joyce Reyes against Pearl [Warren]."[33] They felt it necessary "to unite all Indians in Seattle," and the Service League, led by Warren, was reluctant to apply for federal funding of Indian services.[34] In 1970 an influx of new membership voted Joyce Reyes (Yakama), Whitebear's sister-in-law, into the Service League's presidency.[35]

The lure of new government funding opportunities underlay this challenge to Warren's leadership but had other important impacts as well. Agencies and programs receiving federal funds could not discriminate on race, religion, gender, or other grounds. The gains of the national feminist movement thus had a negative impact on the Service League. This discrimination rule challenged the Service League's organizational structure since a member needed only two qualities: to be Indian and female. (Nonvoting associate members, however, could be male or non-Native.) Rather than change the American Indian Women's Service League's basic character as a women-only group, they voted to split off the Seattle Indian Center as an independent organization.[36] After this structural change, federal funds could be acquired by the Seattle Indian Center, and it grew enormously.[37]

Elizabeth Morris (Athabascan) replaced Pearl Warren as the Center's director, and within three months the group received approval for grants for youth and legal assistance programs totaling $87,000. Morris's five previous years as an active Service League member surely influenced her goals—larger facilities, increased funding, and program development. Morris tapped into new government monies and is credited with developing twelve new social and health programs and increasing Seattle Indian Center staff from four to fifty.[38]

Morris's thumbnail analysis of modern Indian issues, given in 1973 to *Ms. Magazine*, shows pride in Indian culture similar to the early Service League women. Morris said: "The white dominant culture seemed to think that once the Indians were off the reservations, they'd eventually become like everyone else [but] when the Indian-ness is drummed out of them nothing is in its place. Our land has been taken away from us; we can't make it in the old ways. But we can't be white either."[39]

President Lyndon Johnson's War on Poverty (1964–1970) was used to address the economic aspects of Indian issues but brought an unforeseen change to the Service League and the Seattle Indian

Center. Federal monies and regulations meant professionals now performed Center work previously done by Service League members and volunteers. Social workers, counselors, and administrators needed qualifications such as degrees, training, and professional experience, sidelining the many capable and productive women of the Service League who originally built the organization. Agency programs funded by the federal government displaced the Service League's caring, grassroots, self-help approach even as the Indian Center they founded lived on.[40]

Service League influence also continued as part of the Seattle Indian Services Commission (SISC), a new agency formed in the Fort Lawton settlement of 1973 to coordinate space, facilities, and funding needs of local Indian groups. The Commission included two representatives from the Service League, the United Indians, the Seattle Indian Center, and the Seattle Indian Health Board—the leading Indian organizations in Seattle at the time. Coming together in this way allowed SISC to receive Seattle "Model Cities" monies to purchase the 2nd and Cherry Building.[41]

The Seattle Indian Center programs built under Elizabeth Morris's leadership operated out of the 2nd and Cherry Building located in Seattle's downtown. The growth of the Seattle Indian Health Board and the United Indians, also housed in the building, complemented Indian Center development. At this time period there were enough funding sources for the many innovative and important Indian programs.[42]

This new building, this Indian space, engendered conflicts within Seattle's Native community. Fighting over organizations and space has often emerged, argues Joseph P. Gone, because they are so central to the construction of urban Indian cultural identity.[43] The Indian Center's third director, Gregory Frazier (Crow) saw another round of contests over control of place and space. The Service League's guaranteed representation on the Indian Center governing board increased conflict with Frazier. After a flurry of intrigues, factionalism, personal harassment, and lawsuits, the Service League withdrew from the Indian Center's board, completely cutting ties with the agency they had founded.[44]

The Service League's representation on the SISC brought further battles with Frazier. As director of the Indian Center, Frazier also managed the 2nd and Cherry Building.[45] Paying tenants had moved out, extensive renovations were needed to bring the building to code, and, according to Frazier, the Service League paid no rent for its Indian art shop while the Indian Center paid approximately 10 percent of grant revenues in annual rent. After a series of confrontations Frazier ran out of allies and options as the other Indian groups in the SISC closed ranks to oppose him.[46] Frazier moved the Indian Center to another building and lost most staff members during the conflicts. When even a local oversight hearing about federal funding could not remedy the situation, he left the Indian Center in 1978.[47] Woodrow Delorme (Coeur d'Alene) replaced him in February 1979 and, by emphasizing unity and consensus, won back many program grants given to competing agencies during Frazier's troubled tenure.[48]

Seattle's discord replicated nation-wide trends of conflict in other cities' Indian centers.[49] Yet despite these divisions over identity, programs, and philosophy, James LaGrand argues in *Indian Metropolis*, there often remained a "common emphasis on self-determination, Indian pride, and identity politics [that] would survive a time of trouble."[50] Native activists in Seattle shared the ideological vision LaGrand outlines but differed on leadership, organizational structure, and strategies.

Politics and the Service League

Contests within the Native community should not distract attention from the very real political contributions the Service League made in the 1960s and 1970s. One of its major strategies was educating the Indian community and their wider Seattle contacts about treaty rights and sovereignty issues. Almost every issue of the *Indian Center News* in the 1960s and the *Northwest Indian News* that replaced it in the 1970s printed important stories, resources, and other information to help preserve and protect Indian peoples' civil rights, tribal sovereignty, and treaty rights as their historically specific and unique governmental relationship.[51]

For example, the *Indian Center News* followed the federal termination issue closely and argued for tribal continuance. Both the anti- and pro-termination groups appealed to off-reservation tribal members when Washington's Confederated Colville tribes struggled with the issue of termination. Should the reservation land continue as the tribes' political homeland, or should it be sold and profits distributed to tribal members?[52] In this specific case urbanized Colville Indians supported the successful faction, led by Lucy Covington, that sought to maintain the tribal land base and the cultural heritage it represented.[53]

The Service League also had a direct impact on local politics. The city of Seattle, King County, the state of Washington, the federal Bureau of Indian Affairs, and various social service agencies went to the Service League's women for input on Indian issues, representation on boards, involvement in needs assessments, and service provision.[54] In response the United Good Neighbors, the locally based fundraising program for social services and precursor to today's United Way, funded 80 percent of the Indian Center's budget after only two years of existence and continued to do so for many years.[55]

The Service League influenced Northwest tribal politics by launching the careers of numerous Indian women. When many Northwest tribes assumed self-administration of reservation programs following the Indian Self-Determination Act of 1975, the knowledge, skills, and connections many Native women gained from founding and administering urban Indian programs proved useful to their tribes.[56]

While new opportunities came with the growth of federal funding, the reluctance of Indian Center director Pearl Warren to rely on government grants proved prophetic. Accepting federal funding for Indian Centers and Indian programs meant a loss of control over goals and structure, she had argued. The golden opportunities of government funding lasted little more than a decade. Richard Nixon continued federal support for many of the Indian programs established under Johnson's War on Poverty.[57] A recession undercut funding by President Jimmy Carter. As federal monies went to the states in the form of block grants under Ronald Reagan's New Federalism, urban Indian services competed with other programs and constituencies.[58] The numerically small American Indian population received less than needed.

Yet some Indian agencies managed to survive in Seattle. A 2002 overview highlighted the Indian Center, the Seattle Indian Health Board, and the United Indians of All Tribes Foundation. They were "commanding a combined annual budget exceeding $8 million and employing more than 250 peoples, offering much-needed social, cultural, educational and health services [and providing] a sense of community for Native people."[59]

Continuing Legacy

As time passed, the rancor of earlier years quieted in Seattle. In a sign of healing the Seattle Indian Services Commission and the Seattle Indian Health Board recognized the leadership of Pearl Warren in the American Indian Women's Service League and the early Seattle Indian Center by naming their new facility (at 606 12th Avenue South) the Pearl Warren Building.[60]

The Service League's legacy lives on in other ways. The group's vision continued to influence many Indian women active in Seattle and the Puget Sound region. Certainly Ramona Bennett's 1976 election as Puyallup tribal chairwoman provides a useful example of that trend.[61] Bennett relates: "When I first got started in Indian politics and services and learning how to be an advocate, [Pearl Warren] was the one that trained me. They used to call me 'Minnie Pearl.' I liked that." She also remembers writing "mountains" of grant applications that helped support many of Seattle's Indian (and later Puyallup tribal) programs.[62]

In another fight over Indian place and space Bennett helped mastermind the takeover of the former Cushman Hospital on Puyallup lands. The facility, being used by the state of Washington for a juvenile program, became Puyallup Headquarters after the takeover. The successful challenge brought the land lost in 1939 back into tribal hands. Today the tribe's casino and hotel occupy the site.[63]

Bennett provided leadership in the Pacific Northwest fish-ins as her commentary reflects in the 1990 documentary *Full Circle: The Indians of Washington State*.[64] She helped obtain support for the passage of the Indian Child Welfare Act in 1978 and worked to implement it as head of the Indian Center's foster care program in the 1980s and as founder of Rainbow Children and Family Services in the 1990s.[65]

Few of the Service League women equaled Bennett's highly visible leadership role, but their continuing involvement in the Seattle Indian community confirm the long-term importance of the Service League's vision. Many used their exceptional organizational experience and their connections with government decision makers and funding agencies to generate innovative programs. For instance, Pearl Warren had an extensive social service career after leaving the Service League and the Seattle Indian Center. She held offices at the state and national levels during "The Year of the Woman" and in the emerging field of services for the elderly.[66]

Ella Aquino provides another sterling example. Her contributions began with the Service League's *Indian Center News* (1960–1970). She continued her famous "Tee Pee Talk" columns in, and later became editor of, the *Northwest Indian News* (1970–1980). A 1987 film documentary, *Princess of the Powwow*, honored her life, her participation in the Fort Lawton invasion, and her general leadership in the Seattle Indian community.[67]

Julie Johnson (Makah) headed the Seattle Indian Center's Social and Health Services division for eight years, where she directed one of the first urban Indian youth programs in the nation. She went on to manage social services, write major grants, work in planning departments, and serve the Makah, Lower Elwha S'Klallam, Lummi, and other Northwest tribes.[68]

We could add to this preliminary list of urban activists with a closer look at many other former Service League members' careers and their influence in the Northwest. Luanna Reyes (Colville) and Jo Ann Kauffman (Nez Perce) established urban and reservation-based Indian health care programs. Mary Jo Butterfield (Makah) and Lee Piper (Cherokee) contributed to Indian education in various programs and a number of institutions.

The vision and leadership of these and other Indian women continues to inspire into the twenty-first century. Recipients of the Enduring Spirit awards, given by the American Native Women's Leadership Development Forum for 2002, 2003, and 2004, included a majority of American Indian Women's Service League members. Maiselle Bridges, Adeline Garcia, JoAnn Staples Baum, Gina George, and Jeannie Halliday (posthumous) received the 2002 Enduring Spirit awards. Marilyn Wandrey, Joy Ketah, Virginia Cross, and Ramona Bennett accepted the 2003 awards. The 2004 awards honored Johanna Cabuag, Lillian Chappell, Julie Johnson, and Marie Zackuse.[69]

Many younger Indian women emulate the wisdom and carry on the activism of these important women. The historic importance of the Service League women has generated several academic theses, but the most current and potentially most accessible work is by a Native woman. Teresa Brownwolf Powers (Standing Rock Sioux) is producing the video *Legacy of Pride* honoring the Service League.[70]

The varied contributions of the Service League women to a thriving Seattle Indian community built on traditional Indian gender roles — where women cared for families and the sick, educated the young, fed and welcomed others, influenced politics, and managed economic resources — all re-interpreted into a modern urban context. Their actions confirm scholarly assessments of Indigenous women's importance and power.[71] Historical studies broadly define Indian women as "negotiators of change" who balance the pressures of contact with the strengths of tradition, using their agency to resist colonization.[72]

Critical investigations by Native women writers, scholars, and activists find that Indian women's modern roles, identity, and importance revolve around working for their peoples' needs, for sovereignty and cultural pride.[73] The women of the Service League reinforce these paradigms of Indian women's power and importance within the community.

Formation of the American Indian Women's Service League and the Seattle Indian Center demonstrate how central activism was to these women's lives and to their community. They brought history, pride, and accomplishments as Native people to a celebration and renewal of Native culture. Their programs, classes, advocacy, and public and community events contributed to the emergence of pan-Indian cultural practices, awareness, and identity in Seattle. They worked to bring changes in the larger society's perceptions of Native Americans and increase recognition of Indian civil and treaty rights. They changed the provision of social and health services for Indigenous people in urban areas. They provided a foundation for many Native women's careers leading to even further changes for Indian people. As they reclaimed Native place and space in Seattle, these Indian women did more than negotiate or mediate change—they created change.

Notes

The author, who is non-Native, would like to thank the Institute for Ethnic Studies in the United States for funding and Teresa Brownwolf Powers (Standing Rock Sioux) for her assistance on the project as a Mary Gates Undergraduate Research Scholar at the University of Washington.

1 Adeline Garcia Memorial Service, March 2004, Green Lake Presbyterian Church, Seattle, Washington; eulogy by Rev. Michael Kelly; author's collection.

2 Seven women signed the Articles of Incorporation: Ella Aquino (Lummi/Yakama), Hazel Duarte (Makah/Clallam), Theresa Gibbs (Lummi), Dorothy Lombard (Clallam), Leona Lyness (Lummi/Haida), Meredith Mummy (Makah), and Pearl Warren (Makah).

3 James Taylor Carson, "Ethnogeography and the Native American Past," *Ethnohistory* 49:4 (2002): 769–88; Tracy Neal Leavelle, "Geographies of Encounter: Religion and Contested Spaces in Colonial North America," *American Quarterly* 56:4 (2004): 913–43.

4 James Duncan and David Ley, eds., *Place/Culture/Representation* (London: Routledge, 1993), "Introduction," 1–21, "Epilogue," 329–34, quote on 13; Robert Rotenberg, introduction to *The Cultural Meaning of Urban Space*, ed. Robert Rotenberg and Gary McDonogh (Westport CT: Bergin & Garvey, 1993), xi–xix.

5 Margaret V. Daly, "Great Vacations in America's Restored Cities: Seattle," *Better Homes and Gardens*, October 1978, 183, 196; Archie Binns, "Puget Sound and Fury," *Argus*, May 27, 1960, 4; Gary McDonogh, "The Geography of Emptiness," in Rotenberg and McDonogh, *Cultural Meaning of Urban Space*, 3–16.

6 Binns, "Puget Sound," 4.

7 Binns, "Puget Sound," 4; Karin M. Enloe, "Helping Indians Help Themselves, An Urban American Indian Success Story: Identity, Activism and Community Building in Seattle, 1958–1972" (master's thesis, Western Washington University, 1999).

8 Quote in *Indian Center News (hereafter ICN)* 1:1 (February 19, 1960); Open House, *ICN* 1:7 (August 9, 1960); board and officers listed in American Indian Women's Service League, *Old and New Indian Recipes* (Kansas City: North American Press, undated), 18, 18–21. The Center's move to 1900 Boren Avenue in April 1963 was announced in *ICN*, 3:10 (March 14, 1963). An incomplete collection (1960–71) of the *ICN* is housed in the University of Washington's Manuscripts, Special Collections, University Archives (hereafter MSCUA).

9 *ICN*, 1:1 (February 19, 1960): 1.

10 Ramona Bennett, videotaped interview by Teresa Powers, December 6, 2000.

11 *ICN* 1:8 (September 10, 1960); Bernie Binns, "Rain in Pioneer Place," *Argus*, May 27, 1960, 6.

12 Adeline Garcia, videotaped interview by Teresa Powers, May 24, 2000; *ICN* 1:4 (May 7, 1960).

13 "Free Medical/Dental Clinic," *Northwest Indian News* (hereafter NWIN) 1:1 (June 1971): 6–7; *Seattle Times Sunday Magazine*, November 7, 1971, 12–13.

14 Daniel Cohen, "Indians Caring for Indians," *Seattle Sun*, May 10, 1978), 9, 11; NWIN, 2:3 (September 1972): 4; NWIN 5:11 (April 1976): 4; NWIN 10:5

(March 1980): 4; also see the Seattle Indian Health Board Web site, http://
www.sihb.org/about_SIHB.html.

15 NWIN 2:3 (September 1972): 4; NWIN 5:11 (April 1976): 4; NWIN 10:5
(March 1980): 4.

16 ICN 3:10 (March 14, 1963), 3:17 (March 1964), 4:/25 (February 19, 1965),
5:1 (September 1966); NWIN 10:6 (April 1980): 4.

17 Mildred Tanner Andrews, Woman's Place: A Guide to Seattle and King County
History (Seattle: Gemil Press, 1994), 187–89.

18 ICN 4:21 (October 5, 1964), 5:29 (October 5, 1966), 2:12 (March 1962), 2:13
(April 1962). See also Pearl Warren, "Statement of Mrs. Pearl Warren,
Executive Director, Seattle Indian Center, Seattle, Washington," Hearings
before the Special Subcommittee on Indian Education of the Committee on
Labor and Public Welfare, United States Senate, Ninetieth Congress (Wash-
ington DC: Government Printing Office, 1969), 211–18.

19 "10th Anniversary," ICN 3:6 (February 1970): 1–2.

20 "City and Sound: Indian Giver," Seattle Magazine, April 1967, 15–17 (emphasis added).

21 Arthur Denny and party are historicized in Emily Inez Denny, Blazing
the Way, or, True Stories, Songs and Sketches of Puget Sound and Other Pioneers
(Seattle: Rainier, 1909). Charles J. Kappler, comp. and ed., Indian Affairs:
Laws and Treaties, vol. 2: Indian Treaties (Washington DC: Government
Printing Office, 1904); available online at http://digital.library.okstate
.edu/kappler/Vol2/.

22 Alexandra Harmon, Indians in the Making: Ethnic Relations and Indian
Identities around Puget Sound (Berkeley: University of California Press,
1998); Coll Peter Thrush, "The Crossing-Over Place: Urban Indian Histories in Seattle" (PhD diss., University of Washington, 2002).

23 See ICN 5:28 (1965), 5:1 (September 1966); NWIN 10:6 (April 1980): 4.

24 For some news footage of the Fort Lawton take-over see Princess of the Powwow, video, prod. Derek Creisler and Nancy Johnston (Seattle: Running
Colors Production, 1987); "Ella Aquino, Indian Leader," SPI, November
4, 1988, D14.

25 Julie Johnson, personal communication with the author, August 2004.

26 "House Passes Fort Lawton Bill," Seattle Post-Intelligencer (hereafter SPI),
August 11, 1970, 1, 4; "Indian Group Asks Senator Jackson for Surplussed
[sic] Fort Lawton," ICN 8:7 (March 1970): 7; "United Indians of All Tribes
Fort Lawton," ICN 8:8 (April 1970): 1–2.

27 "Important Site Decision to Be Made at AIWSL Meeting," NWIN 1:7 (January

1972): 1; "Options for Building," NWIN 1:10 (May 1972): 1; "New Inroads Made on the Indian Front," NWIN 1:9 (April 1972): 1; Johnson, personal communication.

28 "A Proud Day," SPI, May 12, 1977, A-11; "2000 Turn Out for Daybreak Star Dedication," NWIN, 6:11 (May 1977): 5.

29 Whitebear and the United Indians built a network of government-funded services. Bernie Whitebear, "Taking Back Fort Lawton: Meeting the Needs of Seattle's Native American Community through Conversion," *Race, Poverty and the Environment*, Spring–Summer 1994, 3-6; Claudia Kaufman, interview by the author, July 11, 2000.

30 "War Dancers Tour Europe," ICN 7:3 (November 1968): 6; "500 Gather to Honor Northwest Indian Leader," SPI, July 21, 2000.

31 "500 Gather."

32 "Indians Invade, Lay Claim to Fort Lawton," SPI, May 9, 1970, 1; "Whitebear Leads Indians to Victory in Fort Lawton Battle," SPI, December 5, 1971, A-14.

33 Lawney L. Reyes, *Bernie Whitebear: An Urban Indian's Quest for Justice* (Tucson: University of Arizona Press, 2006), 103–4.

34 Ironically, the ICN publicized this meeting to discuss "unity" and in the same issue spoke of the SIC's long-term plans for the longhouse. See ICN 3:6 (February 1970): 2, 3.

35 Reyes, *Bernie Whitebear*, 103–4.

36 "League Votes Major Change: To Incorporate Indian Center," NWIN 1:4 (September 1971): 2; "From the Indian Center Director's Desk," NWIN 1:6 (December 1971): 2. However, the AISWL continued to guide the Center, having eight seats on the fifteen-member board of directors.

37 "Joyce Reyes Report," NWIN 1:3 (August 1971): 3; ICN 9:9 (May 1971): 1.

38 Johnson, personal communication, 1, 4. On Morris's appointment, see the *Argus*, 78:19 (May 7, 1971); "Joyce Reyes Report," 3; ICN 9:9 (May 1971): 1.

39 "Found Women," *Ms. Magazine* 1:7 (January 1973): 50.

40 Karen Tranberg Hansen, "American Indians and Work in Seattle: Associations, Ethnicity and Class" (PhD diss., University of Washington, 1979) 162–67; Enloe, "Helping Indians Help Themselves"; Donald Fixico, *The Urban Indian Experience in America* (Albuquerque: University of New Mexico Press, 2000), 129–33, 137–40.

41 Gregory W. Frazier, "Building Alternatives for the Seattle Indian Center: A Report Prepared for the SIC Board of Directors" (typescript, 1976), 28, University of Washington Libraries, MSCUA.

42 UIATF programs, NWIN 5:2 (June 1975): 5; NWIN 6:9 (March 1977): 6.

43 Joseph P. Gone, "American Indian Identity," in *Mental Health Care for Urban Indians: Clinical Insights from Native Practitioners*, ed. Tawa M. Witko (Washington DC: American Psychological Association, 2006) 55–80.

44 "Settlement Reached in Board Controversy," NWIN 5:7 (November 1975): 1; Ella Aquino, "Teepee Talk," NWIN 7:/2 (September 1977) 2. "Angry Affiliate Groups Quit Indian Center," SPI, August 17, 1977, D1. Karen Tranberg Hansen, who observed some of the conflicts firsthand, analyzes the Service League and Seattle Indian Center turmoil in her "Ethnic Group Policy and the Politics of Sex: The Seattle Indian Case," *Urban Anthropology* 8:1 (1979): 29–47.

45 "Broderick Building Now Indian Center," SPI, April 14, 1973, A-9; "Open House," *Seattle Times* (hereafter S-T), March 18, 1973.

46 "Indians Debate Future of Building," S-T, June 17, 1976, A-10; "SIC Removed as Manager of the Indian Center Building," NWIN 5:5 (September 1975): 5; Gregory W. Frazier, *Urban Indians: Drums from the Cities* (Denver: Arrowstar, 1993), 115–33.

47 NWIN 7:2 (September 1977): 1.

48 NWIN 9:7 (February 1979): 2; Frazier, *Urban Indians*, 118, 124. Delorme recognized staff members' contributions, NWIN 10:2 (August 1979): 3. SIC programs listed in the *Indian News* included foster care, Urban Indian Education center (GED and basic education), legal department, and job services under CETA. NWIN 10:3 (December 1979): 7; NWIN 10:5 (March 1980): 6.

49 Deborah Davis Jackson, *Our Elders Lived It: American Indian Identity in the City* (DeKalb: Northern Illinois University Press, 2002), 32–52; James B. LaGrand, *Indian Metropolis: Native Americans in Chicago, 1945–75* (Urbana: University of Illinois Press, 2002).

50 LaGrand, *Indian Metropolis*, quote on 218–19; see 183–246 for the new form of activism and its institutional consequences.

51 Eventually a new group, Indians into Communications, published the paper. NWIN 1:2 (July 1971): 2.

52 "A people, a place, a sense of place, and control of place" are the characteristics that define a homeland according to Richard L. Nostrand and Lawrence E. Estaville Jr., "The Homeland Concept," *Journal of Cultural Geography* 13:2 (1993): 1–4.

53 See, for example, ICN 1:4 (May 7, 1960), 2:11 (February 1962), 3:11 (April 20, 1963); Kathleen A. Dahl, "The Battle over Termination on the Colville Indian Reservation," *American Indian Culture and Research Journal* 18:1 (1994): 29–53.

54 In 1968 Pearl Warren listed her commitments as "the Council on Aging, the legal aid program of the Office for Economic Opportunity (OEO), the Seattle-King County Board of the OEO, the Human Rights Commission for the Catholic Archdiocese, and the community aid program." Warren, "Statement," 212.

55 *ICN* 2:6 (September 1961); "City and Sound," 16.

56 Francis Paul Prucha, *The Great Father: The United States Government and the American Indians,* abridged ed. (Lincoln: University of Nebraska Press, 1986), 376–80; Bruce G. Miller, "Women and Tribal Politics: Is There a Gender Gap in Indian Elections?" *American Indian Quarterly* 18:1 (1994): 25–41; Bruce G. Miller, "Women and Politics: Comparative Evidence from the Northwest Coast," *Ethnology* 31:4 (1992): 367–83.

57 George Pierre Castile, *To Show Heart: Native American Self-Determination and Federal Indian Policy, 1960–1975* (Tucson: University of Arizona Press, 1998).

58 The author directed a senior citizen program in the early 1980s and experienced these destructive funding battles firsthand. Also see Fixico, *Urban Indian Experience,* 120–21; Samuel R. Cook, "Ronald Reagan's Indian Policy in Retrospect: Economic Crisis and Political Irony," *Policy Studies Journal* 24:1 (1996): 11–26.

59 N. Iris Friday, "Making the Invisible Visible," *Native Americas* 19:1 (2002): 48.

60 Eric Scigliano, "International District: Eastward Ho, the Growth of Greater Chinatown," *Seattle Weekly,* December 11, 1985, 26, 28.

61 "Puyallup Tribe Hits Stride [Bennett Elected]," *Tacoma News Tribune,* July 4, 1976, A3/1.

62 Ramona Bennett, presentation to author's University of Washington class, December 6, 2000; videotaped by Teresa Powers, author's collection. "Ramona Bennett," *Native American Women: Biographical Dictionary,* ed. Gretchen M. Bataille and Laurie Lisa, 2nd ed. (London: Routledge, 2001), 30–31.

63 NWIN 5:3 (July 1975): 8; NWIN 5:4 (August 1975): 1; NWIN 10:9 (August 1980): 1, 3; Charles L. Carson, "Rising from the Ashes: The Puyallup Indians, Assimilation, Culture & Self-Determination" (master's thesis, University of Washington, 2003), 39–42.

64 *Full Circle: Indians of Washington State,* prod. and ed. John deGraaf and Maria Garguilo (video, University of California Extension Media Center, 1990).

65 "Statement of Ramona Bennett, Chairwoman, Puyallup Tribe," Indian Child Welfare Act of 1977, Hearing before the U.S. Senate Select Com-

mittee on Indian Affairs on S. 1214, 95th Cong., 1st sess. (Washington DC: U.S. Government Printing Office, 1977), 163–68; Don Hannula, "Drums of Dissent at the Seattle Indian Center," *s-t*, November 11, 1987, A-10; Ramona Bennett, presentation to author's University of Washington class, December 7, 1998.

66 "Pearl Warren," *s-t*, January 25, 1986, D-10.

67 *Princess of the Powwow* includes an excerpt of her television commentary. Also see "Ella Aquino," in Bataille and Lisa, *Native American Women*, 16–17.

68 Julie Johnson, program biography, Enduring Spirit 2004 conference; written communication, author's collection.

69 Enduring Spirit conference programs and media announcements, author's collection.

70 *Legacy of Pride*," video, prod. and dir. Teresa Powers (master's in communication, University of Washington, 2006).

71 Lillian A. Ackerman and Laura F. Klein, eds., *Women and Power in Native North America* (Norman: University of Oklahoma Press, 1995).

72 Nancy Shoemaker, ed., *Negotiators of Change: Historical Perspectives on Native American Women* (New York: Routledge, 1995); Theda Perdue, ed., *Sifters: Native American Women's Lives* (Oxford: Oxford University Press, 2001).

73 Devon Abbott Mihesuah, *Indigenous American Women: Decolonization, Empowerment, Activism* (Lincoln: University of Nebraska Press, 2003), esp. 143–71.

9 What Came Out of the Takeovers

Women's Activism and the Indian
Community School of Milwaukee

SUSAN APPLEGATE KROUSE

Alcatraz, the Trail of Broken Treaties, Wounded Knee—these
are the well-known sites of "takeovers" by American Indian
activists, mostly members of the American Indian Movement or AIM, in the 1960s and 1970s. AIM began in 1968
in Minneapolis–St. Paul, when urban Indians organized to
protect their rights and preserve their traditions. Indian activism spread across North America, with other takeovers, sit-ins,
and demonstrations.

Recent studies of American Indian activism have been welcomed for their contribution to our understanding of a crucial
period in recent Indian history. Paul Chaat Smith and Robert
Allen Warrior's history, *Like a Hurricane: The Indian Movement from Alcatraz to Wounded Knee*, and Troy Johnson, Joane
Nagel, and Duane Champagne's edited collection, *American
Indian Activism: Alcatraz to the Longest Walk*, in particular have
prompted discussion and re-examination of events, participants, and causes of recent Indian activism.[1] However, most
of these studies have focused on the very visible, public figures
of the Red Power movement, virtually all of whom have been
men. Women's activism, while less visible, has been crucial to
sustaining Indian communities, particularly in urban areas,
and to maintaining the momentum begun in the heady days
of the 1960s and 1970s. We need to look more closely at the
contributions of women to those activist movements.[2]

In this chapter I examine the role of women in the takeover of the United States Coast Guard Station in Milwaukee, Wisconsin, in 1971 by supporters of the American Indian Movement, and how women parlayed that takeover into a longstanding community organization, the Indian Community School. Leaving the political issues largely to men, women here turned their attention to the needs of their children, ultimately creating a center that is now funded by Indian gaming and serves the entire urban Indian community of Milwaukee. Their success is not acknowledged by AIM, and the Milwaukee takeover itself is rarely mentioned in histories of Indian activism.

The Milwaukee Indian Community and the Indian Community School

Wisconsin's Indian population includes seven tribes: Ho-Chunk or Winnebago, Menominee, Ojibwe or Chippewa, Oneida, Potawatomi, Stockbridge-Munsee, and a small group known as the Brothertown Indians.[3] The Oneidas were the first of Wisconsin's Native people to move in large numbers to urban areas, particularly Green Bay and Milwaukee. They came primarily seeking employment, beginning in the 1920s.[4] Census figures indicate a rapid increase in Milwaukee's Indian population in the last eighty years. The 1930 census reported 291 Indians living in Milwaukee, with 1,939 by 1960 and 3,717 by 1970. More recent estimates have ranged as high as 6,000 in 1973 and 8,000 by 1989.[5] The urban Indian population in Milwaukee today is probably about 10,000, but it defies accurate estimation, due to its shifting and transient character. Many Milwaukee Indians maintain strong ties to their home communities, and there is a great deal of visiting between the reservation and the city.[6]

As more Indian people moved to Milwaukee, a need grew for support groups within the urban setting. In the spring of 1937 several Indians living in the city joined together to form the Consolidated Tribes of American Indians, an organization to provide aid to newcomers and a focus for social activities. This remained the sole Indian organization in Milwaukee until the late 1960s, when other groups began to proliferate. United Indians of Milwaukee organized in the summer of 1968, with members of each tribe in the city electing representatives to the new group. Other intertribal organizations emerged, with different purposes and constituencies, ranging from social service agencies to religious groups and including the Indian Community School.[7]

The school began quietly in the fall of 1970, when three Oneida mothers, Marge Funmaker, Darlene Funmaker Neconish, and Marj Stevens, started holding classes for ten Indian children in the living room of one of the mothers. Frustrated with problems in the Milwaukee Public Schools, the women simply decided to teach their children themselves, combining academics with pride in their own Indian cultures. Enrollment quickly reached seventeen students, and the women moved the school to the basement of the Church of All People. By January 1971 the school incorporated formally as a nonprofit educational institution. The staff consisted of the three founding mothers and several other volunteers. In a publication issued by the Milwaukee American Indian Information and Action Group, the school staff outlined their goals, the primary one being "to restore American Indian dignity and pride in Indian youth through cultural education, social activities and through channeling the natural talents of Indian youth toward making contributions to their community."[8]

In the spring of 1971 a Menominee Indian education student from the local university, Dorothy LePage, arranged to do her student teaching at the school and found herself recruited as the first director. Other local college students, both Indian and non-Indian, volunteered their services as teachers and aides. Enrollment increased to twenty-six, and the need for quarters more suitable than a church basement became acute. An opportunity soon presented itself.

The Takeover of the Coast Guard Station

Early on the morning of Saturday, August 14, 1971, about twenty members of the Milwaukee chapter of the American Indian Movement, mostly men, staged a takeover of the abandoned Coast Guard

Station along Lake Michigan near downtown Milwaukee. The Indians claimed the site under the 1868 Treaty of Fort Laramie, which, they argued, provided that abandoned federal property would revert to Indians.[9] Takeovers in other places, most notably Alcatraz Island in San Francisco Bay, were justified under the same treaty, unfortunately all of them without historical or legal validity.[10] The occupiers planned to use the station as an Indian center, with programs for education, housing, employment, and health. Federal and local officials did not immediately act, and the takeover proceeded quietly.[11]

Several of the women involved in the Indian Community School were members of the Milwaukee chapter of AIM, including serving on the AIM board of directors and heading various committees.[12] Four days after the initial takeover, on August 17, 1971, the women of the Indian Community School arranged to hold children's classes at the Coast Guard Station, in Indian crafts and storytelling. Then, as September approached, with the beginning of a new school year, they decided to move the school into rooms at the Coast Guard Station, enrolling 40 students initially. Within the first month enrollment expanded to 52 students and grew to 70 by the end of November.

Men ran AIM and its programs, including a halfway house for drug and alcohol abusers, and women ran the Indian Community School. The school's presence gave the takeover a legitimacy it would not otherwise have enjoyed.[13] The Bureau of Indian Affairs (BIA) intervened on behalf of the Indians, requesting that the Coast Guard Station be acquired as an Indian center, including the school.[14] AIM could claim a victory, but it was the school that allowed AIM to keep the Coast Guard Station. Nevertheless, relations between the Indian Community School and AIM began to deteriorate as the school entered its second year at the Coast Guard Station.

Funding for the school in these first years was always tenuous. None of the teachers received any pay, and there was no tuition. Dorothy LePage, the director, managed to secure funds from a variety of programs and organizations. Monies for heat and utilities came from private donations and small grants from churches. The school lunch program was funded through the Wisconsin Department of Public Instruction. Other money came from some creative interpretations of funding sources. In the spring of 1972 the school received its first major grant, under the Safe Streets Act, a federal program designed to keep juvenile delinquents off the streets.

The school acquired more stable funding in the summer of 1972 through the Title IV program of the Indian Education Act. This remained its principal source of monies for the next ten years, allowing the school to function, albeit on a shoestring budget. Other funds came from the state's public instruction agency, the federal Comprehensive Employment and Training Act (CETA) program, and grants from philanthropic organizations such as the Wisconsin Council of Churches. Enrollment remained steady at about 70 to 75 students in all grades, and the school was able to hire certified teachers as money became available for salaries.

As the school prospered, ties with AIM became more strained. Members of AIM stayed at the school in the fall of 1972, during their march to Washington DC on the Trail of Broken Treaties. AIM members destroyed property and stole students' Indian crafts projects. The local press covered the story, quoting LePage's concerns that the school might have to find another location: "We do not want to stay around here in the type of atmosphere which [AIM members] have created. We want to return the correct Indian values to our children."[15]

Further complications ensued when monies requested by AIM for the school were cut off, following the takeover of the BIA building in Washington DC in November 1972.[16] These funds from the Office of Economic Opportunity never arrived, and gradually AIM's involvement with the school became virtually non-existent. The men who had been involved with the takeover of the Coast Guard Station went on to other, more dramatic, activist activities. One of the leaders of the Milwaukee chapter of AIM was charged with conspiring to transport firearms to Wounded Knee during the occupation by AIM in 1973 (the charges were later dismissed). He took part in the occupation of the Alexian Brothers Novitiate in Gresham, Wisconsin, by the Menominee Warrior Society in 1975 and was later arrested and found guilty of possession of explosives.[17] By the third anniversary of the Coast Guard Station takeover, another man from Milwaukee AIM claimed that the takeover had been a moral victory but meant little to the Indian community.[18] However, for the 75 local students, for their families, and for their teachers, the takeover meant that they had a school. AIM began the takeover, but the women of the school retained the site in what would become one of the longest of the Indian takeovers of the 1970s.

Following the Takeover

The Indian Community School eventually began using most of the rooms in the two buildings of the former Coast Guard Station. The students also had access to the grassy area around the station on the lakefront. The buildings, however, were never intended to be used as a school, and the rooms were not designed to be classrooms.

Through the 1970s enrollment grew to 100 students, with a teaching staff of seven to ten. Students were initially grouped into four levels: primary, middle elementary, junior high, and senior high, rather than by grades. Teachers tried to relate academic subjects to Indian culture and history, creating an awareness in their students of their rich Indian heritage. By 1974 all the academic teachers had college degrees, and most held Wisconsin teacher certification. One or two of the academic teachers were Indian, and all of the Indian language and culture teachers were Indian. In addition, virtually all the school's support staff were Indian, as were the members of the board of directors. Throughout the 1970s the majority of teachers, staff, and members of the board were women, and most of them were Indian women.

In 1978 the federal General Services Administration turned the Coast Guard Station site over to Milwaukee County, with the provision that the county find a suitable place for the Indian school within two years, while the school remained a rent-free tenant.[19] The school staff and board, still led by Dorothy LePage, pressed for another site, and in 1980 they were able to acquire a former school building from the county. The building was obtained through a complex set of transactions. After the U.S. General Services Administration awarded the former Coast Guard Station to Milwaukee County, with the stipulation that a new site be found for the Indian Community School, the city of Milwaukee, acting for Milwaukee Public Schools, deeded the former Bartlett Avenue School to the county. Next, in exchange for the school, Milwaukee County gave Milwaukee Public Schools a parcel of land next to a local high school. Then Milwaukee County could deed Bartlett Avenue School to the Indian Community School.

The school, however, did not immediately acquire the deed to Bartlett, since there was a dispute over its terms. The city of Milwaukee wanted to require that when the land and buildings were no longer used by the school, they would revert to the city. The school opposed this provision but went ahead with the move to Bartlett Avenue.[20]

At the new site the school expanded to 120 students, from elementary through high school. Funding remained primarily through Title IV of the Indian Education Act. Parents continued to send their children to the Indian Community School for two reasons: to learn about their heritage and to escape the pressures of public school, including overcrowded classrooms and lack of individual attention.[21] According to the school's cultural coordinator, "The parents wanted their kids to learn their history and culture, to reinforce their Indian values before they were completely lost."[22] The Bartlett Avenue site, however, was not ideal for the school. There was no playground area, and the building needed extensive repairs.

Federal funding cutbacks under the Reagan administration led to a reduction in funds available for Indian education for the 1983–1984 academic year. For the first time in ten years, the Indian Community School did not receive funding from Title IV. While the school had been anticipating this reduction, they were unable to secure funding from any other source. Consequently the Indian Community School closed in the fall of 1983.

This was the school's lowest point: their major funding source was unavailable, they had lost their original school site at the Coast Guard Station, their title to the new school building was in dispute, and the school's staff, including the original director, Dorothy LePage, left, since there were no longer any jobs. A new group of urban Indian women, headed by Loretta Ford (Bad River Chippewa), rose to the challenge and took over the leadership of the school board.[23] The women included mothers and grandmothers of children in the school, as well as community members without such personal ties to the Indian Community School.

The new school board, with a core of five women, was able to acquire title to the school building and then sell it to a developer. They applied the proceeds from this sale toward the purchase of an 11.5-acre campus site, just west of downtown Milwaukee. The campus was the former site of Concordia College (now Concordia University), a Lutheran undergraduate institution. The property included a classroom building, dormitories, library, gymnasium, administration building, and a sixteen-unit apartment building. The campus had been vacant for seven years, and many of the buildings were in disrepair. The classroom building was in the best shape and became the home of the new Indian Community School, which opened in January 1987 with classes for kindergarten through eighth grade.[24]

The following fall the school opened the apartment building as housing for elder Indians and one dormitory for local college and technical school students. The plan was to use income from the apartments and dormitory rooms to provide funding for the school, although high utility bills and less than total occupancy prevented any sizeable income from being generated.[25] A day-care center took over two rooms in the classroom building early in 1989, providing some additional rent monies. A fourth building was renovated and opened in 1990, housing administrative offices for the school as well as offices for several other Milwaukee Indian organizations.

The school fought a continuing battle for funding, again utilizing a variety of grants and donations. The school board, with its five core urban Indian women, was able to secure a teacher-training grant through Title IV of the Indian Education Act. This grant provided support money for twenty Indian teachers-in-training and a coordinator, as well as some operating expenses for the school. Additional funds came through the Wisconsin Department of Public Instruction and private foundations. For the first year and a half in the new location, the school maintained grades kindergarten through eight, with up to 130 students, and eight academic and Indian language and culture teachers. Because of mounting expenses, in 1988 the school board cut back to grades one to three, with 32 students, two academic teachers, and three part-time Indian language and culture teachers. For academic year 1989–1990 the board added grade four and one additional teacher. The plan was to expand one grade each year, up to grade eight, so that students who started at the Indian Community School would be able to continue.

The women of the school board knew that they would have to find a more stable source of income. As early as 1983 they sought to ally with one of the Wisconsin Indian tribes to secure Bureau of Indian Affairs funding for education. Then, the 1980s brought a new source of income to Indian tribes—high-stakes bingo and gambling. Under federal law, states that permit bingo or gaming in any form may not regulate the stakes in games played on reservations, which are federal trust lands. The right for tribes to conduct gaming on federal trust lands was upheld by the U.S. Supreme Court in *California v. Cabazon Band of Mission Indians*, 1987. Limitations to the right were formalized in the 1988 Indian Gaming Regulatory Act (Public Law 100-497), which specified that tribes must enter into compacts with states to determine the forms of gaming permitted on trust land.[26] With few options open to them, the Indian Community School board turned to gaming as a last alternative. In 1988 the women signed an agreement with the Forest County Potawatomi Community of northern Wisconsin to take over the campus land, with the expectation that it would be placed under federal trust status. Milwaukee is located on territory ceded by the Potawatomis in 1833, lending a historical claim to the proposed new reservation. Trust status would allow the school and the tribe to operate a high-stakes bingo operation, which would help to fund the school.

The agreement immediately came under fire from residents in the school's neighborhood, who objected to the possibility of using the land for other than residential purposes, particularly bingo. In an effort to allay neighborhood fears, the Indian Community School board changed the initial plans and obtained an option to purchase a two-acre tract in an industrial area of Milwaukee's Menomonee River Valley. This would then be the location for high-stakes bingo, while the campus site would be dedicated to educational and community services, leased back to the school by the tribe. Further, the tribe, the school, and the city of Milwaukee drafted a series of agreements to ensure that all city and state laws, with the exception of those applying to gaming at the industrial valley site, would apply to both parcels of land when put into trust. Because of the high initial capital outlay for the bingo operation, the tribe and the school sought outside investors to help finance the project. When the city and the Bureau of Indian Affairs raised objections to one of the investors' possible ties to organized crime, a second set of investors was found, and new agreements were drafted. A local developer became the primary investor, forming a corporation known as Omni Bingo. At every step, the Indian Community School obtained the approval of the city, a requirement for securing final approval on trust status from the BIA.[27]

Objections to granting trust status came from many quarters, fueling tension surrounding the Indian Community School's presence in the neighborhood. Local residents who had initially opposed bingo on the school site now opposed trust status, and signs appeared on lawns proclaiming "No Trust Status." A new organization formed in the neighborhood—Citizens Against Urban Reservation Status, whose acronym was pronounced "cares."[28] A second group of residents who supported the school organized into "Neighbors Trusting

Neighbors," which helped to sponsor some outreach activities at the school. City and state officials went on record as opposing trust status and began lobbying the BIA with their objections. Even some Milwaukee Indians raised questions about who would benefit from a high-stakes bingo operation, and whether the Potawatomi tribe had any historic claim to land in the Milwaukee area.[29] Internal strife contributed to the school's problems, as two former board members raised allegations of financial improprieties within the school's board of directors.

As the school and the Forest County Potawatomi Community drew closer to attaining trust status, adverse publicity and hostility increased. Letters to the editor and articles in the Milwaukee newspapers expressed opposition to the introduction of high-stakes bingo, saying it would reduce attendance at other bingo games run by Catholic parishes and charitable groups.[30] Local congressional representatives publicly opposed trust status for the industrial valley site.[31] On Sunday, June 18, 1989, a fire was set in garbage cans at the rear of the school building. The fire spread to the rear doors and stairway, breaking glass and spewing smoke throughout the building. No one was arrested in connection with the fire, but many people associated with the school felt it was another expression of opposition to the school and its efforts. The school struggled through the 1989–1990 academic year with minimal funding from the investors, Omni Bingo, and ultimately ended classes two weeks early when funding ran out.[32]

On July 25, 1990, both the 11.5-acre campus site and the industrial site in the Menomonee River Valley were placed in trust for the Forest County Potawatomi Community by the federal government. Under an agreement with the Potawatomi tribe, the Indian Community School continued to manage the campus site. Potawatomi Bingo opened at the valley site on March 7, 1991, providing 460 new jobs and a payroll of $6.5 million in its first year of operation. Monies from the gaming operation were originally split three ways, with the school and the tribe sharing 60 percent of the total profits, and Omni Bingo taking 40 percent.

The decision by the women of the Indian Community School to pursue trust status and gaming proved to be the correct one, providing both tangible and intangible benefits. The most obvious effect was financial security for the school. For the first time in twenty years the school's funding was assured, bills were paid on time, and funds became available for improvements. Teacher salaries increased, and health benefits became part of their compensation. The school was able to add support staff, buy computers, renovate buildings and improve curriculum. Less tangibly, the school had a secure home, providing a sense of identity and belonging in the community. Without revenue from gaming, the school would not have continued past its twenty-year anniversary in 1990. There were simply too many expenses and no foreseeable source of income. Other private schools for Indian children, such as the Heart of the Earth Survival School in Minneapolis, had federal funding reduced again in 1992–1993 and ultimately could not continue.[33]

Early on, the Indian Community School board, under Loretta Ford's direction, anticipated that gaming might eventually be limited by the state of Wisconsin or the federal government. Consequently the school began investing, rather than spending, a substantial portion of its share of the profits. And, indeed, in 1996 the Indian Gaming Regulatory Commission ruled that the Potawatomi tribe could not split proceeds with the school, although the tribe could donate funds to the school. That arrangement was made but will not continue past 2010, when the school's lease with the tribe runs out.

The urban Indian community and the city of Milwaukee benefited as well from gaming. The Indian Community School supports a number of local urban Indian organizations, with office space and with grant monies, including the Indian Elderly Center, Indian Manpower, and the Gerald Ignace Indian Health Center. An alternative high school with an Indian-influenced curriculum uses space in one of the Indian Community School campus buildings. The city of Milwaukee receives a substantial annual payment from the gaming operation, which expanded to a full-scale casino. In addition, the school, the Forest County Potawatomi Tribe, and Omni Bingo, contributed $250,000 to fund new American Indian exhibits at the Milwaukee Public Museum, among other smaller grants. The Indian Community School gave the University of Wisconsin–Milwaukee one million dollars to endow a chair in urban Indian education. Less direct economic benefits come to the city in the form of increased tourism revenue and in reduced unemployment.

In the last few years the Indian Community School has gone through turbulent times, with changes in the board and staff. However, the school is now financially stable and serves some 350 students in pre-kindergarten through eighth grade, with programs in both academics and Indian cultures. Its funding is secure for the next several years, as profits from the expanded gaming operation provide payments of $27 million per year to the school, at least until 2010.[34] In 1998 the school hired an education professional to serve as its chief executive officer, Dr. LindaSue Warner (Choctaw), bringing a new era of urban Indian women academics to the Indian Community School. In September 2007 the school moved once again, to a suburban location on 175 acres, south of Milwaukee, with a more natural environment.

Conclusion

Indian Community School initially benefited from the actions of AIM members who took over the Coast Guard Station, which provided the school with its first permanent home. It was the women who ran the school, however, who managed to hang on to that site and use it to acquire a permanent home. It was a new group of women who formed a new school board and negotiated precedent-setting agreements to obtain trust status and secure the future of the school. Other Indian women led the school to its new location. Indian Community School survived and prospered under the guidance of urban Indian women. Its founders, its board, its directors, its teachers, its staff, and its volunteers have all been largely women. They remained focused on their goal of providing a school that would serve their children and their community, perhaps the most successful outcome of all of the takeovers of the Red Power movement.

Notes

Funding for my original research with the Indian Community School came from an Advanced Opportunity Fellowship through the University of Wisconsin–Milwaukee. More recent funding for continued research has been provided by the Intramural Research Grants Program of Michigan State University. Earlier versions of portions of this paper were presented at the American Anthropological Association annual meetings in 1992 and in 2001. My thanks go to the women of the Indian Community School, who have been a continuing source of inspiration for me. I have identified by name only the three "founding mothers" of the school and the directors or CEOs. Many other women have made tremendous contributions to the school over the last thirty years but are not public figures in the same sense, so I have chosen not to identify them, in order to respect their privacy. The history of the school presented here and any errors therein are fully my responsibility.

1 Paul Chaat Smith and Robert Allen Warrior, *Like a Hurricane: The Indian Movement from Alcatraz to Wounded Knee* (New York: New Press, 1996); Troy Johnson, Joane Nagel, and Duane Champagne, *American Indian Activism: Alcatraz to the Longest Walk* (Urbana: University of Illinois Press, 1997).

2 Devon Mihesuah begins this work of examining the roles of Indian women activists in her collection of essays, *Indigenous American Women: Decolonization, Empowerment, Activism* (Lincoln: University of Nebraska Press, 2003).

3 For basic overviews of Wisconsin's Native peoples, see Patty Loew, *Indian Nations of Wisconsin* (Madison: Wisconsin Historical Society Press, 2001), and Nancy Oestrich Lurie, *Wisconsin Indians* (Madison: Wisconsin Historical Society Press, 2002).

4 Nancy Oestrich Lurie, "Recollections of an Urban Indian Community: The Oneidas of Milwaukee," in *The Oneida Indian Experience: Two Perspectives*, ed. Jack Campisi and Laurence M. Hauptman (Syracuse NY: Syracuse University Press, 1988).

5 Great Lakes Resource Development Project of Americans for Indian Opportunity, *Facts about American Indians in Wisconsin* (Washington DC: Ameri-

cans for Indian Opportunity, 1973); and U.S. Bureau of the Census, 1980 Census.

6 Little research has been published on the Milwaukee Indian community. See Lurie, "Recollections"; Robert Ritzenthaler and Mary Sellers, "Indians in an Urban Situation," *Wisconsin Archaeologist* 36 (1955): 147–61.

7 Information on the early history of Milwaukee's urban Indian organizations comes from files maintained by the Milwaukee Public Museum, including newspaper articles, newsletters, programs, flyers, and posters. Information specific to the Indian Community School comes from the school's files and from my own fieldwork at the school and participation in school activities from 1988 to the present.

8 American Indian Information and Action Group, *Milwaukee Indian Community Resource Handbook*, n.d.

9 Alex P. Dobbish, "Indian Squatters Vow to Stay Put," *Milwaukee Journal*, August 15, 1971, 1, 10.

10 Smith and Warrior, *Like a Hurricane*, 10.

11 Walter W. Morrison, "Militant Indians Seize Old Coast Guard Site," *Milwaukee Journal*, August 14, 1971, 1, 11.

12 *American Indian Movement Newsletter*, February 1971 (Milwaukee Public Museum files).

13 A similar situation occurred near Santa Rosa, California, in November 1970, when Indians took over a former federal broadcast station. A nonprofit educational corporation, Ya-Ka-Ama Indian Education and Development, assumed responsibility for developing the land, which was formally transferred to them from the federal government. See *Ya-Ka-Ama Indian Education and Development*, brochure (Forestville CA, 1991).

14 Thomas J. Hagerty, "For These Indians, a Feast of Mourning," *Milwaukee Journal*, November 25, 1971.

15 Rick Janka, "Center Official Reveals Indian Vandalism Here," *Milwaukee Sentinel*, November 17, 1972, 5.

16 Janka, "Center Official." The Red School House, an Indian survival school in St. Paul, Minnesota, also had federal funds withheld in 1973 because of its ties to AIM. The funds were released the following year, and the school maintained its affiliation with AIM. See Dorothy Lewis, "Indian School Fights for Survival, *St. Paul Dispatch*, October 3, 1974, 6; and Dorothy Lewis, "Indian School Has Direction, *St. Paul Dispatch*, September 6, 1976, 17–18.

17 "Powless Held in Arms Case," *Milwaukee Sentinel*, March 5, 1975; "Powless

Charges Dismissed," *Milwaukee Sentinel*, April 5, 1975; and "Powless, 3 Others Sentenced," *Milwaukee Sentinel*, June 14, 1976.

18 "Indians Still Hold Facility after 3 Years," *Racine Journal Times*, August 29, 1974.

19 "County Gets Possession of Indian School," *Milwaukee Sentinel*, February 27, 1978.

20 "Indian School May Lose Its Building," *Milwaukee Journal*, October 25, 1984, 1, 7.

21 Karen Rothe, "School Teaches Past, Present of Indian Life," *Milwaukee Sentinel*, September 21, 1981.

22 Linda Steiner, "Indians Lost More Than a Building When School Closed," *Milwaukee Journal*, June 13, 1984.

23 Cynthia Denny, "Her Devotion to Native Roots Pays Off at Last," *Milwaukee Journal*, November 27, 1986.

24 Robert Anthony, "Reopening of Indian School Is Resurrection of a Dream," *Milwaukee Sentinel*, January 26, 1987.

25 Robert Anthony, "Center Opens Apartments for Elderly," *Milwaukee Sentinel*, November 9, 1987.

26 For an overview of the history of Indian gaming, see Eduardo E. Cordeiro, "The Economics of Bingo: Factors Influencing the Success of Bingo Operations on American Indian Reservations," in *What Can Tribes Do? Strategies and Institutions in American Indian Economic Development*, ed. Stephen Cornell and Joseph P. Kalt (Los Angeles: American Indian Studies Center, University of California, Los Angeles, 1992), 212–16.

27 David E. Umhoeferr, "Indians Win and Lose in Bid for Land," *Milwaukee Journal*, November 18, 1988, 1, 3B.

28 Jacquelyn Mitchard, "Neighbors Divided: Indian Campus Plan Worries Some Whites," *Milwaukee Journal*, March 13, 1988, 1, 5B.

29 Robert Anthony, "Indian School Gets OK to Buy Valley Land; Bingo Eyed at Site," *Milwaukee Sentinel*, October 10, 1986, 6; and Ted Vogel, "Forest County Indians Have No Land Claim Here," *Milwaukee Journal*, September 26, 1988. Interestingly, no objections were raised by local Indian people about the propriety of gaming itself, unlike controversies that have erupted in other places, such as among the Senecas and Mohawks in New York State and Quebec.

30 See, for example, "Readers Say Indian 'Gambling Hall' Will Hurt Catholic Schools," *South Side Spirit*, July 23, 1989, 1, 30; Chester Sheard, "Church Fears Big-Money Bingo," *Milwaukee Sentinel*, August 1, 1989; and "Thompson Must Say No," *Milwaukee Sentinel*, September 13, 1989.

31 David Staats, "Kleczka, Moody Oppose Valley Bingo Site," *Milwaukee Sentinel*, August 17, 1989, 1, 8.

32 Amy Rinard, "Bingo Hall Investors Halt Indian School Funding," *Milwaukee Sentinel*, May 11, 1990, 5; and Dennis McCann, "Children Lose in This Gamble," *Milwaukee Journal*, June 6, 1990.

33 "Native Leaders Rage at Bush's $ Cuts," *News from Indian Country*, late August 1992; and Jeff Armstrong, "Heart of the Earth and AIOIC Sue for Federal Funds," *Circle*, September 9, 1999, 6. The Heart of the Earth School has been revived in the form of a charter school, separate from the original survival school. See Jean Pagano, "Heart of Earth School Comes to Life Again," *Native American Press/Ojibwe News*, November 22, 2002, at www.press-on.net/.

34 Susan Lampert Smith, "Milwaukee's Indian Children Find a School Where They Are Free to Learn and Be Indians," *Wisconsin State Journal*, July 25, 2002, A1.

10 Telling Paula Starr

Native American Woman
as Urban Indian Icon

JOAN WEIBEL-ORLANDO

Paula Starr and I met for the first time at the Los Angeles American Indian community's 1978 New Year's Eve Powwow. That year the urban Indian tradition was held at Ford Park in Bell Gardens, one of three adjacent cities in south central Los Angeles County in which the 1970 census indicated that American Indians constituted at least 1 percent, and as much as 2.6 percent, of the total population of each city.[1] The 1978 New Year's Eve powwow was a total success. The community center's multipurpose auditorium was filled to overflowing with dancers in traditional and fusion dance regalia and four or five drum groups. Spectators both in and out of dance regalia filled the bleachers on both sides of the gym floor, and business was brisk at the dozens of craft vendor tables and food booths in an adjoining room.

Those revelers who grew restless, or in need of a break from the relentless drumming and singing within, found respite, restrooms, and friends, had a smoke, caught up on community gossip, or accepted the invitation of drinking buddies "to down a few" among the clusters of friends on the walkways and in the parking lots surrounding the community center.[2] If participants were too exhausted to be good company, or if, having "downed a few too many" already, they were not in the mood to talk, laugh, flirt, or fight with nondancing New Year's Eve urban Indian partiers, they could find solitude, safety, and sleep in the privacy of their cars.

To this day, I am conflicted about my appropriate status and role at such urban Indian events. Should I forever restrict myself to outsider observer/ethnographer status when I have always harbored a personal willingness to get caught up and non-analytically involved in the sheer and joyous communion of such rites of intensification? That festive night, total cultural immersion held sway. However, I later wrote several pages of notes about that New Year's Eve's powwow highpoints.

Among my field notes of the evening were a few lines about meeting Paula Starr. I described her as "a warm, gracious, young woman who looked very much the college student in her jeans, tee-shirt and dance shawl." Moving with elegant, sunny assurance around the dance floor, Paula seemed well known to the other attending powwowers. I had also noted that she was not to be found among the secular smoking, drinking, gossiping, flirting groups of revelers outside. Although still young (twenty-four at the time) she clearly had made the choice to present herself as a cultural "traditionalist" in the ritualistic/spiritual/sacred arena of the powwow.[3]

I was sitting in a lawn chair at the foot of the filled-to-capacity bleachers next to Charlotte Standing Buffalo Ortiz (Lakota), one of my best friends, and one of the most respected elders in the Los Angeles Native American community, when Paula Starr and I first exchanged greetings.[4] I remember remarking to Charlotte, at that time, that Paula had a "presence" and bore watching. The usually hypercritical Charlotte readily agreed.

Twenty years later in 1998, when I began to prepare an updated second edition of my book about the Los Angeles Native American community, I elected to contact John Castillo, the executive director of the Southern California Indian Center (scic). John readily agreed to report on his community service organization's history of struggles and successes in its attempts to provide a wide range of social services to the 80,000 or more Native Americans living in Southern California during the 1990s, and given the decade's pervasive climate of budget reduction at all levels (federal, state, and local) of public spending. He had one provision, however. He cautioned me that the interview should not be about him, but about SCIC: "We are a group effort after all. I only execute decisions made by our board of directors." To underscore his personal shunning of the limelight, he asked if he could have Paula Starr, SCIC's assistant director, sit in on the interview. I happily agreed. It had been a while since Paula and I had talked. Things had definitely changed for her.

It was clear from her contributions to the interview that she was just as involved in the administration of the day-to-day SCIC operations as was John Castillo. Twenty years after our first encounter she was still someone who bore watching. The following year John Castillo left the directorship of SCIC to finish a doctoral dissertation in business administration. With his departure, the SCIC Board of Directors appointed Paula Starr as its interim director. Within four months she was formally installed as executive director. She has acted in that capacity ever since.

In the thirty years I have known her, Paula has risen from relative obscurity to become among the most effective, influential, and respected women in the Southern California American Indian community. Therefore, when asked to contribute a chapter to this volume about the leadership experience of a Native American woman in Los Angeles, I immediately knew about whom the article should be written. All of my "Paula Starr watching" over the years finally had a focus and rationale. I looked forward to discovering how this gentle young woman had not only survived but actually thrived in the treacherous waters of twenty-first-century social service delivery in an urban ethnic community. I also wondered how she has been able to maintain personal balance, even serenity, as well as a true sense of her Indian core self.

The Nature of Our Relationship and the Problematics of Sharing and Constructing a Life History Narrative

Although impressed with the pleasant, respectful, and self-assured young Cheyenne woman I met on New Year's Eve in 1978, ultimately

I would not have the opportunity to enlist her as a research assistant at that time. She had been an undergraduate student at UCLA in the mid-1970s, but by 1979 Paula transferred to UC–Irvine, where she completed her bachelor of arts degree the same year. Throughout the 1980s I would see her periodically at powwows. I watched with interest as she introduced her darling toddler, Starr, to powwow dancing. We would nod, exchange pleasantries, and share career moves and accomplishments. We were casual acquaintances. It could not be said that we shared the intimacy and long-term commitment often found between ethnobiographic collaborators and anthropologists.[5]

Rather, our relationship and eventual collaboration on this life history evolved slowly, from an admiring if cautious distance, and from positions of personal achievement and shared and mutually appreciated competencies. When my book *Indian Country, L.A.* was about to be published in 1991, I sent a copy of the chapter on the L.A. powwow scene to Paula for her expert comments and critique. A few years later, when she and her Indian community colleagues thought it a good idea to search out academic advisement about a developing community health research program, they invited me to participate in a program development conference hosted by the SCIC staff.

As Gelya Frank has pointed out in her writings about the collection and construction of life histories, the willingness to share one's personal history and most private thoughts and experiences with another person for possible and widespread broadcast is not an easily arrived-at state of confidence.[6] In fact, the process of information sharing and personal narrative construction can be fraught with psychological tension and even stress. From the moment I decided to ask Paula to share her life history with me I knew that the creative process would also have to be shared. Our product would not be one in which a conventionally educated scholar/translator/author told the story of his or her relatively uneducated key informant's life history. The urban Indian experience of the last fifty years has changed that relational inequality dramatically.

Paula Starr is no naive repository of Native American cultural lore or experience. She had completed all but her master's thesis in theater arts when she left the graduate program at California State University at Long Beach to become fully involved in social service delivery to the Southern California Native American community. She has written more funded grant proposals than I ever had or will have in all of my years of academic research and publication. She is at the center of an impressive, even enviable, network of social service program designers and facilitators. Her contacts are situated at all levels of government and private involvement. Our taped discussions were routinely interrupted by "must take" calls from major television network executives, the president of the Indian Chamber of Commerce, a federal Department of Labor administrator, or a community member needing a medical or employment referral. I am continually impressed by the serenity and assurance with which Paula multitasks. I therefore knew, from the moment of her acceptance of this project, that personal agency (both hers and mine) would have to be addressed and shared.

We handled the issue of agency equity in a number of ways. Although I had a set of personal history questions I thought needed asking, our conversations were free flowing. Paula agreed that we should video-record our conversations. We began each conversation (three 90-minute sessions) with a topical premise to which Paula would respond in whatever manner she chose and for as long as she wished to talk about that particular topic. Between each interview session I reviewed the previous conversation and made notes about its possible narrative themes or areas that needed greater exploration or clarification. Those topics, then, provided the initiating premises for our next talk.

During the summer of 2005 Paula shared not only her personal life history with me but also her ongoing administrative life. I went to meetings of an Indian program development committee, a SCIC board of directors meeting, and SCIC's annual fundraising pow-wow. At every event Paula Starr was a major actor/facilitator of the community activity. Finally, as this narrative began to take shape, I shared it with Paula to ensure that the facts of her life were presented accurately, and that Paula's privacy and trust were not violated by the narrative's disclosures. This also helped me to minimize my inclination for anthropological paradigm building and tendencies toward generalizing perceived cultural patterns from individual experience, and to focus on being consistent with Paula Starr's own sense of the lessons to be learned from this de- and re-construction of her personal life history narrative.

Childhood, Family Background and Relocation

In 1954 Paul and Sharon Sullivan Starr's first child was born in the Indian Health Service Hospital in Claremore, Oklahoma. Paula does not remember much about her Oklahoma childhood. She lived there with her parents for less than four years before her dad, a full-blood Cheyenne and grandson of Chief Black Kettle, made the decision to take the Bureau of Indian Affairs (BIA) up on its offer to facilitate his relocation to Los Angeles.[7] In 1958 the Starr family made its way to Los Angeles and economic opportunity.

Paul Starr was sixteen years older than his Irish American bride. He had enlisted in the U.S. Navy during World War II and had received training as a machinist while serving his country. In contrast with many of the descriptions of Native American relocatees in the early scholarly literature on Native urbanization, Paul Starr was not without marketable work skills.[8] However, little employment opportunity existed for men trained in aeromechanics in post–World War II Oklahoma. There was employment for a person with such skills in the burgeoning aerospace industry in Los Angeles. Paul Starr had chosen his destination city well. Within days of the family's arrival in Los Angeles, Paula's dad had secured a steady, fairly well-paying job in an aerospace plant in South Central Los Angeles, just a few miles from Ford Park in Bell Gardens where I would meet Paula for the first time twenty years later.

Paula does not recall much about those first days in Los Angeles:

"I remember that the hotel the BIA placed us in while Dad looked for work was at the corner of Hoover and 11th Street. . . . Our room was on the top [of the building] and there was a bar beneath it."[9] The Starrs did not stay in this hotel very long. When Paula's dad secured work, the family moved to a small rental in Norwalk, about ten miles southeast of Downtown Los Angeles and close to his place of employment. Within a couple of years the family saved enough to make a down payment on a house. By the early 1960s, the Starrs were living the all-American dream. They were owners of a small home in middle-class Norwalk. By then Paul had secured even better-paying work at Aerojet in the neighboring city of Downey. In Paula's words, "We were just like everybody else."

Socially and culturally, things were looking up for the relocated Starrs as well. By 1958 Native Americans had moved to Los Angeles in such numbers that several member-funded Indian hospitality centers, as well as tribal culture groups and Indian Christian congregations, had formed. These groups were providing volunteer hospitality, spiritual guidance, and a continuity of community tribal customs in Southern California.[10] Brought up to be proud of his cultural heritage and membership in an illustrious Cheyenne family, Paul Starr was well versed in Cheyenne ceremonial traditions. "Oh yes, my dad was brought up in the traditional ways. He was fluent in his language. He taught me certain things about Cheyenne ways. But, then, he would say, 'Don't talk about it. Just keep it to yourself.' So, I never talked with anybody about those things my dad had told me about Cheyenne traditions." Almost upon arrival Paul Starr had been in contact with other relocated Native Americans in Los Angeles. He relished and sought out their companionship and continuing practice of their tribal cultural forms. As Paula recalled,

In the '60s my dad would go to a powwow almost every weekend. He was a member of the Drum and Feathers Drum Group that Mitch Murdock started. Drum and Feathers was made up of mostly southern-style drummers and singers. Since my dad was from the Southern Cheyenne tradition, he knew all the songs the Drum and Feathers group sang and drummed. He fit right in.

And my mom and I would go along with him. I learned pow-wow dancing and etiquette when I was really young. I grew up in the powwow tradition.

The Starr family quickly integrated into the L.A. Indian community's weekly schedule of social and cultural events.

From the onset of our conversations Paula Starr's trust in our friendship seemed complete. Without hesitation, she confided that her memories of the weekend powwows of her childhood are decidedly mixed. On one hand, she had enjoyed the music, dancing, food, and friendships she experienced at the weekly social and cultural gatherings. On the other hand, she, her mother, and, later, her younger siblings would grow apprehensive, even loathing, of the inevitable after-hours powwow-going outcomes:

> It was a drinking culture. Everybody drank at the powwows in the 1950s and '60s! And after hours, we'd go down to the Tombs or the Shrimp Boat and drum, sing, and drink some more. But people would always end up fighting. Everybody fought! I hated the fights! I just couldn't understand why friends would do that to each other. . . . And there we would be, the kids, in the back of the car, scared stiff and wishing our parents would stop drinking or fighting and take us home so that we could go to bed and get some sleep. And then people would sober up, until the next weekend, the next powwow, bowling tournament, or softball game. And then the drinking and fighting would start all over again. It was just constant![11]

Paula Starr certainly knows the devastation alcohol abuse can bring to family life from personal and, eventually, professional experience.[12]

Her dad's drinking was confined to "downing a few" with his weekend powwow or athletic league drinking buddies for only a short period of time. By the mid-1960s his alcohol consumption was clearly out of control. He began to lose jobs. As his inconsistent work record reputation began to precede him, it became increasingly difficult for him to secure employment in his field of expertise. Paula's mom, who until then had been a stay-at-home mom, began to work outside of their home to help with the family finances. Paul was often unemployed for stretches of time, and his drinking and violence found locus in their home.

By 1970 the Starr family home life had become intolerable. Unwilling to endure her husband's abuse when he was intoxicated, Paula's mother asked him to leave the family household. Within two years Paul Starr, grandson of Cheyenne nobility, died on the mean streets of Los Angeles from medical complications associated with alcoholism. He died alone and without family to mourn his passing.[13] Paula's childhood memories of family life are too personally painful for her to relate more graphically here. We will share with you only certain personal outcomes of that experience.

From the start, Paula was an average-to-good student. She won awards for perfect attendance in both the third and fourth grades. Her early school experience was such that she made it her responsibility to attend school as much as possible. Paula now talks of school as one of several "escape mechanisms" she developed over the course of her childhood to cope. When in fifth grade Paula developed asthma, her health was so compromised by the illness that, at ten years of age, she was hospitalized for a month. Upon her medical release, her parents were advised that she needed to recuperate at home for an even longer period of time.

Her doctors informed her mother that Paula's asthmatic condition had developed in part from her susceptibility to certain allergens in her environment (her parents and most of their friends were heavy smokers). However, the adult, highly educated Paula believes that having been exposed to second-hand smoke as a child was only one of two powerful and illness-producing irritants. Her asthma, she assumes, was just as much if not more a reaction to the psychological stresses of a dysfunctional home life in childhood.

While her dad's departure from the family home relieved certain obvious tensions, it created other and equally painful stresses. Her mother's limited education (she had dropped out of high school in her senior year) and work training made her ill-equipped to be the family's financial head of household. The work she could secure rarely paid wages sufficient to cover the family's household expenses. As a consequence, in 1970 their Norwalk home went into fore-closure. The family turned to Paula's grandparents. "Luckily, my [maternal] grandparents had moved out to L.A. at the time. When we lost our house in Norwalk, we moved in with them for a while. But it was really crowded. They had only two bedrooms — one for them and one for my mom and the four of us kids. We eventually found a place for ourselves. But then we would have to move again. . . . We moved a lot. I went to four different high schools because we kept having to move." Always willing to view her life from a glass half-full, rather than a half-empty perspective, Paula offered: "I have to admire my mom for trying to keep us together as a family. She made sure I finished my education. . . . And my grandparents who were out here at the time . . . because we could have easily ended up in foster homes, easily." Things could have been worse, Paula rationalizes.

In 1970 her mother, three siblings, and she were still together as a family. They still had relatives who could provide a safety net for them when things got too bad. And they were not the only Native American relocatees to have their families torn apart by substance abuse. Things could have been worse. There were still reasons for sixteen-year-old Paula Starr to go on.

Surviving Childhood, Turning Points, and Defining Moments

Paula also used the phrase *turning point* a number of times when describing certain life course–changing events and moments of clar-ity in the telling of her life history. She clearly remembers making the decision (when she was fourteen or fifteen years old and in the tenth grade) that "I was not going to end up like my mom!" She had no high school diploma, worked for minimum wages, and endured for years an alcoholic husband's abuse because she did not think she had any other, viable choices in her life. As Paula entered high school, she knew that getting an education could be her personal salvation.

Paula, however, acknowledges that she lost so much academic momentum when she had her first bout with asthma that it was years before she was able to recapture her earlier achievement. And then there were all of those residential moves and changes of schools during her high school years. Paula felt, at the time, she would never catch up scholastically with her assorted and shifting classmates. She remembers feeling that she would forever be able to attain only "average" student status because of her early and traumatic academic setback.

Compensating

All of her elder relatives (including her dad when still in the home) had impressed upon Paula the absolute need to complete her education. Paula readily agreed with this dictate. However, from her first days in school she had found ways other than outstanding academic achievement to relieve the stresses of her dysfunctional family environment. Ever the resourceful psychosocial survivalist, Paula readily admits, "I escaped a lot. I was always over at a friend's house when I had homework to do. I got involved in Girl Scouts. I got involved in a local church. I had a pretty good singing voice. So the choir director taught me how to do it right. I sang in the [church] choir for a while." And she tried to "blend in." Paula tells about being the only Native American in her Girl Scout troop, elementary and junior high school classes, and even into high school: "It was OK. I really didn't look like a stereotypical 'Indian.' I could have been a Gypsy or an Egyptian or a Mexican. I didn't want to identify myself as an Indian. All through junior high and high school I tried very hard to just 'blend in.'" Denial of one's ethnicity and individuality in the interest of appearing "just like everyone else" or "normal"—could this sort of psychosocial survival strategy ever have a positive outcome?

To this day Paula understands the reasons why she had done so, but she has deep reservations about the ultimate efficacy of this survival strategy. She therefore works tirelessly to educate and to encourage young, third- and fourth-generation urban Native Americans to find reasons to be proud of their tribal heritages and themselves. While having accepted the dictum of a completed and higher education, Paula also tried to have some fun and to create her own brand of personal happiness. For example, she "liked Girl Scouts and getting those little badges. That was fun. I think my mother still has the band with all of the badges I earned sewn onto it. . . . And I like to sing. The common theme in all four high schools I attended was my ability to get into the choir. And then in my senior year, when I was able to join the Drama Club, I really found my niche."

On Niche Building and Finding (and Following) One's Passion

Paula adored the fantasy world of high school theater production. Life always had a happy ending by the end of a musical production's third act. And because she had considerable and proven singing and dancing skills, she was guaranteed a part in every production for which she auditioned. She was having fun. She was the center of attention for the first time in her life. She received training and excelled in every aspect of theater production. Paula Starr had found her passion and personal niche. By her senior year in high school she experienced a second turning point and self-defining moment. She would apply to college and there acquire the skills necessary to fashion a professional career for herself in music and theater production.[14]

Paula Starr elected to apply to and was accepted at Cerritos College. Her reasoning was impeccable. Cerritos had both excellent music and theater arts programs. Cerritos offered the training she would need to fulfill her dream of a career in the theater at a price her family could afford. While there she "tried it all on for size." She took music theory courses. She learned music composition, how to do film orchestration and score adaptation. She continued to love and be drawn to the performance aspects of theater. Then she discovered that there were careers to be had for women in the technical aspects of theater production. She loved the "techie" life. She took up lighting design. Within a year she was being offered real, paying jobs as a production lighting designer in professional theater productions.

Paula giggled when revealing she had stayed at Cerritos College for four years rather than the usual two years before transferring to a four-year, BA degree–granting institution because "I was having so much fun being a theater 'techie' at Cerritos I didn't want to leave." By 1975 Paula Starr was well on her way to a sort of positive personal agency. Personal ambition eventually prevailed. Convinced that a Bachelor of Arts was within her intellectual capacity and that the University of California system was not only affordable but had well-respected theater and music programs, Paula applied to UCLA. An added incentive to being at UCLA was its close proximity to the major theater venues on L.A.'s West Side and in the Downtown District. She reasoned that while at UCLA she could find professional work in her area of expertise to augment her student loans and BIA stipend. Paula applied to and was accepted into the Theater Arts Program at UCLA in 1976.

Paula readily acknowledges that her UCLA period was a major turning point of her life. She had hit the "big time," to use a theatrical term. While at UCLA she won the 1977 L.A. Drama Circle's award for lighting design for her work in Ray Bradbury's production of The Martian Chronicles. Her writing skills were honed to professional standards by leading scholars at UCLA. And Native American scholars such as Charlotte Heth, the director of the American Indian Studies Center at UCLA at the time, provided positive role models for her. "I learned that it was all right to be a woman; it was all right to be Native American and not drink, to get an education. I learned at it was OK to be Indian and not do what all of the other people in my [and my parents'] social circle were doing." And while at UCLA, Paula learned that personal agency and career success may not be enough to affect complete self-actualization.

Political Activism and the Longest Walk

It may have been a synergistic concurrence of the mid-1970s Anglo and Native American political climate, the liberal leanings of the faculty at UCLA, and the pro-activism of her cohort of Native American students at UCLA that prompted her to think politically for one of the first times in her life. When Paula entered UCLA in 1976, her earlier wish simply to blend in, perfect a marketable craft, and stay out of "Indian politics" would have gotten her labeled as an "apple."[15] Her activist fellow Native American students at UCLA resolutely challenged her personal political awareness and zeal. In 1976 it was no longer tenable for Native Americans "just to blend in, not to make waves, to be good little Indian boys and girls." By then, Native American agency required more than being pro-active with regard to maximizing one's personal well-being. Indian pro-activism demanded speaking out on behalf of tribal Americans everywhere.

Seasoned firebrands of the American Indian Movement (AIM) at UCLA found a willing and receptive student in Paula Starr. She explained: "It started by going to the sweats that Ernie Peters and his wife conducted. I learned a lot about myself during that time. I learned it was okay to pray. It was okay to be Indian. I learned that the government was trying to abrogate our treaties. I knew the consequences of that. If it passed, we no longer existed as a people. I didn't think that was right. So, I went to meetings, especially at DQ University, and got involved in planning the Longest Walk."[16] By the time the Longest Walk of 1978 started in earnest, Paula Starr was among its most fully empowered and invested participants.

She and Toni Goodin, her Chippewa roommate at UCLA, requested and received stipends from the Tribal American Corporation (coordinating L.A. agencies) to act as reporters on the Longest Walk for *Talking Leaf*, the local Native American monthly newspaper. At the end of the UCLA academic quarter (June 1978), the two young women joined the walkers, who by that time had reached Ohio. The month of total physical and mental commitment to a social cause was, Paula and I agree, one of the most important and defining experiences of her life. In a number of ways Paula Starr came back to Los Angeles from "the Walk" a changed woman. Career goals had been transformed. Work would not only have to be "fun," it would also have to be meaningful and contributory, not only to Paula but to her wider and intertribal community.

Love, Marriage, Motherhood, an MA, and Community Commitment and Service

Paula fairly gushes when she talks about involvement in "the Walk." It was a defining moment and major turning point, her Maslowian "peak experience."[17] Paula was inspired by the congregation of thousands of Native Americans: "It was just like our great tribal convocations in the past—everyone coming together for a common good." She also stressed the educational as well as the political outcomes of the trek: "We didn't confront. We educated. When people would come into the campsites to see what we were doing, we would take the time to explain to them what the political issues were and what needed to be done about them. They learned a lot about our people, and we found out a lot about ourselves in the process." Paula also found love on the Walk.

Although she had been peripherally associated with AIM since she entered UCLA, "the Walk" totally changed her relationship with that American Indian activist group. Assigned to camp security upon her arrival in Ohio, when the walkers arrived in Pennsylvania she met and worked with Richard Robideau, another Longest Walk security officer and a veteran AIM activist. By the time the walkers reached Washington DC, Paula and Richard were in love, planning a marriage, and thinking about parenthood.

When Paula and I met for the first time on New Year's Eve of 1978, she had been back in L.A. for about six months and was not only back in school, but also pregnant. The college students who participated in "the Walk" had pledged to finish their educations. Paula meant to keep her word as she only had another year of course work to complete before receiving her BA. Therefore, in 1979 she transferred to the communications program at the University of California in Irvine (UCI) and finished her undergraduate work there that year. Paula did so because she had found the theater arts program at UCLA "too theoretical," and she "wanted the hands-on training the UCI theater program provided." That same year, Paula's daughter, Starr, was born as well.

Consistent with her life-long belief in the efficacy of a good education, Paula entered the master's program in theater arts at California State University in Long Beach the following year. She had completed her graduate course work when her years of community activism became the catalyst for yet another pivotal life decision. She found the esotericism of literary criticism no longer held her attention. Restless to "be out there and making a difference," Paula left her graduate program with only a thesis to write and never looked back.

It was at this point in her life that Paula began to fulfill another commitment she had made following the Longest Walk, to use her skills and education for the good of the Native American community. In the early 1980s she found employment for the first time in Native American social service centers. She worked as a health educator for three years at the Downtown L.A. Indian Free Clinic. She made a lateral move to a satellite American Indian service center in Hollywood the following year. By the mid-1980s Paula had become so adept at Native American social services delivery planning and administration that when John Castillo took over the executive directorship of SCIC in 1986, he invited her to join his support team as a proposal writer, and the rest is history.

On Good Community Stewardship

Historically, certain governance issues have consistently plagued the social service organizations of the culturally diverse and geographically dispersed Los Angeles Native American community. The first, of course, is how to go about choosing responsible and sufficiently trained executives to administer effectively its hard-won community service programs. The second and equally problematic issue is how to ensure that proper community oversight is in place so as to prevent entrenchment of self-absorbed executive leaders who become so isolated from or indifferent to both the will and needs of the community they were chosen to serve that they ultimately are viewed by their constituents as "the problem, not the solution."[18] Paula Starr's SCIC stewardship since 2000 appears to have avoided these sociostructural and political pitfalls.

I asked Paula for her insight into why her administration seems to be immune to such organizational viruses. She repeatedly underscored a number of leadership qualities she felt were vital to SCIC's continuance as an effective social service umbrella agency. Responsibility, commitment, dedication, a focus on service to the community, and team effort came up consistently in her evaluation of her leadership style and the SCIC way of doing things. She also emphasized her conviction that her and her staff's "passion for the work" has carried them through the rough spots. Paula laughed sardonically when I asked her what the personal "perks" of her job are and if they compensate for the fifty- to sixty-hour weeks she routinely puts in.

> Take a look around [she made a circling gesture about her document- and computer-filled but otherwise spare office]. There's no padding here. We haven't had raises in six years. I'm driving an eight-year-old car. Other CEOs [with similar responsibilities in mainstream service organizations] make two and three times what I make. No, we're not in it for the money here. It's to see that we get services to our community members. That keeps us going.[19]

Paula's tone changed dramatically, however, when I asked about how she went about making difficult executive decisions on behalf of SCIC, coping with the stresses of multitasking, and just getting through the daily demands of her community stewardship. She quietly offered, "I start each day with a prayer. You see, I have this *huge responsibility* [Paula's emphasis]. And so I have what I call my office feather." Paula then showed me the items that she keeps in a desk cubby above her computer and that she uses in her daily, deeply personal and orienting prayers. Reverently, she explained the meaning and use of the perfect eagle feather with which she had been gifted some years ago. She took out and lovingly fingered another older, worn eagle feather that "is here to remind me of my peoples' struggles." Included in her prayer item collection is a small rock her father gave her when she was a child, to remind Paula of another order of Native American struggle, I suspect. She took out her braid of sweet grass and explained the cleansing properties inherent in its burning. She also talked about burning cedar bark and sage in the large scallop shell she kept among her prayer objects. She explained, "So I start my workday with a prayer. Sometimes I use smoke to cleanse, purify, and tranquilize the area. It's my responsibility to do this—to keep these feathers and the staff reenergized." With that life-transforming and action-validating recognition of and reliance on powers both within us and beyond our understanding, Paula Starr is the ultimate multitasker.

Not only is she the politically savvy, administratively adept, skilled fundraiser and longtime and respected executive director of SCIC; she is also its spiritual vessel. She understands her and the SCIC staff's work and responsibility to their community as sacred mission. Paula, humbly and not without some trepidation, feels herself bound to take on and sustain the organization's spiritual and moral superiority through the regular practice of traditional Native American forms of prayer and sanctification. What a powerful, even subversive thought, to validate the nonseparation and vital synergism of sacred direction and public service. Paula Starr is convinced (as is most of the SCIC staff/family) that their community service is validated by criteria other than career advancement, impressive income, or personal power. They do what they do because it is the people's and the ancestors' work.

Auto/Ethnobiography as Social Paradigm

Paula Starr's life history gives us reason to hope. It also provides a few clues about how individuals, despite seemingly overwhelming odds, find their paths to positive personal agency and self-actualization. Every adult in her immediate family stressed the importance of getting an education. Therefore, no matter how stressful family life became, Paula knew she had a personal survival plan. She would and did educate herself. Children of a particular household do not necessarily have identical family culture experiences. Birth order, sex, and parental preferences can all shape an individual's family experience and sense of self. Paula was the oldest of four siblings. By the time she was six or seven she had already taken on the role of family babysitter, mother's helper, sibling protector, and "mother hen," roles that allowed her an acceptable way of removing herself from the more negative aspects of her early and at times negative familial and cultural scene, and for which their ultimate and continuing expression bring her admiration and community respect.

Contemporary urban contexts provide not one but a range of social models and behavioral templates that individuals can adopt or reject wholly or in part, only to go on and experience, experiment with, or reject and adopt other cultural forms. Individuals make cultural choices all the time. Paula rejected early on the drinking culture that as a child she conflated with "being Indian." It would take a decade or more for her to learn that "being Indian" did not have to be a negative experience but a positive, rewarding, and even necessary experience.

Having learned that lesson, Paula did the remarkable. She found ways to translate personal experience and choice into positive community action. Convinced of the efficacy of education, she ensures that scic provides educational preparation, access, and reward to her community members. She has also found ways to provide her community with health education and assistance and with access to health service locations. Alcohol and drug abuse intervention and HIV education are but three of the health issues addressed in intervention programs for which she has written grants, secured funding, and administrated. And for the last decade, perhaps driven by the awful memory of the possibility that she and her siblings could have been placed in foster homes because of the breakup of her family, Paula and her SCIC colleagues have worked to prevent the placement of Native American children in non-Indian foster homes and to establish a Southern California network of Indian foster parents and grandparents. Paula Starr continues to work her community service alchemy. In expressions of social and political agency she transforms personal experience into positive community action. Charlotte Ortiz and I were right, nearly three decades ago: Paula Starr indeed bore (and still bears) watching.

Some Concluding Thoughts: Cultural Templates and Individual Choice

It would have been so easy (and I really did attempt to resist the desire to do so) to make meta-theoretical leaps from what seemed meaningful comparisons and obvious parallels between the particulars of Paula's life and the frequency with which those kinds of experiences have been discussed in the urban Indian literature of the last forty years. In certain clear and already documented instances Paula's life narrative is both microcosmic and iconic. In a number of ways it exemplifies assumptions about contemporary urban American Indian life—that confusion of ethnic identity accompanies urban relocation, and that the outcomes of that dislocation necessarily include poverty, recreational drinking that escalates into alcoholism, family dysfunction, disruption, and collapse, and premature deaths from unnatural causes.[20]

In other and equally meaningful ways, Paula's life is unique. It is a shining refutation of the tyranny of cultural context and its assumed capacity to shape individual experience. The potency of the telling of Paula Starr's life is in its microcosmic power to inform about additional and more positive American Indian truths. Paula's successes are emblematic of the range of the urban Indian experience as well as tenacity of personal agency. She grew up in a drinking culture but does not drink. Though her early family life was chaotic and provided little in the way of positive role modeling, Paula is married and happily enjoying grandmotherhood. While many Native American youths never finish high school, Paula has a bachelor's degree and has completed all but the thesis for a master's degree.

Given such contrasts between expected cultural forms and actual personal experience, of what worth is this or any ethnobiography to the anthropological project? Is there any ethnological lesson to be learned here? Between 1972 and 1977 I completed my graduate work in anthropology at UCLA. At the time, anthropology was just beginning a self-critique and redefinition. I remember feeling more confused than informed by Robert Edgerton's seminar admonishments that future generations of anthropologists would have to be very careful about generalizing about a group of people from what one, a few, or an opportunistic sample of them had to say about the culture in which they were imbedded. His illustrations of the extent to which intelligence tests scores, skin color, size, and height can range widely across an ethnic group and what those findings tell us about the relative significance of intra- versus intergroup variation were as disturbing as they were informative.

Those were sage admonishments, as salient today as they were unsettling thirty years ago. The culturally integrated ethnographic village in which cultural norms are easily identified and recognized by both the indigene and the ethnographer may, in the long run, be largely fiction or at most only partial truths. With such individual experiential variation in contemporary urban and globalized society, perhaps life history narrative and an indigene's experience and point of view are as close as we come to sociocultural verity.

Adopting Paula's ability to see the half-full glass, we argue that the negatives of the urban Indian experience do exist, but they only partially represent the sociohistorical context and narrative of urban American Indian life. The personal and communal successes, the evolved and effective survival strategies, the evolving plans and prognoses for the future of one's ethnic community—these positive elements of the contemporary urban Indian experience require public exposure and acknowledgment. Indeed, they need telling in order to construct more meaningful and thickly descriptive urban Indian ethnographies.[21] The new urban Indian narrative is informed by this collection of urban Indian women's stories and this telling of Paula Starr's story.

Notes

1 Bell and Cudahy are the other two south central Los Angeles County incorporated cities with concentrations of Native American residents. In 1970 Bell Gardens, with a Native American population of 762, which constituted 2.6 percent of its total population, had the largest proportion of Native American citizens in all of the incorporated cities in Los Angeles. Neighboring Cudahy, with its 476 Native American residents (2.1 percent of its total population), ran a close second. The 196 Native American residents of Bell constituted 1.3 percent of its total population in 1970. For details, see Joan Weibel-Orlando, *Indian Country, L.A.: Maintaining Ethnic Community in Complex Society*, 2nd ed. (Urbana: University of Illinois Press, 1999), 25.

2 A viewing of the 1961 quasi-ethnographic film *The Exiles* establishes that "binge drinking" was an early, continuing, and routine element of the weekly Los Angeles urban Indian powwow scene; dir. Kent Mackenzie, *The Exiles*, USC, 1961. By 1973, when I began attending powwows in Los Angeles, the community was vigorously self-regulating its drinking during powwows and especially when they were held at government-regulated public locations. In 1978 large posters requesting people not to drink while on the powwow grounds were prominently placed both within and outside of the gymnasium. Consequently, for those for whom New Year's Eve celebrations are incomplete without drinking, "downing a few" took place outside of the park building and in the shadows of the surrounding walkways, athletic fields, and parking lots. For in-depth ethnographic accounts of L.A.-based powwows, see Joan Weibel-Orlando, "Miss America and Powwow Princess: Icons of Womanhood," *Urban Resources* 4:3 (L.A. ed., 1988): 1–8, and Weibel-Orlando, *Indian Country, L.A.*

3 For a full discussion of the secular/sacred dimensions of the powwow arena, see Weibel-Orlando, *Indian Country, L.A.*, chapter 8.

4 Charlotte Ortiz was not only an L.A. Indian community leader but was also one of my research assistants at the time. In 1978 I was a research anthropologist at the Alcohol Research Center at UCLA. As a co-principal investigator of an ethnographic study of urban Indian drinking patterns, I was interested in locating college-educated Native Americans to hire as community-based fieldworkers on the project.

5 The relationship between Paula and me was not, for example, like that between quadriplegic collaborator Diane De Vries and anthropologist Gelya Frank, which was described with such candor, sensitivity, and, yes, love in their book, *Venus on Wheels: Two Decades of Dialogue on Disability, Biography, and Being Female in America* (Berkeley: University of California Press, 2000). Nor did our collaboration have the dynamic intensity of the mother/daughter-like tie shared by the older, successful, Korean American woman mentor Dora Yum Kim and her younger, Korean American woman aspirant, admirer, and biographer Soo Young Chin, as described in their collaborative life history narrative, *Doing What Had to Be Done: The Life Narrative of Dora Yum Kim*, Asian American History and Culture Series (Philadelphia: Temple University Press, 1999). Nor was Paula's and my relationship shaped by the writing of focused biographies of Native American women by non-Native American writers such as David Jones's *Sanapia: Comanche Medicine Woman* (New York: Holt, Rinehart and Winston, 1972), or Florence Shipek's description of her confidante's "ethnobotanic contributions" in *Delfina Cuero: Her Autobiography: An Account of Her Last Years and Her Ethnobotanic Contributions* (Menlo Park CA: Ballena Press, 1991), or Diana Bahr's examination of acculturative shifts across three generations of Cupeno women in Los Angeles in *From Mission to Metropolis: Cupeno Women in Los Angeles* (Norman: University of Oklahoma Press, 1993).

6 L. L. Langness and Gelya Frank, *Lives: An Anthropological Approach to Biography* (Novato CA: Chandler and Sharp, 1981).

7 Paula's paternal grandmother, Nettie Black Kettle Starr, was the daughter of the historically important Cheyenne peace chief Black Kettle. Black Kettle headed the Cheyenne band that was nearly annihilated during the Sand Creek Massacre of 1864. For more, see E. Adamson Hoebel, *The Cheyennes: Indians of the Great Plains*, 2nd ed. (Fort Worth TX: Harcourt Brace, 1978), 113. Paula's mother is of Irish American descent. Paula suspects, however, that her mother may have some (if undocumented) Seminole family background.

8 See, for example, John Price, "The Migration and Adaptation of American Indians to Los Angeles," *Human Organization* 27 (1968): 168–75; Lynn Simross, "The Plight of Native Americans on the 'Urban Reservation,'" *Los Angeles Times*, April 16, 1986, part 5:1, 4; Alan L. Sorkin, *The Urban Indian* (Lexington MA: Lexington Books, 1978); Jack O. Waddell and O. Michael Watson, *The American Indian in Urban Society* (Boston: Little, Brown, 1971).

9 Hoover and 11th is located just west of downtown Los Angeles in an area now known as the Pico-Union District. It is currently a lower-working-class neighborhood with residents who are largely from Mexican and Central and South American cultural backgrounds. All of Paula Starr's quotes in this chapter are taken from the three recorded interviews/discussions she and I had in June and July of 2005. In the interest of conserving space and avoiding redundancy, I do not cite the source of each quotation.

10 The 1950 U.S. Census identified 19,943 Native American residents of Los Angeles County. In 1960 that population had doubled to 39,014. See Weibel-Orlando, *Indian Country, L.A.*, 13. For in-depth and historical discussions of the development of the Los Angeles Native American community organizational structure over time, see Wayne G. Bramstedt, "Corporate Adaptations of Urban Migrants: American Indian Voluntary Associations in the Los Angeles Metropolitan Area" (PhD diss., University of California at Los Angeles, 1977), and Weibel-Orlando, *Indian Country, L.A.*

11 The Tombs refers to an open area underneath a highway intersection in East Los Angeles where powwow enthusiasts would gather after hours on weekends to continue their tribal drumming, singing, and dancing. The Shrimp Boat was the name of a twenty-four-hour fast food diner in downtown Los Angeles. The diner was situated at the front of a large parking lot where weekend powwowers would congregate after hours to continue their tribal songs, and Native Americans often frequented the food stand for midnight snacks. The Shrimp closed in the mid-1990s.

12 The degree to which alcohol and drug abuse has impacted Native American families and communities has, over the last fifty years, been graphically documented in hundreds of research reports, articles, and books as well as in Indigenous literary works and films, such as N. Scott Momaday, *A House Made of Dawn* (New York: Harper and Row, 1968); N. Scott Momaday and Richardson Morse (screen adaptation), *House Made of Dawn*, dir. Richardson Morse (Washington DC: Film and Video Center, National

Museum of the American Indian (NMAI), distrib., 1972); or, more recently, Sherman Alexie (writer), *Smoke Signals*, dir. Chris Eyre, prod. Shadow-Catcher Entertainment, 1998.

13 In a follow-up interview, Paula explained that the family had lost contact with her father in the last years of his life. In many Native American tribal groups, being without family at death is one of the worst possible human conditions as there is no one to pray for you and your spiritual peace when you have gone to be with the ancestors. Paula learned of the circumstances of her father's death in 1972 more than twenty years later when, ironically and serendipitously, her Indian community friend, former UCLA student adviser, and future husband, Gene Herrod, in his capacity as a licensed private investigator, uncovered the circumstances of Paula's dad's death in 1995.

14 In 1972, when Paula initiated the college application process, the local and public junior college systems were well established in California. The two-year college programs that culminate in associates of arts degrees at minimal tuition costs—one of the most positive and far-reaching public services California offers its citizens—have made it possible for hundreds of thousands of economically disadvantaged young people to acquire a college education.

15 An "apple" is a pejorative term for a person who is "red on the outside but white on the inside," referring to a Native American who wishes to emulate (be) an Anglo.

16 DQ University, a two-year tribal college founded in 1971, closed in 2006. The Longest Walk references the traumatic Native American trek of the Navajo in 1864, when they were forced at military gunpoint to remove from Fort Laramie and walk three hundred miles to Bosque Redondo, lands designated by the U.S. government as the new area of Navajo concentration. The 1978 five-month, three-thousand-mile trek from Alcatraz Island in San Francisco Bay to Washington DC, in which thousands of Native Americans and their political and philosophical supporters participated, was meant to dramatize the refusal of Native Americans to allow the federal government to abrogate their rights of tribal sovereignty. By co-opting the negative imagery of an earlier act of political disempowerment and repression, and by reworking that imagery and action into an expression of positive political protest, resistance, and agency, the Longest Walk of 1978 was an inspired, highly successful, and politically potent rite of reversal.

17 A. H. Maslow labeled as a "peak experience" an event in a person's life

so profoundly moving or iconic that it forever shaped or altered the person's worldview and behaviors. *Toward a Psychology of Being*, 2nd ed. (Princeton NJ: Van Nostrand Reinhold, 1968).

18 See chapter 14 in Weibel-Orlando, *Indian Country, L.A.*, for discussion of the sociostructural tensions that led to the closing of the Los Angeles–based Indian Center.

19 On January 9, 2006, while Paula and I met at her office to discuss her reactions to the rough draft of this chapter, she amended the record here: "I think you should know that, with continuation of one of our major service grants, core staff will be receiving raises this fiscal year for the first time in five years!"

20 See, for instance, Theodore Graves, "Drinking and Drunkenness among Urban Indians," in *American Indian in Urban Society*, ed. Jack O. Waddell and O. Michael Watson (Boston: Little, Brown, 1971), 274–311; and Simross, "Plight of Native Americans."

21 Clifford Geertz, *The Interpretation of Cultures* (New York: Basic Books, 1973), 3–30.

Contributors

GRANT ARNDT studied cultural anthropology at the University of Chicago and now teaches anthropology and American Indian studies at Iowa State University. He is currently writing a book based on his doctoral research on Ho-Chunk powwows and related cultural performances in Wisconsin. His previous writings on urban issues include "Relocation's Imagined Landscape and the Rise of Chicago's American Indian Community" in the edited volume *Native Chicago*.

DARA CULHANE is an associate professor of anthropology at Simon Fraser University. She is the author of *An Error in Judgment: The Politics of Medical Care in an Indian/White Community*; *The Pleasure of the Crown: Anthropology, Law and First Nations*; and co-editor with Leslie Robertson of *In Plain Sight: Reflections on Everyday Life in Downtown Eastside Vancouver* (winner of 2006 George Ryga Award for Social Issues in Literature). Her current research focuses on experimental ethnography, particularly articulation between fine and performing arts in community-based methodologies.

HEATHER A. HOWARD is adjunct assistant professor of anthropology at Michigan State University and holds a research status appointment with the Centre for Aboriginal Initiatives at the University of Toronto. Her research interests include urban Native community organizing, socioeconomic class, citizenship, and sovereignty, with a particular focus on health, labor, and gender in Canada and the United States. She has served as a consultant for tribes in the Great

Lakes region and California on land claims and resource use. She is completing a monograph, *Lineage, Land and Labor: The Northfork Mono and the San Joaquin Valley, California*, and an edited collection on Aboriginal peoples in Canadian cities. She is co-editor of *Feminist Fields: Ethnographic Insights* and *The Meeting Place: Aboriginal Life in Toronto*.

NANCY JANOVICEK is assistant professor in the Department of History at the University of Calgary. She is the author of *No Place to Go: Local Histories of the Battered Women's Shelter Movement*.

SUSAN APPLEGATE KROUSE (Oklahoma Cherokee) is associate professor of anthropology and director of the American Indian Studies Program at Michigan State University. Her current ethnographic research focuses on urban American Indian communities, and she is completing a monograph on the Indian Community School of Milwaukee. She has also published on historic and contemporary images of American Indians. She is the author of *North American Indians in the Great War*, which examines Joseph K. Dixon's visual and written documentation of Indians in World War I.

MOLLY LEE retired in 2008 from her positions as curator of ethnology at the University of Alaska Museum of the North and professor of anthropology at the University of Alaska, Fairbanks. Her research interests include the art and material culture of northern peoples and the anthropology of art. She lives with her husband, Michael Krauss, in Fairbanks and is at work on a book about Yup'ik Eskimo basketry.

SUSAN LOBO is a cultural anthropologist who has worked for years with Indian community-based nonprofits. She has taught at the University of California at Berkeley and at Davis, at Merritt College, and at the University of Arizona. She is currently a distinguished visiting scholar in American Indian Studies at the University of

Arizona. Her books include *A House of My Own: Social Organization in the Squatter Settlements of Lima, Peru; Native American Voices: A Reader; American Indians and the Urban Experience; Urban Voices: The Bay Area American Indian Community;* and *The Sweet Smell of Home: Leonard F. Chana, Tohono O'odham Artist.*

ANNE TERRY STRAUS retired from the University of Chicago, where she taught and practiced action anthropology, focusing on the Chicago American Indian community. Much of her work has involved collaborating with community people, including Debra Valentino, the co-author of her contribution to this volume.

DEBRA VALENTINO (Oneida/Menominee) currently serves as president of the board of directors of the American Indian Center of Chicago, the oldest urban American Indian center in the country. She has held various leadership roles in the Chicago American Indian community. She was one of four founding members and the executive director of Chicago's Urban Indian Retreat and was a founding member of the Native American Foster Parents Association, which became a model throughout the nation.

JOAN WEIBEL-ORLANDO is a recent emerita professor from the Department of Anthropology at the University of Southern California. There she taught both a year-long research methods and practicum seminar to anthropology majors as well as upper-division courses in Native American cultures and their visualizations for nearly thirty years. Her book *Indian Country, L.A.* and numerous journal articles, edited book chapters, and teaching videos are largely focused on the contemporary Native American experience.

MARY C. WRIGHT teaches in American Indian studies at the University of Washington, with interests in gender, space, Indian gaming, and the Plateau cultural area. She received a PhD from Rutgers, The State University of New Jersey in 1996.

Index

Ablon, Joan, x
Aboriginal rights movement, 57, 89
abused women. *See* violence
Ackerman, Lillian, 6, 8, 12
activism, political: aboriginal rights
    and, 60–63; Alaska Federation
    of Natives, 99–102; Alcatraz
    Island occupation, 29, 146,
    149; American Indian Women's
    Service League, 125–26, 127–29,
    131, 134–36; Canadian Aborigi-
    nal identity and, 58–60, 70–71,
    72–73n15; Civil Rights move-
    ment and, 29–30; economic
    issues and, 99–102; education
    and, 30; expansion of opportuni-
    ties for women through, 46–49;
    against family violence, 56–58,
    63–70; gambling and, 154–58;
    gender and, x, 32–33, 34–37;
    incipient, xix; Longest Walk
    and, 176–78, 187n16; Native art
    and, 100–102; Native lands and,
    130–31; Paula Starr and, xix–xx,
    176–77; poverty and, 80–81,
    132–33, 136; Red Power move-
    ment and, 29, 108, 126–27, 146;
    Seattle Indian Center, 131–34;
    social welfare and, 46–50; South-
    ern California Indian Center,
    178–80; sovereign power and, 41;
    studies of, 146; takeover of the
    U.S. Coast Guard Station and,
    148–51; Urban Clan Mothers
    and, 14–15, 16; urban indigenous
    identity and, 61–63, 118–20;
    volunteerism and, 118–21;
    women's visibility and, 76–77,
    83–89, 87–88. *See also* Chicago
    American Indian Center
affluent Native people, 110
Alaska Federation of Natives, 93–94;
    crafts fairs, 93–96, 99–102;
    founding of, 94; links to Native
    Americans, 93–94; political
    activism and, 99–102; rural
    in-migration to urban areas,
    97–99, 100, 102–3n3; subsis-
    tence debate and, 97–99
Alaska National Interest Lands Con-
    servation Act (ANILCA), 98
Alaska Native Claims Settlement Act
    (ANCSA), 98
Alcatraz, occupation of, 29, 146, 149
Alcoholics Anonymous, 128
alcoholism, 128, 170–71, 181–82,
    184n2, 186n12
Alexian Brothers Novitiate, 151

All-American Indian Dancers, 131
American Anthropological Association, xxi
American Indian Activism: Alcatraz to the Longest Walk, 146
American Indian Chicago conference, 28
American Indian Economic Development Association, 30
American Indian Lodge, 38
American Indian Movement (AIM), 29, 31, 146, 176; takeover of the U.S. Coast Guard Station, 148–51
American Indian Quarterly, xiv, xxi
American Indians and the Urban Experience, xxii
American Indian Welfare Council (AIWC), 39
American Indian Women's Leadership Development (WLD) project, 31, 47
American Indian Women's Service League, 125–29, 131; legacy of, 136–39; politics and, 134–36
American Native Women's Leadership Development Forum, 138
America's Most Wanted, 82
Anchorage Daily News, 101
anchor households, 12
Aquino, Ella, 130, 137
Argus, 127
Arndt, Grant, xx, xxii, *Native Chicago*, xxii
assimilation, x–xi, 4, 57, 61, 106

Batisse, Ludie, 28
Baum, JoAnn Staples, 138
Bay Area American Indian community: fieldwork on, 2–3; fluidity and mobility of, 6–8, 9–10; key households in, 8–18; social structure, 3–6
Bearskin, Ben, 24, 26, 27, 37
Bearskin, Betty, 26
Beaucage, Josephine, 115–16, 120
Beaver Tales, 118
Beck, David, xii, 49
Beendigen hostel, 56–58, 63–70
Ben, Jesse, 32
Bennett, Ramona, 136–37, 138
Black Kettle, Chief, 168, 185n7
Bonvillain, Nancy, 6, 10–11
Brass, G. M., 80
Breaking Free: A Proposal for Change to Aboriginal Family Violence (ONWA), 69
Bridges, Maiselle, 138
Bureau of Indian Affairs (BIA), 52n16, 135; education and, 149, 154; Indian gaming and, 154–58; relocation policies and, 25–26, 40, 42, 168
Butterfield, Mary Jo, 138

Cabuag, Johanna, 138
California v. Cabazon Band of Mission Indians, 154
Carner, Lucy, 39
Carter, Jimmy, 136
Castillo, John, 164–65, 178
Cerritos College, 174–75
Chadwick, Bruce A., xi
Champagne, Duane, 146
Chappell, Lillian, 138
Chicago IL: growth of Native population in, 23–24, 37; Indian

Fellowship League of, 23–24;
Natives viewed as maladjusted
in, 38–39, 42; need for social
services in, 22–28
Chicago American Indian Center,
30, 32; Bureau of Indian Affairs
and, 25–26, 40; counseling
services offered by, 45; funding
of, 42–44; leadership, 22, 25–28,
47–48; programs, 40–41, 43;
social welfare work by, 35, 37–45,
49–50; staff, 43–44, 48; Welfare
Council and Community Fund
and, 42–45, 47–48
Chicago American Indian Community Organizations conference, 30
children, Native, 65–70, 86–87;
education of, 148–59
choice, individual, 182–84
citizenship, 118–20
Citizens Plus, 58
Civil Rights movement, 29
class, xv–xvi
Cobe, Al, 25, 37–38, 40
colonialism and imperialism, xviii,
76, 81, 109, 126
Colville reservation, 12
compensating, 173–74
Comprehensive Employment and
Training Act (CETA), 150
cooperatives, housing, 15–16
Covington, Lucy, 135
craft fairs, xix, 93–96, 99–102,
116–18
Cross, Virginia, 138
csi: Crime Scene Investigation, 83
Culhane, Dara, xviii, xix, xx
cult of true womanhood, 36–37

cultural templates, 182–84

Daybreak Star Cultural Center, 131
deaths in urban Indian communi-
ties, 17–18, 86–87, 171, 187n13
Delgado, Louis, 30
Delorme, Woodrow, 134
Denny, Arthur, 129
Department of Indian Affairs,
Canada (DIA), 58, 65, 107
Dion Stout, Madeleine, xiii–xiv
Dosman, Edgar, xi, 110
Dowling, John H., xi
Downtown Eastside Women's
Memorial March, 76
drug abuse, 77–80
Dubec, Bernice, 60–61, 62, 64–65,
67

Eaton, Mrs. John D., 119
economic issues in urban Indian
communities: craft fairs and,
93–96, 99–100; education and,
149–50, 152–58; employment of
Native women and, 84–85, 96,
99–100, 107–11; gambling and,
154–58; middle-class identity
and, 106, 108–11, 118–20; subsistence debate and, 97–99
Edgerton, Robert, 183
education, 116; college, 174–76, 178;
funding, 149–50, 152–58; gambling and, 154–58; Milwaukee
Indian community and, 148–59;
school boards and, 153–54, 157;
value of, 172–73; of women,
28–32, 107–8, 111–13, 172–73,
174–76, 178

families: children in, 65–70, 86–87;
    multigenerational, 86; violence,
    56–58, 63–70
Fastwolf, Phyllis, 30
feminism. *See* women's rights move-
    ment
Fiske, Shirley J., xi
Fixico, Donald, 4
fluidity of urban Indian communi-
    ties, 6–8; key households and,
    8–18; migration patterns and, 56
Fogel-Chance, Nancy, 96
Fort Lawton, Washington, 130, 131,
    137
Frank, Gelya, 166
Frazier, Gregory, 133–34
*Full Circle: The Indians of Washington
    State* (1990), 137
Funmaker, Marge, 148

gaming, Indian, 154–58
Garcia, Adeline Hannah Skultka,
    125, 138
gender: activism and, x, 32–33,
    34–37, 46–50, 61–63; leadership
    and, xix, xx–xxi, 28–33, 32–37,
    46–49, 136–39; migration pat-
    terns and, 56; traditional roles
    and, 1–6, 13–14, 18, 35–37
George, Gina, 138
ghettos, 4–5
Gilbeau, Audrey, 61, 63, 65–66, 67
Gone, Joseph P., 133
Goode, Judith, 78
Goodin, Toni, 176–77
Grand Council Fire of American
    Indians, 24
Green, Rayna, xiv

Halliday, Jeannie, 138
Harris, Anna, 23
health care, 22–23, 128, 138, 157;
    alcoholism and, 128, 170–71,
    181–82, 184n2, 186n12; HIV/
    AIDS and, xviii, 77, 80
Heth, Charlotte, 175
Hirabayashi, James, xi
HIV/AIDS, xviii, 77, 80
Hoikkala, Paivi, 11
households: anchor, 12; children
    in, 65–70; housing cooperatives
    and, 15–16; key, 8–18; multiple,
    10–11; relocation programs and,
    26, 40, 42, 52n16; violence in,
    63–70
Howard, Heather A., xv–xvi, xx, xxi
Hull House, 38
Hurt, Wesley R., Jr., x

*I Am Nokomis, Too: The Biography of
    Verna Patronella Johnston* (Van-
    derburgh), 105–6
identity, Native, 60–63, 109, 118–20,
    133–34
illegal drugs, 77–78
imperialism. *See* colonialism and
    imperialism
Imperial Order of the Daughters
    of the Empire (IODE), 118–19,
    119, 120
incarcerated Native women, 114–15
incipient activism, xix
Indian Act, Canada, 58–60, 71n1
Indian Center News, 134–35, 137
Indian Child Welfare Act of 1978, 137
Indian Council Fire, 24
Indian Country, L. A., 166

Indian Education Act, 152, 154

Indian enclaves, 4–5

Indian Fellowship League, 23–24

Indian Metropolis, 134

Indian Rights for Indian Women
   (IRIW), 59

Indian Self-Determination Act of
   1975, 135

Indian Service League, 25

Indians' Service League, 38

indigenous identity, urban, 60–63,
   118–20

individual choice, 182–84

invisibility of Native people, 76

Janovicek, Nancy, xvi, xxi

Jennings, Peggy, 119

Johnson, Julie, 130, 137–38, 138

Johnson, Lyndon, 132

Johnson, Troy, 146

Johnston, Verna Patronella, 105–6,
   111–12, 114, 120; *Tales of Nokomis*,
   112

Jojola, Theodore S., 5, 6, 13

Jones, Dorothy, 116–17, 120

Kauffman, Jo Ann, 138

Kemnitzer, Luis, xi

Ketah, Joy, 138

key households, 8–18

Kingston Prison for Women, 114–15

Kipling, Gregory D., xiii–xiv

Kirkness, Verna J., xi

Kirmayer, L. J., 80

Kitka, Julie, 99, 101

Knack, Martha C., 6

Krouse, Susan Applegate, xvi–xvii,
   xix, xx, xxi

LaGrand, James, 134

LaMere, Willard, 23, 24, 25, 27, 37

LaPearl, Cleo, 38

leadership and gender, xix, xx–xxi,
   28–33, 32–37, 46–49, 136–39

Lee, Molly, xvi, xix, xxi

Legacy of Pride, 138

LePage, Dorothy, 148, 149, 152, 153

Liebow, Edward D., xii

life history narratives, 165–68,
   181–82

*Like a Hurricane: The Indian Move-
   ment from Alcatraz to Wounded
   Knee* (Smith and Warrior), 146

Lobo, Susan, xii, xv, xxi, xxii, 4, 6

Longest Walk, 176–78, 187n16

Los Angeles Native American
   community: growth of, 169–70;
   powwows, 163–64, 186n11; problems facing, 178–79; Southern
   California Indian Center and,
   164–65, 178–80

MacLeod, Linda, 67–68; *Wife Battering in Canada*, 68

Margon, Arthur, xi

Maskovsky, Jeff, 78

McGregor, Lillian, 113–14

McNickle, D'Arcy, 29

medical services. *See* health care

men, Native: education of, 32; family violence and, 63–70; leaders,
   22–28, 37–38

Menominee Warrior Society, 151

Metcalf, Ann, xiii

middle-class Native people, 106,
   108–11, 118–20

migration patterns: Native identity

migration patterns (*cont.*)
and, 109; rural to urban, xvi,
97–99, 100, 102–3n3, 105–6,
127–28, 147–48. *See also* mobility
patterns
Million, Dian, 69
Milwaukee Indian community: education in, 148, 151–59; following
the takeover of the U.S. Coast
Guard Station, 151–59; gambling
and, 154–55; population growth,
147; takeover of the U.S. Coast
Guard Station, xvii, 148–51
Milwaukee American Indian Information and Action Group, 148
Minea, Russell A., 24
mobility patterns, xv–xvi, 6–8, 9–10,
56, 118–20. *See also* migration
patterns
Montezuma, Carlos, 22–23, 24, 28
Monture-Okanee, Patricia, 68
Morris, Elizabeth, 132, 133
Ms. Magazine, 132
multigenerational kinship groups, 86
murder, 82–83, 91n19

Nagel, Joane, 146
Nagler, Mark, 110
narratives, life history, 165–68,
181–82
National Association of Social Workers, 44
National Congress of American
Indians (NCAI), 28
National Endowment for the
Humanities (NEH) grants, 129
National Federation of Settlement
and Neighborhood Center, 44

National Indian Youth Council
(NIYC), 29
Native American Committee, 30
Native American Educational
Services College (NAES College),
30, 32
Native American Foster Parents
Association (NAFPA), 30–31
Native American Rights Fund, 99
Native American Urban Indian
Retreat (CNAUIR), 30
Native Canadian Centre of Toronto,
106, 108, 111, 113–14, 116–17, 119;
Ladies' Auxiliary, 106, 114–15,
117–18, 119–20
Native Chicago (Strauss and Ardnt),
xxii
*Native Hubs: Culture, Community,
and Belonging in Silicon Valley
and Beyond* (Ramirez), xxii
Native People of Thunder Bay
Development Corporation, 63
Neconish, Darlene Funmaker, 148
niche building and finding, 174–76
Nixon, Richard, 136
North American Indian Club, 106,
108, 112, 114–15
North American Indian Council
(NAIC), 24, 37–38
North American Indian Mission, 24
Northwest Indian News, 134–35, 137

Oakland Intertribal Friendship
House, 22
Ontario Native Women's Association
(ONWA), 57–58, 62, 69; *Breaking
Free*, 69
Ortiz, Charlotte Standing Buffalo,
164, 182

Ortner, Sherry, 110
Owen, Philip, 82

Perales, Joseph, 32
Peters, Ernie, 176
Peters, Evelyn, 118
Peters, Kurt, xii, xxii
Pickton, Robert William, 82–83,
    91n19
Piper, Lee, 138
Podlasek, Joe, 32
politics. *See* activism, political
poverty, 80–81, 132–33, 136
Powell, Peter, 27, 46
Powers, Teresa Brownwolf, 138
Powless, Eli, 25
Powless, Meriville, 38
powwows, 163–64, 169–70, 184n2,
    186n11
Price, John A., xi
Princess of the Powwow (1987), 137
prisons, 114–15
prostitution, 77, 78, 81–86, 92n24

Ramirez, Renya, xxii, 7, 8, 11; *Native
    Hubs*, xxii
Reagan, Ronald, 136
Red Cloud, Bill, 27
Red Cloud, Margaret, 28
Redmond, Millie, 115, 120
Red Power movement, 29, 108,
    126–27, 146
relocation programs, 26, 40, 42,
    52n16
reservations, 5–6, 11
Reyes, Joyce, 131
Reyes, Lawney, 131
Reyes, Luana, 128, 138

Riley, Denise, 36
Robbins, Theresa, 25, 39
Robideau, Richard, 177–78
Rosenthal, Nicolas G., xiii
Rush, Ella, 111, 112, 115, 120
Ryan, Joan, xi

Saint Augustine's Center (Chicago
    IL), 27, 30, 46–47
Salo, Matt, 6, 9
*San Francisco Bay Area American
    Indian Resource Directory*, 3
Satzewich, Vic, 109
Save Our Ancestors Remains and
    Resources Indigenous Network
    Group, 32–33
Scott, Ken, 32
Sealey, D. Bruce, xi
Seattle WA: American Indian Wom-
    en's Service League, 125–26, 127–
    29, 131, 134–36; Indian Health
    Board (SIHB), 128, 136; Indian
    Services Commission (SISC),
    133; legacy of women leaders in,
    136–39; medical services in, 128;
    Native identity in, 133–34; Native
    lands in, 129–30; Native migra-
    tion to, 127–28; political activism
    in, 130–31; skid row, 128. *See also*
    Seattle Indian Center
Seattle Indian Center, xvi–xvii;
    cultural programs, 129; funding
    of, 132; growth of, 125–26; lead-
    ership, 131–32; location, 126–27,
    129–30; medical services,
    128; political activism, 131–34;
    services provided by, 127–29,
    132–33. *See also* Seattle WA

Seattle Indian Health Board (SIHB), 128, 136
Segundo, Thomas, 26, 28, 42
Seligman, Linda J., 100
sex workers, 77, 78, 81–86
shelters, women's, 56–58, 63–70
Shoemaker, Nancy, xii, 35
Skenadore, Amy Leicher, 27, 46
Smith, B. B., 116
Smith, Faith, 30
Smith, Paul Chaat, 146; *Like a Hurricane*, 146
smudging, 87, 92n25
social fluidity. *See* fluidity of urban Indian communities
social structure of urban Indian communities, 3–6
social welfare work: Chicago American Indian Center and, 22–28, 37–45, 49–50; family violence and, 63–70; incarcerated women and, 114–15; Native people viewed as maladjusted and, 38–39, 42; need for, 35–38; North American Indian Club and, 114–15; Southern California Indian Center, 178–80; in Toronto, Ontario, 108, 111–18; in Vancouver, British Columbia, 85–86, 88–89; welfare reform and, 89; women's opportunities and, 46–49
Sorkin, Alan L., xi
Southern California Indian Center (SCIC), 164–65, 178–80
sovereign power, 41, 134–35
spousal abuse, 56–58, 63–70
St. Regis Mohawk Reservation, 11

Stanbury, William T., xi
Standing Bear, Joseph, 33
Starr, Paul, 168–71
Starr, Paula: childhood, family background and relocation of, 168–72; collaboration with Joan Weibel-Orlando, 165–68, 185n5; compensating by, 173–74; cultural templates and individual choice by, 182–84; defining moments and survival of, 172–73, 181–82; education of, 166, 167, 174–76, 178; love, marriage and motherhood of, 177–78; New Year's Eve powwows attended by, 163–65, 166; niche building and finding by, 174–76; political activism of, xix–xx, 176–77; Southern California Indian Center and, 178–80
Starr, Sharon Sullivan, 168–72
Statement of the Government of Canada on Indian Policy, 58
State Subsistence Law, Alaska, 98
Stauss, Joseph H., xi
Stevens, Marj, 148
Straus, Anne Terry, xix, xxi, xxii, 6, 34, 35; *Native Chicago*, xxii
subsistence debate, 97–99
Switzer, Elaine, 43–44, 48
Sylvester, Hettie, 113, 117–18, 120

Tait, C. L., 80
Tales of Nokomis (Johnston), 112
Talking Leaf, 176
templates, cultural, 182–84
Thomas, Robert, 42
Thunder Bay, Ontario: classification of Native people in, 71n1; migra-

tion patterns of Native people in,
56; population growth, 60
Thunder Bay Anishinabequek:
Beendigen shelter and, 56–58,
63–70; organization of, 56–57;
political activism and, 59–60,
70–71; traditional movement
and, 60–63; women's activism
and, 60–63
Thunder Bay Indian Friendship
Centre, 60–63
Thundercloud, Scott, 24, 37
Toronto, Ontario: community building in, 118–20; education in, 107–
8, 111–12; employment of Native
people in, 107–11; middle-class
Natives in, 107–11; migration to,
105–6; national identity and citizenship in, 118–20; native urban
class mobility in, xv–xvi, 118–20;
women's lives and organizational
development in, 111–18
Toronto Native Community History
Project, 108, 111
Toronto Native Times, 114–15
traditional movement and urban
indigenous identity, 60–63
Trail of Broken Treaties, 150
Treaty of Fort Laramie, 149
Tribal American Corporation, 176
Tribally Controlled Community Colleges Act, 32
Turner, Patricia, 113
turning points, life, 172–73,
187–88n17

UCLA, 175–76
United Good Neighbors, 135

United Indians of All Tribes Foundation, 131, 136
United Indians of Milwaukee, 148
United Way, 135
Upward Bound grants, 129
Urban Clan Mothers: defined, 1;
fieldwork on, 2–3; fluidity and
mobility patterns of, 6–8; in key
households, 8–18; role of, 5–6,
13–14, 18
urban Indian communities: affluent, 110; alcoholism in, 128,
170–71, 181–82, 184n2, 186n12;
assimilation of, x–xi, 4, 57, 61,
106; class in, xv–xvi; colonialism and imperialism effects
on, xviii, 76, 81, 109, 126; craft
fairs and, xix, 93–96, 99–102,
116–18; cultural templates and
individual choice in, 182–84;
deaths in, 17–18, 86–87, 171,
187n13; economic issues facing,
84–85, 93–99; education in,
28–32, 32, 107–8, 111–12, 113,
116, 148–59, 172–73; fluidity
of, 6–8; gambling and, 154–58;
health care in, 22–23, 128, 138,
157; key households in, 8–18; life
history narratives in, 165–68,
181–82; middle-class, 106,
108–11; migration and mobility
patterns, xv–xvi, xvi, 6–8, 9–10,
56, 97–99, 100, 102–3n3, 105–6,
118–20, 127–28, 147–48; military
veterans in, 24; Native identity
in, 60–63, 109, 118–20, 133–34;
poverty in, 80–81, 132–33, 136;
powwows, 163–64, 169–70,

urban Indian communities (*cont.*)
184n2, 186n11; proximity to
reservations, 5–6; Red Power
movement, 29, 108, 126–27;
relocation programs and, 26, 40,
42, 52n16; research on, ix–xv,
xxi–xxii; social structure of, 3–6;
sovereign power and, 41, 134–35;
traditional gender roles in, 1–6,
13–14, 18, 35–37; traditional movement, 60–63; uniqueness of, 2;
viewed as maladjusted, 38–39,
42; volunteer work in, 118–21
urban indigenous identity, 60–63,
109

Valentine's Day March (Vancouver,
British Columbia), xviii, 76–77,
84–88
Valentino, Debra, xix, xxi, 6, 31, 34,
35
Vancouver, British Columbia:
deaths in, 78–80, 82–83, 87–88,
91n19; drugs, violence, and sex
in, 77–84; inner-city neighborhoods of, 77–78; invisibility of
Native people in, 76–77, 87–88,
89; media attention on violence
in, 82–83; politics, 88–89;
population of Native people in,
79, 90–91n6; poverty in, 80–81;
prostitution in, 77, 78, 81–86,
92n24; social services in, 85–86;
Valentine's Day March, xviii,
76–77, 84–88
Vanderburgh, Rosamund, 105; *I Am
Nokomis, Too*, 105–6
violence: family, 56–58, 63–70,

171; against women, xvii–xviii,
78–80, 82–83, 87–88, 91n19
visibility, struggle for, 76–78, 87–88,
89
volunteer work, 118–21

Wandrey, Marilyn, 138
Warner, LindaSue, 158
War on Poverty, 132–33, 136
Warren, Pearl, 125, 127, 131–32, 135,
144n54; legacy of, 136, 137
Warrior, 45
Warrior, Robert Allen, 146; *Like a
Hurricane*, 146
Weibel-Orlando, Joan, xii, xix–xx,
xxi–xxii, 165–68, 185n5
Welfare Council and Community
Fund, 42–45, 47–48
Welfare Council of Chicago, 25
welfare reform, 89
Wesaw, Leroy, 27
White, Joe, 27
White, Ted, 28, 40
Whitebear, Bernie, 130–31
White Paper, Canada, 58
*Wife Battering in Canada: The Vicious
Circle* (MacLeod), 68
Willard, William, xi
women, Native: compensating
by, 173–74; craft fairs and, xix,
93–96, 99–102, 116–18; cult of
true womanhood and, 36–37;
deaths of, 17–18; education
of, 28–32, 107–8, 111–13, 116,
172–73, 174–76, 178; employment of, 84–85, 96, 99–100,
107–11; expanded opportunities
for, 46–49; festivals celebrat-